L.A.'s Legendary Restaurants

Celebrating the Famous Places
Where Hollywood Ate, Drank, and Played

George Geary

Foreword by Barbara Fairchild

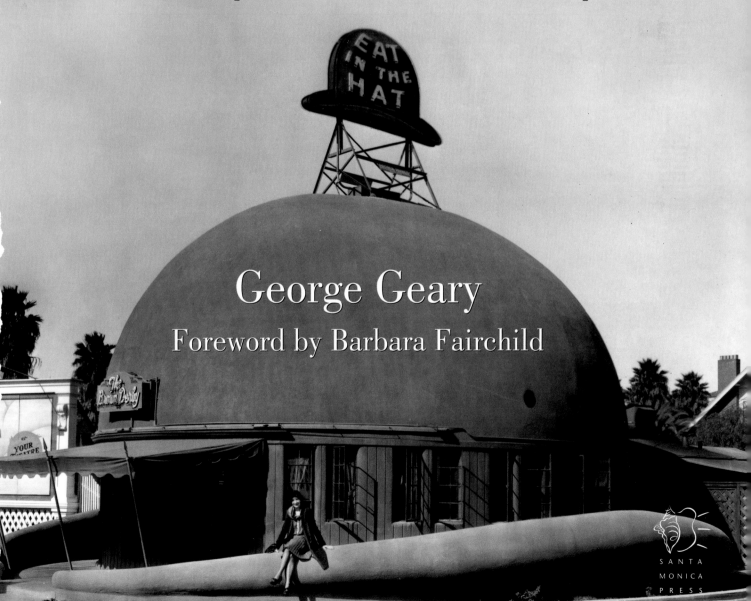

SANTA
MONICA
PRESS

Published by:

Santa Monica Press LLC
P.O. Box 850
Solana Beach, CA 92075
1-800-784-9553
www.santamonicapress.com
books@santamonicapress.com

Printed in Canada

Santa Monica Press books are available at special quantity discounts when purchased in bulk by corporations, organizations, or groups. Please call our Special Sales department at 1-800-784-9553.

This book is intended to provide general information. The publisher, author, distributor, and copyright owner are not engaged in rendering professional advice or services. The publisher, author, distributor, and copyright owner are not liable or responsible to any person or group with respect to any loss, illness, or injury caused or alleged to be caused by the information found in this book.

ISBN-13 978-1-59580-089-3

Library of Congress Cataloging-in-Publication Data

Names: Geary, George, author.
Title: L.A.'s legendary restaurants : celebrating the famous places where   Hollywood ate, drank, and played / by George Geary.
Description: Solana Beach, CA : Santa Monica Press LLC, [2016]
Identifiers: LCCN 2016006759 (print) | LCCN 2016021904 (ebook) | ISBN   9781595800893 (hardcover) | ISBN 9781595807991 (PDF ebook) | ISBN   9781595808004 (Kindle) | ISBN 9781595808011 (Epub)
Subjects: LCSH: Los Angeles' legendary restaurants | Cooking--California--Los Angeles. | Restaurants--California--Los Angeles. | Motion picture actors and actresses--Homes and haunts--California--Los Angeles--History--20th century. | LCGFT: Cookbooks.
Classification: LCC TX714 .G43 2016 (print) | LCC TX714 (ebook) | DDC 641.59794/94--dc23
LC record available at https://lccn.loc.gov/2016006759

10 9 8 7 6 5 4 3

Cover and interior design and production by Future Studio

Cover photo: **The Brown Derby, 1927.**
Back cover photo: **C. C. Brown's on Hollywood Boulevard, circa 1960s.**

Saimon 1.00

Ripe or Green Olives ...40

Assorted Hors d'Oeuvres 75
  with Caviar 1.00

Filet of Marinated
  Herring 65

Fruit 75

Avocado 75

Tomato Juice on Ice ...25

Clam Juice on Ice 35

Sea Food Cocktail 85

Cherry Stones
Derby Oyster
Fried Eastern
  Half Shell in
Baked Oysters
  Any Style

Roast Beef

Pan Fried Ch

Boston Bake

Fresh Veget

Creamed Ch

Ragout of F

Stuffed Mus

Breaded Ve

Veal Sweeth

Whole Brea

Broiled Calf

en Bouillon
...... .25

...... 1.00

...... .90

...... 1.00

...... 1.35

...... .90

...... 1.25

...... 1.35

...... 1.35

...... .90

...... .95

...... 1.10

...... 1.25

Dedication

To Mom, who became a carhop—the second-hardest job
besides being a mother—at Marty's Drive-In in Santa Monica at
age thirteen.

Also, to my grand-
mother, Gammie, and Aunt
Bea, who both worked at
Van de Kamp's, and my
grandfather, Coley, who, in
1946, was one of the best
executive chefs in Las Vegas when it was just a spot
in the Nevada desert.

Lastly, to every person
who has worked as a wait-
er, chef, or any other job in
the food industry. Everyone
should, at one time or another; it humbles you, and
you'll tip better afterward.

FROM THE CHINESE KITCHEN

Chicken Chow Mein .... 1.00   Chicken Fried Rice 90
Chicken Chop Suey .... 1.00   Eggs Foyoung 90
Fried Shrimp 75   Special Chinese Pork 75
Pork Chop Suey 90   Yakomein 70

All Chinese Dishes Prepared by a Chinese Chef. This Department is Fully Stocked to Serve Any Chinese Delicacy You
Might Desire.

PASTRY SPECIALS

RITA CAKE 25
MPKIN PIE 25
colate or Cocoanut Sponge Cake 25
e or Chocolate Pudding ..... .25
und Cake 25   Cup Cake 15
eese Cake 25   Assorted Pies 25
nch Pastry 25   Caramel Custard 25

ICE CREAMS, SHERBETS

Mocha or Fresh Strawberry Ice Cream ....
Vanilla or Chocolate Ice Cream ....
Orange or Pineapple Sherbet ....
Parfaits, Assorted ....
Sundaes, Assorted ....
Fresh Fruit Sherbet ....

Contents

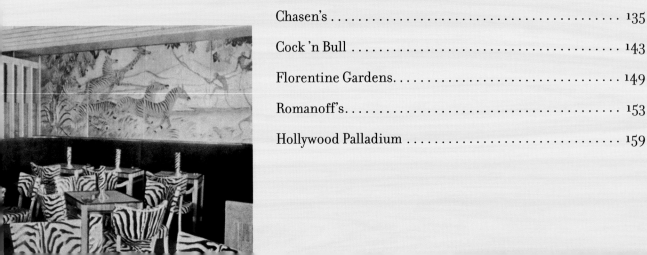

Recipes

WHILE I WAS PUTTING THIS BOOK TOGETHER, ONE BIG QUESTION I WAS OFTEN ASKED WAS WHERE I GOT THE RECIPES. Many of them came from the *Los Angeles Times* food section archives, which go as far back as the 1920s. Old books from the restaurants themselves were another source. Many food magazines also had columns that highlighted recipes from the establishments. I even watched old television programs featuring the restaurants' chefs, and took down notes to reconstruct the recipes.

Many of the restaurants happily sent me their recipes. There were, however, a few places that couldn't provide theirs, and I had to improvise. One of these recipes was C. C. Brown's Hot Fudge Sauce, which is manufactured and owned by Lawry's Restaurants. I've indulged in the gooey topping both in the 1970s and today at Lawry's The Prime Rib, and I've also purchased a jar of the sauce. All three versions tasted different to me. Was it because I wasn't eating it out of a silver goblet at C. C. Brown's? Maybe. In any case, I created my own milk chocolate sauce recipe for this book, trying my best to get as close to the original as possible.

For very popular dishes that I couldn't obtain recipes for, I chose not to include them in the book—such as Chasen's chili. In my research, I found about seven versions of the restaurant's famous spicy chili. Since I've never eaten it myself (or had it flown to me on a movie set), I had no reference for choosing the most authentic version. After I obtained the recipes for each of the eateries, I tested each one using the exact same ingredients if at all possible. For some of the recipes—such as those including MSG—I made substitutions. I now invite you to try these recipes yourself and taste the same delectable dishes once enjoyed by the stars of this bygone era.

Chef Keith Hull in the kitchen at Miceli's.

Foreword by Barbara Fairchild

OUR FAMILY MOVED FROM NEW YORK TO LOS ANGELES WHEN I WAS A KID. My dad was a character actor, and we went where the work was. At the risk of dating myself—and this definitely will—there were great roles to be had for him on TV shows like *Perry Mason, Dr. Kildare, Bewitched, The Twilight Zone,* and many, many others. In the meantime, my mom also got a job, and my sisters and I went off to school, lost the New Yawk accent, and eased happily into the sunny rhythm of Southern California.

Later on, I also eased into my teen years, including the important milestone of "Sweet Sixteen." I must have been a budding foodie even then, because to mark the occasion, the farthest thing from my mind was having a big fancy party with a gang of my friends. No, I knew exactly what I wanted to do: go to dinner with my dad and my best friend at Don the Beachcomber, already a Hollywood landmark that somehow seemed both glamorous and decadent. Rumor had it that there was also a rainstorm *inside* every so often. I just had to check it out.

So began my exploration of the "grown-ups'" L.A. restaurant scene, and I haven't looked back. Still an enthusiastic restaurant-goer, I'm also lucky enough to have been to some of the classic spots—both long gone and still open—covered so affectionately here in George Geary's wonderful book. What a terrific (and thorough) job of research he has done! It is all too easy to lose track of time poring over these interesting old menus, not to mention the amazing photos—Marilyn Monroe and Lucille Ball at Ciro's! Jimmy Stewart at Chasen's! Elizabeth Taylor at Romanoff's! Orson Welles at Ma Maison (always)! Who can resist?

But the biggest bonus this book delivers is the recipes. There is everything here from kitsch to classic, all tested (George is a perfectionist, trust me) and all delicious. So many of these recipes are timeless, too. For a summer barbecue or retro cocktail party, I can see myself mixing up a batch of Zombies or some Navy Grog from (where else?) Don the Beachcomber. Or, for breakfast or brunch, bringing to the table a basket of warm popovers from the beloved Bullocks Wilshire Tea Room. For lunch, the Brown Derby's Cobb Salad can't be beat—and it lives on in hundreds of imitations (and iterations) today. And if you don't think that I will make a *lot* of C. C. Brown's celebrated hot fudge sauce, then you don't know just

ZOMBIE

Created at Don the Beachcomber, Hollywood in 1934. Often imitated, but never duplicated.

how much of a chocoholic I am.

Those iconic spots are only memories now, but I'm happy to report that a number of places endure and thrive, among them the Tam O'Shanter, Miceli's, Musso and Frank's, Taix, and Clifton's Cafeteria, which has been revamped and reborn within one of our hottest restaurant neighborhoods these days, downtown L.A. And the cultural glitterati—from the movie biz and beyond—still wheel and deal (and drink and dine) over lunch at La Scala, or dinner at Dan Tana's, Spago (now in Beverly Hills), or Michael's in Santa Monica. These are still places to see and be seen *in*, just as they were when they began.

Yes, there is a long thread of restaurant history here in the City of Angels, and it is an impressive one, indeed. George Geary understands the importance of that history and its legacy. Now, thanks to him, we are fortunate to be able to relive those times—and taste the food—in these fascinating pages. ✗

PI YI

Crushed fresh Hawaiian fruits and light Cuban Rums served in a hollowed-out baby pineapple.

TAHITIAN RUM PUNCH

Exotic tropical fruits admirably blended with Mexican limes and old Cuban Rums.

Introduction

TRENDS IN FOOD, DRINKS, AND RESTAURANTS HAVE CONTINUALLY CHANGED OVER THE DECADES, BUT LOS ANGELES HAS ALWAYS LED THE WAY WHEN IT COMES TO CELEBRITIES, CUTTING EDGE FOOD, AND WILDLY POPULAR DINING SPOTS. *L.A.'s Legendary Restaurants* brings back special memories, detailing the history and lore associated with these establishments.

Such culinary icons as the hot fudge sundae and the tiki bar and its many tropical drinks, as well as striking architectural wonders like the Brown Derby restaurant (shaped like the hat it was named af-

ter), were created here. It was at the Pig 'n Whistle's soda fountain that Shirley Temple enjoyed dishes of ice cream. The Tam O'Shanter Inn on Los Feliz Boulevard was so favored by the film community that it was referred to as the "other" Disney studio commissary. And Hamburger Hamlet was courageous enough to have one of the first mixed-race staffs in the industry.

In the 1940s, dance halls and music venues sprung up to cater to those with less cash to spend. With the growing prevalence of automobiles, the arrival of carhops made dining that much easier. The 1950s brought a television into every house, and with the popularity of hamburgers and sandwiches, dining began to take less time. In the 1970s, new celebrities appeared in the form of chefs. Ma Maison had Wolfgang Puck, L'Ermitage had Jean Bertranou, and Michael's had Michael McCarty. These star chefs began building personal empires, which often resulted in locations around the country and their brands in grocery stores.

L.A.'s Legendary Restaurants reveals the architects who created the legendary locations, from the famous Paul Revere Williams to the movie studio craftsmen who plied their trade outside the walls of the film lot. Architectural styles ranged from the refined elegance of Perino's to the Polynesian theme of Trader Vic's. In this book, you'll feel the textures of the restaurant designs and meet the chefs and owners. You'll rub elbows with the famous stars who dined there and learn what their favorite dishes were and which booths were their favorites. You'll discover the memorable events that took place there. Perhaps best of all, you'll savor the flavors of the dishes that were prepared in the kitchens.

Many of the stories in this book have been told again and again over the years. But which ones are a hundred percent true? Was Lana Turner really discovered at the Schwab's Pharmacy soda fountain counter? Did Elizabeth Taylor actually have Chasen's chili flown to the *Cleopatra* set in Rome? Was Hamptons really backed or owned by Paul Newman? I know some of these stories are true because I saw them with my own eyes (I witnessed Mr. Newman working at Hamptons myself; I believe he was a secondary partner). For the others, I carefully researched the reports, and did my best to separate fact from fiction.

My research led me all over the country: from the Hollywood and downtown Los Angeles library branches, all the way to Texas, and even across the country to Rhode Island. Throughout it all, the various former employees and owners of the restaurants were gracious, helpful, and incredibly supportive that a book was being created that would celebrate their legacy.

Make these recipes for your family and friends. Enjoy the feast, read the stories, and dine like a star. Bon appétit!

George Geary CCP

P.S. Throughout the years, some of the restaurants' addresses have changed, sometimes because the street names themselves have evolved. In 1963, zip codes came into play, and in 1984, West Hollywood became its own city, changing the addresses of many establishments once again. The addresses included in this book are the most up-to-date for their respective venues.

Additionally, for each restaurant, both the original and current (if the business is still in operation) phone numbers are included. Starting the 1920s, phone numbers contained both numbers and letters. The letters told you where the venue you were dialing was located. It was not uncommon for a business to have more than one number. In the 1980s, some of the exclusive restaurants had a separate number for their A-list patrons. These numbers are also included in the book. Today, we have phone and online reservation systems to bypass all of this. ✕

Above: **The patio at the Tam O'Shanter Inn, 1933.** ▪ *Opposite:* **Robert Taylor and Barbara Stanwyck at Ciro's.**

C. C. Brown's

OPEN: 1906–1996

LOCATION: 7007 Hollywood Boulevard
Hollywood, CA 90028

ORIGINAL PHONE: HO 4-9755

CUISINE: Dessert

DESIGN: Meyer & Holler

BUILDING STYLE: Renaissance

CURRENTLY: Clothing Store

FROM 1906 TO 1918, CLARENCE CLIFTON BROWN WORKED ALONE, MAKING HIS RAGTIME CHOCOLATES AT 715 S. FLOWER STREET IN DOWNTOWN LOS ANGELES (NOW MACY'S PLAZA) WITH A LARGE COPPER KETTLE THAT HE HAD BROUGHT WITH HIM FROM OHIO. C. C. Jr. joined his dad in the business in 1918 and began experimenting with the chocolate mixtures, trying to create a sauce that would not harden when exposed to air the way typical candy coatings did.

In 1929, the duo moved their business to 7007 Hollywood Boulevard, next to the newly opened Grauman's Chinese Theatre and across the street from the El Capitan Theatre and the Hollywood Roosevelt Hotel. It took nearly ten more years before the Browns thought their C. C. Brown's Hot Fudge Sauce had reached perfection, finally debuting the concoction in 1938.

To cash in on the Olympic fever of 1932, Clarence opened a C. C. Brown's Candy Store at 3834 Wilshire Boulevard, about two blocks from Western Avenue. It only stayed open for one year. The C. C. Brown's on Hollywood Boulevard, however, became a popular hangout for locals, tourists, and celebrities alike. The shop always had an intense, captivating aroma of chocolate and caramel. Its chocolate-colored booths were thoughtfully elevated to create a sense of private space, a subtle filter so tourists could glimpse—but not intrude upon—the celebrities seated nearby.

Without a doubt, the place had a star-studded following. A teenaged Judy Garland was a server there. Marilyn Monroe called it her favorite date spot. Marlon Brando savored his ice cream in his limo parked out front while his family ate inside, so he wouldn't be bothered. Clark Gable, Mary Pickford, Joan Crawford, Art Linkletter, Bob Hope, and Elvis Presley were regulars. One frequent customer would eventually become president of the United States: Ronald Reagan. (After Hinckley attempted to assassinate President Reagan, C. C. Brown's shipped a case of their famous hot fudge sauce to the White House as a tribute. Mr. Reagan's gracious thank-you note was displayed in a case by the cash register.)

Opposite: Ben-Hur actress Haya Harareet pouring C. C. Brown's famous chocolate sauce on her sundae, 1959.

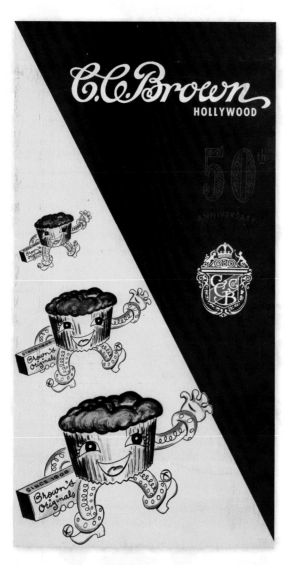

Brown's Unexcelled Ice Cream and Sherbets

ICE CREAM .... .40

Strawberry, Mocha, Vanilla, Chocolate and Special

SHERBET .... .40

Fancy Sundaes and Formulas

OUR WORLD FAMOUS HOT FUDGE or CARAMEL SUNDAE
with Roasted Almonds and Whipped Cream .... .75

HOT GOLDEN MOCHA SUNDAE — Three scoops Ice Cream, Toasted Cashews, Pitcher of Hot Mocha Sauce, and Whipped Cream .... .85

BROWNIE — Banana, Vanilla and Chocolate Ice Cream, Marshmallow and Milk Chocolate Dressing, Ground Nuts, Whipped Cream and Cherry .... .85

BITTER MALLOW — Banana, Chocolate and Vanilla Ice Cream, Marshmallow and Bitter Sweet Topping, Whipped Cream .... .85

BUSTER BROWN — Banana, Vanilla and Chocolate Ice Cream, Roasted Almonds, Pitcher of Hot Fudge, Whipped Cream and Cherry .... .85

CINDERELLA — Melba Peach, Vanilla Ice Cream, Crushed Strawberries, Lemon Sherbet, Pineapple Fruit, Roasted Almonds and Whipped Cream, designed by Ellen Drew .... .85

PEACH MELBA — Strawberry Ice Cream, Pineapple Sherbet, Melba Peach, Marshmallow and Whipped Cream .... .85

BANANA SPECIAL — Banana, Vanilla and Strawberry Ice Cream, Pineapple and Strawberry Fruit, Nuts, Whipped Cream and Cherry .. .85

PINEAPPLE SPECIAL — Vanilla Ice Cream and two Sherbets, Pineapple Fruit, Nuts, Whipped Cream and Cherry .... .85

HAWAIIAN DELIGHT — Strawberry Ice Cream, Vanilla Ice Cream and Sherbet, Pineapple Fruit, Ground Nuts, Whipped Cream and Cherry .... .85

LOVER'S DELIGHT — Banana, Vanilla and Strawberry Ice Cream, Raspberry Fruit, Ground Nuts, Whipped Cream and Cherry .... .85

PETER PAN — Banana, Two Scoops Chocolate Ice Cream, Marshmallow Dressing, Nuts, Whipped Cream and Cherry .... .85

CONEY ISLAND — Vanilla and Strawberry Ice Cream, Sherbet, Pineapple and Strawberry Fruit, Whipped Cream and Cherry ...... .85

CHOCOLATE DROP — Banana, Two Dippers Chocolate Ice Cream, Cold Fudge, Whipped Cream and Cherry .... .85

★　　★　　★

SERVE OUR HOT FUDGE SUNDAES
IN YOUR OWN HOME

Fudge — 13 oz. Can	.80
(6 servings)	
Toasted Almonds	2.00 per pound
Ice Cream	1.40 per quart

The servers wore pristine white uniforms, and the ice cream menu was extensive. The most popular choices were the Hot Fudge Sundae, the Caramel Sundae, the Buster Brown, and the Brownie—the boss's eponymous sundae. The Brownie didn't actually contain brownies, but it did have a sliced banana, scoops of vanilla and chocolate ice cream, marshmallow and milk chocolate sauces, fresh whipped cream, and a sprinkle of chopped roasted almonds. The Hot Fudge Sundae was served in a silver goblet; C. C. claimed that the metal kept the ice cream cold longer. The all-important two-and-a-half ounces of hot fudge sauce were served on the side, in a brown ceramic pitcher. The original hot fudge sauce that Brown and his son had worked so hard to perfect stayed creamy on top of the ice cream without hardening or sliding off.

In 1959, John Schumacher, a close friend of the Browns and a dairy chemist with the Carnation Ice Cream Company, started working at C. C. Brown's and purchased it a few years later. The Schumachers maintained the original recipes and prices. While running the shop, Schumacher and his wife, JoEllen, raised eight children who were always around, either doing homework or working as servers.

In the 1970s and '80s, the neighborhood around C. C. Brown's deteriorated. The El Capitan Theatre was abandoned, and in 1982, a Häagen-Dazs shop opened two doors down, capturing most of what was left of the business. Still, the Schumachers kept doing what they knew best: making the ice cream and hot fudge sauce that everyone loved.

John Schumacher passed away in 1994. In all the years of his ownership, he never missed a day at the shop, wearing his white uniform with the black tie and cooking up fudge sauce in the same vintage copper kettle the Browns had used. JoEllen and her children kept the place open for two more years, but in 1996, the doors of C. C. Brown's closed for good, an event that even the *New York Times* noted.

The old neighborhood has since come back. The Walt Disney Company renovated the El Capitan Theatre and opened an ice cream shop nearby. The Academy Awards were held just a few doors away. The Hollywood Roosevelt Hotel is thriving. For years, the C. C. Brown's space was occupied by a t-shirt shop, with the ice cream parlor's original light fixtures and wallpaper still hanging. Recently, the entire building—which also contained an automobile showroom—was reconditioned into a discount clothing store.

The Schumacher family has continued to produce their famous hot fudge sauce and sell it by mail order and in certain Gelson's grocery stores in the Los Angeles area. In 2003, a small C. C. Brown's ice cream stand existed briefly in the Sunset and Vine Complex, but it was short-lived.

Exactly one hundred years after C. C. Brown's opened in downtown Los Angeles, Lawry's Restaurants, Inc., purchased the rights to its name and recipes. They still produce the hot fudge sauce and sell it in their restaurants and on the company's website. ✕

White-uniformed servers at C. C. Brown's, 1978.

1909 Brownie Sundae

When people came into C. C. Brown's and ordered the Brownie Sundae, the waitstaff had to emphasize that the dessert didn't actually contain any brownies. Rather, it was named after C. C. Brown, because he loved it so much.

Serves 1

1 scoop vanilla bean ice cream
1 scoop chocolate ice cream
3 oz. Milk Chocolate Sauce (recipe follows)
3 oz. Marshmallow Cream (recipe follows)
1 banana, sliced
whipped cream, for topping
roasted almonds, for topping

1. Place the vanilla and chocolate ice cream scoops in a large dish. Top the vanilla ice cream with the Milk Chocolate Sauce and the chocolate ice cream with the Marshmallow Cream.
2. Top with the banana slices and whipped cream and sprinkle with the roasted almonds.

Marshmallow Cream

A staple at C. C. Brown's, this rich, pillowy cream floats atop ice cream beautifully. Pair it with a hot fudge sauce for a Black and White Sundae, or use it along with the Milk Chocolate Sauce (recipe follows) to make a Brownie Sundae.

Makes about 2 cups (6 servings)

1 tbsp. unflavored powdered gelatin
2 tsp. cornstarch
½ cup heavy cream
2 large egg whites, at room temperature
pinch cream of tartar

1 cup granulated sugar
½ cup light corn syrup
½ cup water, at room temperature
2 tsp. pure vanilla extract

1. In a small saucepan, whisk together the gelatin, cornstarch, and heavy cream. Let stand for 5 minutes, then place the mixture in a small saucepan and warm over low heat, stirring until the gelatin dissolves. Do not heat to boiling. Remove from the heat and place a double-folded towel underneath to keep the pan warm.
2. In a mixing bowl fitted with the whisk attachment, whip the egg whites and cream of tartar until soft peaks form, about 12 minutes. Set aside in the mixing bowl.
3. In a small, clean saucepan, combine the sugar, corn syrup, and water. Place over medium heat and bring to a boil. Cook without stirring until the mixture reaches 238°F on a candy thermometer. Remove from the heat.
4. Pour the sugar mixture into the egg white mixture in a steady stream. Add the warm cream and gelatin mixture. Whip the mixture on high speed until it cools to room temperature, carefully touching the bottom of the bowl to gauge the temperature, then add the vanilla.
5. Transfer the sauce to an airtight container and refrigerate for at least 3 hours. Store in an airtight container in the refrigerator for up to 7 days.

TIP: When ready to use, place your stored Marshmallow Cream in a mixing bowl and whip until it reaches the desired consistency.

7A-H3650

Postcard featuring Hollywood Boulevard, with C. C. Brown's pictured on the left.

Milk Chocolate Sauce

This chocolate sauce was the finishing touch on the famous Brownie Sundae.

Makes about 2 cups (6 servings)

16 oz. high-quality milk chocolate, finely chopped
2 tsp. pure vanilla extract

¾ cup heavy cream
2 tbsp. unsalted butter, softened

1. Place the chocolate and vanilla in a medium bowl. Set aside.
2. Place the cream and butter in a small saucepan and set over medium heat until the mixture reaches a low boil. Pour the mixture directly onto the chopped chocolate and whisk until the chocolate is fully melted. Serve hot.
3. To save the sauce for future use, place in an airtight container and refrigerate for up to 7 days.

Note: To reheat your stored sauce, place the sauce in the top of a double boiler over indirect heat and warm until melted. Do not microwave or it will burn.

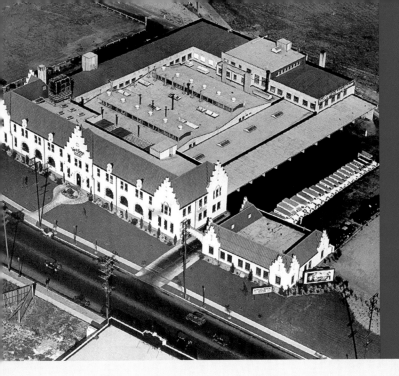

Van de Kamp's Holland Dutch Bakery

OPEN: 1915–1990

LOCATION: 2930 Fletcher Drive
Los Angeles, CA 90039

ORIGINAL PHONE: AL 3-856 and CL 5-0171

CUISINE: Baked Goods

DESIGN: J. Edwin Hopkins

BUILDING STYLE: Dutch Renaissance Revival

CURRENTLY: Los Angeles City College
Van de Kamp Campus

YOU CAN TELL HOW LONG SOMEONE HAS LIVED IN SOUTHERN CALIFORNIA BY HOW THEY REMEMBER THE VAN DE KAMP'S BRAND. Do you remember it as bakery products sold in stores with packaging that featured windmills and bakery girls wearing traditional "Holland Blue" dresses, white hats, and aprons? Or as fish sticks in the frozen-food section? Or do you remember the Van de Kamp's restaurants and coffee shops?

I have a personal fondness for the Van de Kamp's brand. During the holidays, my mother would slice a Van de Kamp's Date Nut Loaf and arrange the pieces in a spiral on a fancy glass plate for the family to enjoy. In the late 1940s, my grandmother worked as a Van de Kamp's salesgirl at a Vons market in Santa Monica, which was also where my mother worked in the snack bar. In 1950, my father came into the market to visit his mother while on military leave, and he met my mother. They married a few years later. My aunt also worked as an area supervisor with Van de Kamp's. While I was in culinary school in 1980, one of our instructors, Mr. Perkowski, was the lead decorator at the Van de Kamp's plant on Fletcher Drive and took all of us on a tour of the three-story building. I got to see the production of butter sprinkle cookies, my favorite as a kid.

In 1915, Theodore Van de Kamp and his brother-in-law, Lawrence "Lawry" Frank, started a potato chip business in downtown Los Angeles called Saratoga Chips, employing their wives, Marion and Henrietta, as the sales staff. Due to a shortage of potatoes, they were soon forced to diversify into other products. Within a year, Van de Kamp's Holland Dutch Bakeries was born, and by 1921, a full-scale retail bakery was in operation at 408 N. Western Avenue, serving made-to-order cakes, cookies, pies, and flaky yeast breads. The family created a total of 140 different recipes for baked goods. Later on, they also founded the Tam O'Shanter Inn in 1922 (see page 45), Lawry's The Prime Rib in 1938, and Lawry's California Center in 1953 (page 197).

Frank and Van de Kamp needed something to catch the attention of the drivers speeding along Western Avenue and draw them into the shop, so they attached a large windmill to the roof of their bakery building, designed by art director Harry Oliver. Following the Dutch theme, the Van de Kamp's salesgirls wore blue dresses, starched laced aprons, and white hats. In 1923, they opened their first coffee shop at 600 S. Spring Street, where the twelve-story Alexandria Hotel annex now sits (it has

Above: The Van de Kamp's central production facility on Fletcher Drive, circa 1945. ▪ *Opposite:* Postcard showing a Van de Kamp's shop in Los Angeles, topped with the bakery's signature windmill, 1947.

Food and Service you'll enjoy!

CAR • COUNTER
DINING ROOM
OUTDOOR TABLES

VAN DE KAMP'S

LOS-ANGELES

FLETCHER DRIVE & SAN FERNANDO RD.

since been converted into lofts).

By 1929, the original Van de Kamp's store had grown into a chain, with more than ninety-five locations in the Los Angeles area. The family then opened a central production facility on Fletcher Drive. Later, they added a coffee shop on the corner of the Fletcher Drive property, the first of a chain of coffee shop locations around Southern California.

When Theodore Van de Kamp passed away in 1956, the Van de Kamp family sold the bakery to the General Baking Company, which also controlled Lawry's Restaurants, Inc., and a number of other food ventures. As a result, Lawrence Frank devoted more time to the Lawry's spices at the California Center and Lawry's The Prime Rib on La Cienega Boulevard. In 1979, the company was sold to private investors.

In September 1990, Van de Kamp's Holland Dutch Bakeries filed for bankruptcy. The original 1929 manufacturing plant on Fletcher Drive closed its doors, putting 500 bakers, plant workers, and office staff members out of work. On May 12, 1992, the building was designated as a Historic-Cultural Monument by the City of Los Angeles. It underwent a $72 million renovation by the Los Angeles Community College District, which opened it as the Van de Kamp satellite campus of Los Angeles City College.

Over the years, the Van de Kamp's brand has been owned by Pillsbury, Aurora Foods, Pet, Inc., and Van de Kamp's, Inc. Today, the trademarks are owned by Pinnacle Foods Group. The Van de Kamp's brand is also used by Kroger, the West Coast's Ralphs chain, for its line of private-label baked goods.

Many of the newer Van de Kamp's coffee shop buildings were designed by architect Wayne McAllister, whose creations ranged from Las Vegas casinos to steak houses. The Van de Kamp's structures, complete with their windmills, could be seen from miles away. They were originally more whimsical-looking, but McAllister updated them, redesigning them in the Googie style. Today, a Denny's restaurant at 7 E. Huntington Drive in Arcadia (on Route 66) now occupies the only fully intact Van de Kamp's restaurant structure left in Southern California. ✕

Right: Regional manager Bernice Miles (*right*) with a salesgirl at a Van de Kamp's shop. ▪ *Opposite top:* The Van de Kamp's float, which won the grand prize in the Pasadena Tournament of Roses Parade, circa 1940. ▪ *Opposite bottom:* The Van de Kamp's bakery on Fletcher Drive, where the first Van de Kamp's coffee shop was opened, circa 1945.

VAN DE KAMP'S BAKERIES GRAND PRIZE
WINNER—PASADENA TOURNAMENT OF ROSES

Van de Kamps

Hot Fudge Sundae

with Real Whipped Cream
and Ice Box Cookie

40c

with Toasted Almonds 50c

*Fudge Served Hot
in an Individual Cup*

ICE CREAM

*Fine Ice Cream Made from Pure Cream,
Sugar, Fruit or Flavoring*

Van de Kamp's Fine Ice Cream 15
Van de Kamp's Fine Sherbet 15

SUNDAES

Fresh Frozen Strawberry Sundae . . . 40
Marshmallow 35
Pineapple 35
Hot Fudge 40   Chocolate 35

*Above Sundaes Served with Real Whipped Cream
Toasted Almonds 10c Extra*

SODAS, MALTS, SPECIALTIES

Grade "A" Pasteurized Milk Used Exclusively

Mellow Malt, Chocolate, Strawberry,
or Vanilla 30
Milk Shake, Choice of Any Flavor 35
Orange Freezer-Teaser
(Delightfully Refreshing) 30

Orange Sherbet Shake 30
Malted Milk, Choice of Any Flavor 35
Double Ice Cream Soda 35
Root Beer, Frosted 30

BAKERY, DESSERTS, SPECIALTIES

Coffee Cake . . . . 10, 12, and 15
Plain or Sugared Doughnut 06
Cruller or Crumb Doughnut . . . 08, 2 for 15
Toast, Butter and Jelly 15
Cinnamon Toast 25
Van de Kamp's Cake 20
Cake a la Mode 35
Cake with Real Whipped Cream 35
Van de Kamp's Pie 20
Pie a la Mode 35
Pie with Real Whipped Cream 35

Your Favorite Malt

*An amazingly smooth creation made from
Van de Kamp's fine ice cream. A variety
of flavors.*

35c

BEVERAGES

Coffee 10   Milk 15
Hot Chocolate . . . 20   Tea 10
Buttermilk (⅓ qt.) . . 15   Coca-Cola . . 10
Root Beer (in a Frosted Mug) 10

4% Sales Tax will be added to all Taxable Items

NO TABLE SERVICE UNDER 25c

Date Nut Loaf

In the 1950s, Van de Kamp's was at the forefront of entertaining. The bakery encouraged home cooks to create a sweet appetizer to brighten a party by sandwiching a little cream cheese between thin slices of its Date Nut Loaf.

Serves 6 to 8

4 oz. pitted dates, finely chopped
1 cup water
1 cup packed brown sugar
¼ cup unsalted butter, melted
1 large egg, beaten

½ tsp. salt
1 tsp. pure vanilla extract
½ cup walnut pieces
1⅓ cups all-purpose flour
½ tsp. baking powder

1. Preheat the oven to 325°F.
2. Spray an 8 x 4-inch loaf pan with nonstick spray.
3. Combine the dates and water in a medium saucepan and bring to a boil over medium heat. Remove from heat and use a handheld mixer to purée the mixture.
4. Place the mixture back over low heat and add the brown sugar and butter. Stir until the sugar melts, then remove from heat.
5. Place the egg in a medium bowl and add a small amount of the warm date mixture in a steady stream while stirring to temper the egg. Slowly whisk the tempered egg mixture into the rest of the date mixture, being careful not to let the mixture overheat and scramble the egg. Add the salt, vanilla, and walnut pieces.
6. In a medium bowl, whisk together the flour and baking powder, then fold into the warm date mixture to combine. Mix just until the batter is smooth.
7. Pour the batter into the prepared pan. Place in the oven and bake until a toothpick inserted into the center comes out clean, 50 to 60 minutes. Remove from the oven, cover immediately and tightly with aluminum foil, and let cool for at least 1 hour before slicing. To store, keep wrapped in foil or a plastic bag in the refrigerator for up to 7 days.

A Van de Kamp's bakery in Glendale, 1925.

Musso & Frank Grill

OPEN: 1919–present

LOCATION: 6667 Hollywood Boulevard
Hollywood, CA 90028

ORIGINAL PHONE: HO-0728 and HO-7-7788

CURRENT PHONE: (323) 467-7788

CUISINE: American

DESIGN: L.A. Smith

BUILDING STYLE: Regency

IN 1919, A RESTAURANT OPENED ON HOLLYWOOD BOULEVARD NAMED FRANK'S FRANCOIS CAFÉ. Four years later, its owners, Frank Toulet and Joseph Musso, changed the name to the Musso and Frank Grill; four years after that, they sold the classic New York-style eatery to restaurateurs Joseph Carissimi and John Moss. Still in operation today, the Musso and Frank Grill has become one of the longest-running restaurants in the Los Angeles area.

After Carissimi and Moss purchased the restaurant in 1927, they began construction to renovate the space. They also refurbished the kitchen and added a state-of-the-art grill with cast-iron grates. Although its bars have bent a bit over the years, the original grill is still used today; all of the steaks prepared at the Musso and Frank Grill are seared on its blackened grates. Burning through about 250 pounds of mesquite wood per week, it can cook up to 80 items at one time, with a daily output of about 550. Its temperature ranges from 300°F to 600°F.

The restaurant has expanded a few times over the years. In 1934, the owners leased what they called the "Back Room," a legendary private space reserved for the Hollywood elite. When the lease expired on the space in 1955, a larger "New Room" was built, modeled after the original Back Room. Everything that could be removed from the Back Room, including the bar, chandeliers, coat racks, booths, and tables, was transferred to the New Room. Whatever could not be transferred was replicated as closely as possible—including the Back Room's skylights, which were recreated as faux skylights in the New Room to maintain the same feel.

Stepping into the Musso and Frank Grill is like walking back into the year 1919. The place remains virtually

Right: Joseph Carissimi, Joseph Musso, and Frank Toulet named their restaurant Frank's Francois Café before settling on the Musso and Frank Grill. ▪ *Opposite:* Legendary bartender Manny Aguirre pours a drink at the Musso and Frank Grill, 2012.

MUSSO & FRANK GRILL

Above: The Musso and Frank Grill on Hollywood Boulevard, 1930. ▪ *Opposite:* The oldest restaurant in Hollywood, 2013.

unchanged. Its high ceilings with tin inlay, its red, high-backed booths, and its dark mahogany wood are all still the same. The coat and hat racks that separate the booths are the same ones that were first installed in 1919. The front bar still has seats attached to it, like what you might see in a diner. The bartenders and waiters don the same short red jackets with black trim, crisp white shirts, neatly tied bow ties, center-pressed black pants, and spit-shined black shoes as they did the day the venue opened. The restaurant's pay phone was the first to be installed in Hollywood; this was where many industry deals were made.

Many claim to have seen and heard the ghosts of past patrons at the bar, such as Orson Welles and Charlie Chaplin. Some have seen faces in the mirrors while dining. Those who sit in booth 1 (Chaplin's favorite spot) sometimes feel a strange presence there, as well as variations in the temperature.

The restaurant was known as a writer's café, since many authors—including regulars like Nathanael West, F. Scott Fitzgerald, and Bill Lippman—created literary works while tucked away in the private, high-backed booths, working undisturbed for hours. On Saturdays, a big group of them would come in and sit around the large table in the Back Room. The *Los Angeles Times* once claimed that if you came to the Musso and Frank Grill every day since its opening day, you would encounter every major writer imaginable.

This place was not meant for the big parties that stars held at other famous establishments like Chasen's or Spago, but for good, hearty, honest food. Stars like Buddy Ebsen, Steve McQueen, Keith

Richards, and Johnny Depp were regulars (and always requested that Sergio Gonzalez be their waiter). Instead of entering through the front door on Hollywood Boulevard, they would use a back entrance and go through the busy kitchen. They could also see what Chef Jean Rue was creating for the day's special.

Like other restaurants frequented by the stars, the Musso and Frank Grill would reserve certain preferred tables for celebrities. Raymond Burr always sat at table 38, never at the bar. Elizabeth Taylor sat at table 34. Nancy Reagan preferred table 36, while Merv Griffin enjoyed table 37 with a glass of wine or a vodka tonic. Al Pacino used to sit in the corner at table 28, so he could see everyone who walked in. George Hamilton enjoyed eating at the bar. Legend has it that Charlie Chaplin once challenged Douglas Fairbanks to a horse race down Hollywood Boulevard, and the winner had to buy lunch at the restaurant. Chaplin won and ordered his favorite dish: grilled lamb kidneys.

Grilled lamb kidneys are still on the menu today, as are lamb shanks, braised short ribs, fillet of sole, and many of the other dishes that Chef Rue developed during his fifty-three years as head chef. It seems that Rue wasn't the only employee to make the restaurant his life's work. Chef Hellman served for thirty-one years. Indolfo Rodriquez has manned the behemoth grill since 1983. Ruben Rueda has been working at the restaurant for sixty years.

The Musso and Frank Grill is home to many generations. Today, the place is run by Musso's three granddaughters and their children. Chef JP Amateau is only the third chef to have held the position since the restaurant opened. It's in his blood; his father, Rod, a Hollywood writer and director, was a regular at the eatery. Waiter Sergio Gonzalez has been working at the Musso and Frank Grill for forty-one years; after stumbling upon the position by filling in for his uncle, it became the first and only job Gonzalez ever held in his life.

Because of the age of the restaurant and the operation of the bar before, during, and after Prohibition, drinks and cocktails are a major part of the dining experience at the Musso and Frank Grill. Behind the bar is Manny Aguirre, who has been the bartender at the establishment for more than twenty years. A star in his own right, he is known as the "Cocktail Ambassador of Hollywood" (and has printed pens to prove it). Once I sat at the bar in the Writer's Room and asked him if he made old-fashioneds. "I invented them!" he replied—and I would not doubt it. Manny can recall the stars' preferred drinks: Bette Davis liked a whiskey sours; Drew Barrymore favors champagne. Once, Francis Ford Coppola asked him why the restaurant didn't serve his namesake wine from Coppola Winery. The next week, it was on the wine list.

In 2013, the *New York Times* declared that the Musso and Frank Grill was one of the top ten "World's Greatest Old Dining Institutions," the only Southern California location on the list. In August 2012, the restaurant's Gibson made the list as one of the top twenty most iconic drinks in Los Angeles. It was also named the number-one spot to order a martini in L.A.

Today, the restaurant's motto is: "The history will bring you in; the food and service will keep you coming back." Nothing could be more true. ✗

Fillet of Sole in White Wine with Mushrooms

This dish is only on the restaurant's menu when fresh sole can be obtained.

Serves 6

2 tbsp. unsalted butter, softened
1 tbsp. freshly squeezed lemon juice
sea salt
12 oz. button mushrooms, sliced

6 fillets of sole
white pepper
½ cup dry white wine
1½ cups White Wine Sauce (recipe follows)

1. In a saucepan over medium heat, sauté the butter, lemon juice, and a pinch of salt. Add the mushrooms and sauté for 4 to 5 minutes, or until lightly golden. Transfer to a bowl and set aside.
2. Season the fish lightly with salt and pepper. Fold each fillet in half. Place one layer deep in the pan in which the mushrooms were sautéed. Add the wine, cover, and bring the liquid to a boil. Turn the heat to low and poach the fish just below the boiling point, until it flakes with a fork, about 10 minutes. Lift the fish out of the broth and place on a platter. Set aside.
3. Bring the leftover broth to a boil and reduce to one-third of the original volume. Stir in the White Wine Sauce, along with the mushrooms, and simmer for a minute or two. Pour over the fish.

White Wine Sauce

Makes 1½ cups

3 tbsp. unsalted butter, softened
2 shallots, minced
2 tbsp. all-purpose flour
½ cup dry white wine
½ cup whole milk, at room temperature
½ cup heavy cream, at room temperature
sea salt
white pepper

1. In a saucepan over medium heat, melt the butter, add the shallots, and cook for about 3 to 4 minutes, until golden. Stir in the flour, then the wine, milk, and cream.
2. Cook for 3 to 4 minutes, until smooth and thickened. Add salt and white pepper to taste. Simmer for 10 minutes.

Right: Charlie Chaplin and his wife, Paulette Goddard, at the Musso and Frank Grill. ▪ *Below:* The "Back Room" at the restaurant, 1934.

Lamb Shanks

Raymond Burr loved the flavor of these lamb shanks so much that the waiters at the Musso and Frank Grill didn't even need to ask the actor for his order when he came into the restaurant. They would simply bring him the dish.

Serves 4

4 lamb shanks
1 clove garlic, minced
sea salt
freshly ground black pepper
8 medium carrots, sliced into 1-inch pieces
8 small white onions
8 medium button mushrooms, caps only
1 stalk celery, sliced
8 oz. tomato sauce
1 cup peas (frozen, canned, or fresh)

1. Preheat the oven to 350°F.
2. Sprinkle the lamb with the garlic and season with salt and pepper. Place in a roasting pan and bake for 30 minutes, turning frequently to brown all sides.
3. Add the carrots, onions, mushroom caps, celery, and tomato sauce.
4. Increase the oven temperature to 375°F and roast for 30 minutes, then add the peas and cook for an additional 15 minutes, or until the meat is tender.

Braised Short Ribs

The chefs at the Musso and Frank Grill begin preparing this dish in the morning, so the ribs are nice and tender for the lunch crowd.

Serves 4 to 6

canola oil
6 lbs. beef short ribs
sea salt
freshly ground black pepper
all-purpose flour
1 large onion, diced
1 large carrot, diced
2 stalks celery, diced
8 oz. tomato sauce
boiling water

1. Coat the bottom of a Dutch oven with canola oil, add the meat, and brown the ribs on each side over high heat. Sprinkle with salt, pepper, and a little flour. Continue to cook until browned on all sides.
2. Add the onion, carrot, celery, and tomato sauce. Pour boiling water over to cover.
3. Cover and cook for 1½ to 2 hours, or until the meat is tender.

HORS D'OEUVRES

Appetizer, Frank ...60	Fruit Cocktail 65	Shrimp Cocktail 1.35
Celery en Branch ...50	Lobster Cocktail ...1.35	Varies, Half 90
Stuffed Celery 80	Crab Cocktail 1.35	Italian Sardines .. 80
Canape Anchovies ...95	Imported Italian	Italian Salami 60
Super Colossal	Antipasto 1.00	Hors d'Oeuvres ...1.75
Olives 50	Finest Sliced Smoked	Marinated Herring
Green Olives 50	Red Salmon in	with Sour Cream
Half Avocado 60	Olive Oil 75	Sauce 75
	Avocado Cocktail ...75	

SALADS

Hearts of Lettuce ...50	Lobster Salad 1.75	Hearts of Artichoke 1.50
Romaine Salad 50	Salad de Luxe 1.40	Shrimp Salad 1.50
Sliced Tomatoes ...60	Stuffed Tomato with	Crab Salad 1.50
Lettuce and Tomato ..60	Chicken or Shrimp 1.35	Shrimp Louie 1.60
Chef's Salad 1.10	Stuffed Tomato with	Crab or Lobster Louie 1.85
Combination Salad ..80	Crab 1.60	Musso-Frank Special 1.75
French Endive 1.35	Fruit Salad 1.00	Dinner Salad with
Chiffonade Salad 70	Avocado Salad 1.35	Roquefort Dressing..70
	Chicken Salad 1.35	

DRESSINGS

Roquefort 50	1000 Island 30	Anchovie 60

STEAKS AND CHOPS

Calf's Liver Steak 2.00	Pork Chops 2.00
Lamb Chops [3] 2.35	Broiled Lamb Kidneys, Bacon 1.85
Club Steak 2.90	Ham Steak 2.15
Sirloin N. Y. Cut 3.65	French Lamb Chops 2.75
Filet Mignon Steak 3.65;	Minute Steak 2.75
a la Frank 3.90	Half Chicken Saute, Jerusalem ..2.25
Tenderloin Steak 4.25	Ground Sirloin Steak 2.25
Double New York Cut ..7.25	Roast Whole Chicken en
Double Tenderloin Steak 8.50	Casserole, Parisienne 4.50

SAUCES

Creole 30	Bearnaise 70	Hollandaise 70
French Bordelaise 50	Fresh Mushroom Sauce ...70	

EGGS AND OMELETTES

Fried or Boiled 65	Ham and One Egg 1.00
Poached Eggs, Benedictine 1.60	Ham and Eggs 1.35
Poached on Toast [2] 70	Omelette with Cheese 1.20
Shirred 70	Ham Omelette 1.25
Scrambled [3] 95	Omelette with Fresh Tomato ..1.20
Bacon and Eggs 1.25	Onion or Parsley Omelette 1.15
Bacon or Sausage and One Egg ..1.00	Spanish Omelette 1.25
Asparagus Tips Omelette ...1.25	Omelette with Fresh Mushrooms ..1.75
Plain Omelette [3-Egg] 95	Eggs, Vienna 1.60

Full Order of Ham or Bacon .....1.35 Side Order of Ham or Bacon 75

Flannel or Wheat Cakes 60 [Served from 11:00 a.m. to 3 p.m.]

POTATOES

Boiled New 20	Mashed 20	Baked 50
Candied Sweet 40	Julienne 35	Hashed in Cream ..50
Long Branch 35	Lyonnaise 45	Cottage Fried 60
French Fried 35	Hashed Brown 40	Au Gratin 50
American Fried 40	O'Brien ... .45	

COLD MEATS (Served with Potato Salad)

Assorted Cold	Corned Beef 1.15	Roast Lamb 1.50
Meats 1.60	Sliced Chicken 1.60	Smoked Beef
Cold Roast Beef .. 2.00	Cold Ham 1.25	Tongue 1.25

SANDWICHES

Smoked Tongue ...60	Imported Sardine ...60	Tuna 65
American Cheese ...50	Ham 75	Chicken or Turkey ...95
Hot Cheese, Toast ... 65	Club House 1.25	Corned Beef 60

HOT SANDWICHES (Served with Mashed Potatoes)

Hot Tongue Sandwich 1.25	Hot Corned Beef Sandwich 1.55
Hot Roast Lamb Sandwich 1.75	Hot Chicken Sandwich 1.50
Hot Beef Sandwich 1.75	Hot Prime Rib Sandwich 2.25

COFFEE, TEA, ETC.

Cup of Coffee 10	Tea with Cream ...15	Glass Pure Cream ...50
Coffee [pot for 1] ...20	Cup of Chocolate 15	Glass of Milk 15
Iced Tea or Coffee ...15	Glass Milk, Cream ...25	Buttermilk 15
Postum, Cup 15	Sanka, Cup 15	

"We Serve Lipton's Tea"

NOT RESPONSIBLE FOR LOST ARTICLES   A FIFTY-CENT CHARGE ON ALL SPLIT ORDERS
We Reserve the Right to Refuse Service to Anyone
No Service Less Than 25c; at Tables 50c   Bread and Butter 15; with Checks under 50c

---

FISH
NO SUBSTITUTIONS, PLEASE

Fried Oysters 1.75	Oyster Stew, Cream 1.85
Oyster Stew ..1.50; ½ & ½ ..1.65	Fresh Half Cracked Crab 1.75
Oysters on the Half Shell ...1.75	Fried Shrimps or Scallops ..1.75
Filet of Sole, Margueri 1.90	Filet of Sandabs, Meuniere ...1.65
Swordfish, Broiled or Saute ...1.50	Fried Filet Sole, Tartar Sauce ...1.25
Filet of Sole au Gratin 1.60	Finnan Haddie 1.50
Baked Halibut, Italienne 1.60	Salmon Steak 1.50
Half Lobster 2.25	Abalone Steak, Saute Meuniere 1.80
Lobster Thermidore 2.50	Cherrystone Clams 1.65
Steamed Clams, Plain or Bordelaise 1.75	
Corvina Saute Meuniere or Broiled 1.50	
Fresh Colorado Mountain Trout, Saute Meuniere 1.85	

SOUP

Puree of Green Peas 30	Consomme with Printaniere 25
Jellied Consomme 30	
Cream of Tomato 30	Onion Soup au Gratin (10 minutes) 50

SPECIAL PLATE

Fried Calf's Liver with Onions, Assorted Vegetables ..1.95

READY ENTREES

Fresh Columbia River Smelts, Fried 1.10	
Fried Filet of Sole, Tartar Sauce 1.25	
Roast Capon with Dressing and Fresh Peas ...1.95	
Braised Short Ribs of Beef with Vegetables ...1.80	
Veal Fricassee with Mushrooms and Peas 1.35	
Roast Loin of Pork with Sweet Potatoes 1.80	
Roast Rack of Lamb, Casserole, Parisienne 1.95	
Pounded Steak with Lyonnaise Potatoes 1.90	
Fresh Mushroom Omelette 1.75	
Macaroni, Fresh Mushrooms ....1.10; au Gratin ..95	
Ravioli, Mushroom Sauce (10 Minutes) 95	
Spaghetti Italienne, Mushrooms or Tomato Sauce 90	
Fresh Vegetable Dinner 1.25 Chicken Enchilada, Chili 90	
Roast Prime Rib Sandwich with Mashed Potatoes ..2.25	

TO ORDER

Veal Scallopini Saute, Marsalla with Peas 2.50	
Broiled Squab with Bacon, Julienne Potatoes 2.90	
Chicken a la King 2.00	
Fresh Mushrooms on Toast 1.50	
Half Spring Chicken Saute, Provencale 2.25	
Lamb Kidneys Saute, Turbigo 1.85	
Grenadine of Beef, Bearnaise Sauce 2.65	
Fresh Shrimps, Sauce Poulette 2.00	
Calf's Brains, Milanaise Style 1.50	
Veal Cutlet, Milanaise Style 1.90	
Calf's Sweetbreads, Jardiniere 2.00	
Chicken Liver Omelette 1.75	
Welsh Rarebit 1.50	

ROASTS

Roast Prime Rib of Beef au Jus 2.80	
Roast Spring Lamb with Mint Jelly 1.80	

VEGETABLES

Fresh String Beans ...30	Zucchini, Florentine ..50	Canned Asparagus,
Corn Saute with	Boiled Onions in	(Hot or Cold) 50
Green Pepper ...35	Cream 40	French Fried Onions ..50
Creamed Spinach ...35	Zucchini Saute 50	Stewed Tomatoes ...30
	Fresh Green Peas 35	Fried Egg Plant 40
		Spinach, Plain 30

Broccoli, Butter Sauce 50; with Hollandaise Sauce 70

DESSERTS

Diplomat Pudding ...30	Custard Pie 35	Cheese Cake 50
Caramel Custard 30	Boston Cream Pie 35	French Pastry 45
Baba au Rhum 50	Black Bottom Pie 50	Zambalione 1.00
Jell-O 30	Pound Cake 30	Butterscotch Sundae .35
Apple Pie 35	Fruit Compote 35	Parfait (all flavors) ..50
Spumoni Ice Cream ..50	Preserved Pineapple 35	Raspberry or
Musso-Franks Torten 50	French Vanilla 30	Pineapple Sherbet 30
Pumpkin Pie 35	Baked Apple 40	Chocolate Ice Cream 30
Old Fashion Strawberry Short Cake 50		

Coconut Custard Pie 35   ½ Cantaloupe 35

CHEESE

American Cheese 30	Camembert Cheese ..40	Cottage Cheese 35
Roquefrot Cheese ...60		Swiss Cheese 40

We Attribute Our Success to Our Quality Meats Colored Poultry and Fresh Eggs Used the Year Around Plus Our Good Cooking from 1919 to 1954

Flannel or Wheat Cakes (Served from 7 a. m. to 3 p. m.)

Toasted French Bread 25c

Cocoanut Grove
at the Ambassador Hotel

OPEN: 1921–1989

LOCATION: 3400 Wilshire Boulevard
Los Angeles, CA 90010

ORIGINAL PHONE: DRexel 7000

CUISINE: California-French Fusion

DESIGN: Myron Hunt (original design);
Paul Revere Williams (extensive interior/
exterior renovations)

BUILDING STYLE: Spanish Revival and Art Deco

CURRENTLY: Robert F. Kennedy Community Schools

THE AMBASSADOR HOTEL WAS ONE OF THE MOST HISTORIC HOTELS ON THE WEST COAST. It was infamous for its celebrity clientele and as the location of Robert F. Kennedy's assassination. With its grand pools and palm-lined property, the twenty-four-acre Ambassador complex was the epitome of the California lifestyle.

The hotel was part of the Ambassador Hotels System, which at one time consisted of sixty-seven properties from coast to coast (the chain was dissolved in the 1930s). A city in itself, the hotel had a whopping 1,200 rooms and bungalows, plus golf courses, tennis courts, and Olympic-size pools. The arcade contained thirty-seven specialty shops, including dress shops, a post office, a hat shop, jewelry shops, a men's cigar shop, an art gallery, and a British and European import shop called the Continental.

Many guests stayed at the property year-round. It was not uncommon for a celebrity to live at the Ambassador while filming or working. Howard Hughes and Charlie Chaplin lived there for a while. In 1927, F. Scott Fitzgerald and his wife, Zelda, moved into one of the bungalows on the property and reportedly trashed it. Rumor has it that they started fires in the bungalow and also burned their bill. Preparing for the 1928 Summer Olympics, Egyptian swimmer Farid Simaika used the Ambassador Swimming Club for his practices. In 1933, Amelia Earhart checked into the hotel for a short stay. In 1945, Emmeline Snively of the Blue Book Modeling Agency, which had offices on the premises, signed Norma Jeane Baker, who later changed her name to Marilyn Monroe. Baker paid $100 for makeup, beauty, fashion, and charm lessons from the agency, all deducted from her first salary.

The World Famous Cocoanut Grove · Los Angeles Ambassador

Above: The sprawling grounds of the Ambassador Hotel, home of the Cocoanut Grove nightclub, 1943. ▪ *Opposite:* Actor and producer Ross Hunter with his date at the Cocoanut Grove entrance, 1948.

The Ambassador also hosted many heads of state from every corner of the globe, as well as seven American presidents. In 1952, vice presidential nominee Richard Nixon wrote his famous "Checkers" speech in one of the suites. It was later broadcast live from the former El Capitan Theatre (now the Avalon Theatre) in Hollywood, with only Nixon and his wife, Patricia, who was off-camera, sitting on the stage.

During the 1920s, countless celebrities frequented the Ambassador's Cocoanut Grove nightclub, including Louis B. Mayer, Douglas Fairbanks, Howard Hughes, Norma Talmadge, Clara Bow, Mary Pickford, Charlie Chaplin, Rudolph Valentino, and Joan Crawford. When the hotel first opened its doors, the owners realized that its Zinnia Grill nightclub was not large enough for both their guests and the locals. Only a few months later, they converted the grand ballroom into the lavish, 1,000-seat Cocoanut Grove. Upon their arrival, guests were led down a majestic staircase into a large ballroom decorated with mechanical monkeys swinging from full-size palm trees, purchased after their use in Rudolph Valentino's 1921 movie *The Sheik*. The nightclub's ceiling was scattered with "stars," and a waterfall flowed in the back of the room. The Grove hosted many famous performers, including Richard Pryor, Barbra Streisand, Judy Garland, Lena Horne, Bing Crosby, Merv Griffin, Nat King Cole, Frank Sinatra, the Supremes, Benny Goodman, Liza Minnelli, Vikki Carr, Sonny and Cher, and Liberace.

The Grove was also a French dinner club where Chef Henri used West Coast staples like citrus fruits and other fresh produce to create a California-French fusion cuisine. Despite the mass quantities of food that came out of the kitchen, the dishes were known for being very inventive and flavorful.

For those wanting something lighter, the hotel also offered the Palm Bar & Coffee Shop, which architect Paul Revere Williams designed with the help of interior designer Don Loper. You can see the final iteration of the Palm in the 1996 film *That Thing You Do*.

In 1930, the Ambassador hosted the second Academy Awards; the hotel would host the event seven more times in the thirteen years that followed. During World War II, the hotel was used for countless fundraisers in the war effort, and the Cocoanut Grove became a hot spot for men and women on leave from the military.

On August 23, 1964, the Ambassador canceled a reservation for the Beatles because the hotel was packed with fans and security could not be guaranteed. Luckily, British actor Reginald Owen rented his Bel-Air mansion at 356 Saint Pierre Road to the Beatles for $1,000. That evening, the Beatles performed a sold-out concert at the Hollywood Bowl.

It wasn't all glitz and glamour at the Ambassador, however.

Left: **Constance Bennett and Marquis Henry de La Falaise at a party for Marion Davies at the Ambassador, 1931.** ▪ *Opposite top:* **Inside the Cocoanut Grove, 1939.** ▪ *Opposite bottom:* **Harold Lloyd and Mildred Davis on the Ambassador's front lawn, 1923.**

It was also the site of a horrific crime that convulsed the nation. On June 5, 1968, Senator Robert F. Kennedy stepped off the podium in the Ambassador's Embassy Room ballroom after a brief victory speech. He had just won the California Democratic presidential primary election. Passing through the pantry area of the hotel's main kitchen on his way to the press area, Kennedy was shot three times, along with five other people, with a .22 caliber Ivan-Johnson Cadet revolver. Palestinian immigrant Sirhan Sirhan was arrested at the scene and later convicted of the murder. Kennedy died from his injuries twenty-six hours later at the Good Samaritan Hospital. The other victims survived. Ever since that incident, the U.S. Secret Service has provided protection for presidential candidates. The hotel's former location on Wilshire Boulevard was renamed "Robert F. Kennedy Parkway."

In another instance of macabre notoriety, the jury members in the Charles Manson trial were sequestered at the Ambassador. The jury's seven men and five women spent a costly 225 days at the hotel during the 1971 trial.

A very special employee at the hotel was Arthur Nyhaden Jr., the doorman who manned the Ambassador's front doors from 1949 to 1989. He was the first person guests came in contact with upon their arrival at the Ambassador, and he could recall the details, preferences, and confidences of thousands of the hotel's long-standing guests from memory. Art wore a black tie adorned with keepsake pins from every point on the globe that guests had brought back to him from their travels. Over the forty years that he worked for the hotel, Art only missed three days of work.

The demise of the Ambassador and the surrounding neighborhood began in the 1970s, when gang and drug problems grew severe. The Cocoanut Grove was renovated in the mid-1970s, but it didn't help. The

hotel checked out its last guest in 1989.

The Ambassador was said to be the most-used filming location that wasn't at a major studio. More than 120 motion pictures, music videos, and television shows were filmed there. In the 1967 film *The Graduate*, the Ambassador stood in for the Taft Hotel, where Mrs. Robinson and Ben Braddock had their affair. In 1990, the hotel established a private company, Ambassador Films, to lease the hotel for film production. In 1992's *Sister Act*, Whoopi Goldberg fled the Mob through the same kitchen where Robert Kennedy had been shot. Two hotel rooms were used as Gary Sinise and Kevin Bacon's "apartments" in *Apollo 13*. Fittingly, *Bobby* was the last film shot there, in 2006, while other sections of the hotel were being demolished.

During this time, private groups and event promoters were allowed to rent out the ballrooms or even the Cocoanut Grove for dances, parties, and other events. In 1992, I was fortunate enough to attend a Halloween party at the Grove. As I wandered the halls of the shopping arcade and the lobby area, I hoped the Ambassador would return to its former glory.

In 2004 and 2005, the hotel was restricted from filming because of a legal struggle between the Los Angeles Unified School District (LAUSD) and Sirhan Sirhan, who wanted to conduct more testing in the

Above: Postcard featuring the Cocoanut Grove, circa 1962. ▪ *Right:* Thelma Todd and Pat DiCicco at the Ambassador before Todd's mysterious death a short time later, 1935. ▪ *Opposite top:* Charles MacArthur, Norma Shearer, Jimmy Stewart, and Helen Hayes MacArthur, 1938. ▪ *Opposite bottom:* On location at the Ambassador for the film *Foolish Wives*, 1921.

pantry where Robert F. Kennedy had been shot. When the hotel was razed beginning in 2005, the pantry was dismantled and placed in storage, where it remains today.

In 1998, after almost ten years of proposing to build the world's tallest building on the site of the Ambassador, Donald Trump blamed the LAUSD for ruining his investment and pulled out of the purchasing talks. The LAUSD had put up a $50 million dollar deposit for the site. Part of the deal of sale to the LAUSD was that many of the elements of historical value in the building would be preserved and used in the new school. These terms were agreed upon, but when demolition started they found that the areas they had planned on saving were not structurally sound.

I personally watched the demolition from across the street a few times in the first part of 2006. The agreement was for the Cocoanut Grove to be saved for the school auditorium, and the Palm Bar & Coffee Shop would be turned into a teachers' lounge and café. Based on what was possible, the original terms of preservation were altered to reflect that they would incorporate "working original elements" into the design of the new campus.

Today, the campus is called the Robert F. Kennedy Community Schools. Six schools sit on the property. The north side of the campus resembles the original hotel façade. The front lawn is now the school's sports field, and there is also a small park with quotes from Kennedy adorning its front gates on Wilshire. ✄

Above: **Henry Fonda making a promotional appearance for** *The Best Man* **at the Ambassador, 1962.** ▪ *Opposite left:* **William Demarest, Jerry Lewis, and William Bendix at a wrap party for** *The Errand Boy,* **1959.** ▪ *Opposite right:* **Guest of honor Claudette Colbert, 1934.** ▪ *Opposite bottom:* **Guests at a 1933 party, including: Josef von Sternberg (***top row, center***); Leo Carillo, Marlene Dietrich, Jean Harlow, and Joan Blondell (***middle row, center***); John Boles (***front row, far left***); and Dolores del Rio, Edward G. Robinson, and Heather Angel (***front row, second, third, and fourth from right***).**

Beef Short Ribs with Brown Gravy

These delicious ribs were a staple on the Cocoanut Grove's menu.

Serves 6

6 (12 oz.) beef short ribs
sea salt
freshly ground black pepper
fresh rosemary
1 cup diced celery
1 cup diced carrot
½ cup red wine
Brown Gravy (recipe follows)

1. Preheat the oven to 350°F.
2. Place the ribs in a shallow baking pan, sprinkle with salt, pepper, and rosemary, and place the celery and carrot pieces around them. Roast for 1 hour.
3. Add the red wine and Brown Gravy to the pan, cover with foil, and roast for an additional 1½ hours, or until the meat is tender when a fork is inserted.

Brown Gravy

Makes about 3 cups

6 tbsp. unsalted butter, softened
6 tbsp. all-purpose flour
14 oz. chicken broth
14 oz. beef broth
1 tbsp. beef concentrate (or one bullion cube)
sea salt
freshly ground black pepper

1. In a saucepan over medium heat, melt the butter and stir in the flour until smooth and pale golden.
2. Whisk in the chicken broth, beef broth, and beef concentrate until blended. Bring to a boil and simmer for 10 minutes. Season to taste with salt and pepper as needed.

C O C O A N U T   G R O V E

Bread Pudding

When the Cocoanut Grove hosted large banquets, this bread pudding was a mainstay of the menu. It was also a very popular late night snack at the Palm Bar & Coffee Shop.

Serves 8

6 large eggs
4 cups whole milk
1 tsp. pure vanilla extract
¾ cup granulated sugar
½ tsp. ground nutmeg
1 lb. white bread, cubed
½ tsp. ground cinnamon
¼ cup sweetened coconut flakes

1. Preheat the oven to 325°F. Butter a 2-quart baking dish and set aside.
2. In a bowl, whisk together the eggs, milk, vanilla, sugar, and nutmeg. Mix in the bread cubes. Place in the prepared pan and sprinkle the top with the cinnamon and coconut.
3. Bake until set, 40 to 45 minutes. Serve warm.

Tam O'Shanter Inn

OPEN: 1922–present

LOCATION: 2980 Los Feliz Boulevard
Los Angeles, CA 90039

ORIGINAL PHONE: OL-0228

CURRENT PHONE: (323) 664-0228

CUISINE: British Pub Fare

DESIGN: Harry Oliver

BUILDING STYLE: Storybook

THE TAM O'SHANTER IS SAID TO BE THE LONGEST-RUNNING SAME-LOCATION, SAME-FAMILY-OWNED RESTAURANT IN LOS ANGELES. Two families, the Van de Kamps and the Franks (of the now-famous Van de Kamp's Holland Dutch Bakeries and Lawry's Restaurants, Inc.), opened the Scottish pub-themed Tam O'Shanter in 1922. The restaurant has been rechristened several times—first named the Tam O'Shanter, then the Montgomery Inn, then the Tam O'Shanter again, then the Great Scot, and then finally the Tam O'Shanter again in 1968.

Motion picture art director Harry Oliver, who worked on such films as *Ben-Hur* and *Scarface*, was commissioned to build the Tam O'Shanter. Oliver, who also designed the famous Witch's House in Beverly Hills, hired carpenters from a nearby studio to char the inn's wooden planks to create a weather-beaten effect. Thanks to this technique, the planks have never had to be painted and only look better with age.

The Tam was built on a dirt road named Tropico Avenue (now Los Feliz Boulevard), in an area that was originally on the outskirts of Los Angeles. The neighborhood around the restaurant soon grew into what the motion picture studios nicknamed "On Location"—off of studio property, but still close by.

Having lunch at the Tam was like being in a backlot commissary. It was not uncommon to spot Mary Pickford, the Keystone Kops, Tom Mix in his leather chaps and ten-gallon hat, or Fatty Arbuckle in his suit and tie. John Wayne was a frequent diner in his later years; his table was number 15 in the Tartan Room.

With the original Walt Disney Studios about half a mile away, Walt Disney himself also had a regular table at the Tam: number 31, which now displays a plaque that reads, "This was a favorite spot of Walt Disney and his Imagineers." Disney was such a frequent visitor that some called the restaurant "the Walt Disney Studios commissary." Today, two of Disney's autographed sketches hang in the lobby: one of Lawrence Frank with Mickey, Minnie, Goofy, Donald, and Tinkerbell, and another of Richard Frank and his son, Richard Jr., sitting at a table with half a dozen Mickeys (one for each decade that both the Tam and Disney had been around). Upstairs, near the employee changing area, are framed photographs of some of Disney's "Nine Old Men" (the Walt Disney Company's famed animators) hamming it up for the camera. These are some of the last pictures taken of them together.

Opposite: A tartan-clad server at the Tam O'Shanter, 1930s.

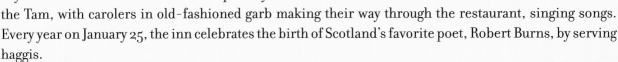

Considered one of the first themed restaurants in the country, the Tam O'Shanter hasn't wavered from its original 1922 vision, featuring medieval weapons, coats of arms, and family crests. Three roaring fireplaces and a large pub welcome you in the lobby. The restaurant's "snug" displays awards won by the eatery, Scottish tartans, and lively decor. A large red display case houses old menus, photos, napkins, and other memorabilia. Because of its historical look and feel, the Tam has been used in many film and television productions—most recently for one of the final episodes of AMC's *Mad Men*, in which it played a steak house where Don Draper ate lunch.

The Tam O'Shanter pulls out all the stops for holiday celebrations. Christmastime is especially festive at the Tam, with carolers in old-fashioned garb making their way through the restaurant, singing songs. Every year on January 25, the inn celebrates the birth of Scotland's favorite poet, Robert Burns, by serving haggis.

The restaurant's menu, which features both British pub fare and American favorites, has not changed much over the years. Baked chicken and ham have always been mainstays. Box lunches, such as burgers with coleslaw, are available for picnicking at nearby Griffith Park. On Dodger game days, the Tam offers special menus with free bags of roasted peanuts, making it easy to get over to Chavez Ravine in time for the first pitch.

Today, meals at the Tam start off with bread hot from the oven—pumpernickel and sourdough. Two of the most popular items on the menu are the prime rib with Yorkshire pudding and the "toad in the hole" (sausages in Yorkshire batter). The creamed horseradish is the same recipe that was served in 1922. After all, when you've found a good thing, why change it? ✂

Above: **Walt Disney's sketch of Lawrence Frank with Disney characters, 1958.** ▪ *Left:* **Walt Disney, Lawrence Frank, and Harry Oliver at the Tam O'Shanter, 1960.** ▪ *Opposite top:* **The dining room at the Tam, 1939.** ▪ *Opposite bottom:* **Postcard featuring the Tam, 1933.**

Coleslaw with Peanuts

This tasty coleslaw is served alongside the Tam O'Shanter's incredible hamburgers.

Serves 4 to 6

4 cups shredded white cabbage
½ cup chopped green onion, including green tops
1 cup chopped celery
¼ cup chopped cocktail peanuts
½ tsp. seasoned salt
¼ tsp. seasoned pepper
⅓ cup Italian salad dressing

1. In a large salad bowl, toss together the cabbage, onion, celery, and peanuts.
2. Sprinkle with seasoned salt and pepper. Toss evenly with the Italian dressing and serve.

Above: The Tam O'Shanter as it appears today.
Opposite: The Tam in 1931, when it offered car service.

Thousand Island Dressing

Arguably the most versatile of dressings, Thousand Island works on everything from hamburgers to fancy Crab Louis salads. The Tam O'Shanter tops its hamburgers with this dressing.

Serves 8 to 10

½ large hard-boiled egg, chopped
¼ cup canned beets, chopped
3 tbsp. minced green bell pepper
1 tsp. chopped black olives
1½ cups mayonnaise
4 tsp. chili sauce
1 tbsp. ketchup
¼ cup tomato juice

1. In a large bowl, combine the egg, beets, bell pepper, olives, mayonnaise, chili sauce, ketchup, and tomato sauce. Refrigerate until needed.

SOUPS

Soup du jour 10

Split Pea with Croutons 15

SALADS
All Salads served with Buttered Toasted Roll

Chef's Salad Bowl 40	Lettuce and Tomato 50
Chef's Salad with Chicken . . .60	Tomato Sliced 50
Chicken 60	Cottage Cheese 40
Sun-Kissed Salad 50	Heart of Lettuce 35

HOT SANDWICHES
Served with Olive and Relish

Hamburger 30

Fried Egg 25

Fried Egg and Bacon 35

WAFFLES
Served with syrup or honey and butter

Waffle 30

Waffle with Walnuts 40

Waffle with One Egg .40; 2 Eggs . . .50

Waffle with Bacon 50

EGGS

Eggs with Bacon 65
Served with Potatoes and Toast

Eggs with Ham 65
Served with Potatoes and Toast

Fried, Boiled or Scrambled 40
With Toast and Potatoes

Poached Eggs on Toast with Potatoes . . .40

Omelette, plain; with Toast and Potatoes . .40

Eggs with Little Pig Sausages 65
With Hash Browned or Mashed Potatoes and Buttered Toasted Roll.

TOAST

Dry or Buttered 10	Milk Toast 30
Dry or Buttered, with Marmalade 20	Milk Toast—Half Milk, Half Cream 35
Cinnamon 25	Dry Cereal with Cream . . .15
French Toast 35	Coffee Cake 10

COLD SANDWICHES (Plain or Toasted)
Served with Olive and Relish

Bacon and Tomato 40

Lettuce, Tomato, and Mayonnaise 35

Peanut Butter 20

Chicken 65

Chicken Salad 40

HOT CAKES
Served with syrup or honey and butter

Hot Cakes 30

Hot Cakes with One Egg .40; 2 Eggs . . .50

Hot Cakes with Bacon 50

DESSERTS

Pie 15

Ice Creams, various flavors . . .15

Sherbet 15

Maple Walnut Sundae 25

Chocolate Sundae 20

Chocolate Nut Sundae 25

Hot Chocolate Fudge Sundae . . .30

DRINKS

Coffe, cup 10	Milk and Churned Buttermilk .10	Ovaltine—Cold, Glass . . .20	Coca Cola 10
Tea, pot 10	Pure Orange Juice . . .15	Postum 10	Root Beer 10
Ice Tea 10	Lemonade 15	Malted Milk 25	
Iced Coffee 10	Fresh Limeade 15	Tam o' Shanter Cooler . .20	Frosted Root Beer 20
Chocolate 15	Ovaltine—Hot, Cup . . .15	Milk Shake 25	Scotch Drink . . . . .FREE

100% Beef . . .

HAMBURGER

The same fine-quality beef that made the Inn renowned since 1922. Freshly-ground, virtually to your individual order.

HAMBURGER STEAK with vegetables 65c

Onions if desired. Hash Browned or Mashed Potatoes and Buttered Toasted Roll

---

CHEF'S SALAD BOWL 40

SUN-KISSED SALAD 50
Segments of Grapefruit, Orange and Avocado, with Buttered Toasted Roll.

WAFFLES, Tam o' Shanter Style . . .30
Served with Syrup (or honey) and butter

SPECIAL SPAGHETTI, Tam o' Shanter Style 50
Allow 12 minutes for cooking Spaghetti. Served with Fresh Mushroom Sauce, Parmesan Cheese and Buttered Toasted Roll.

HOT CAKES Tam o' Shanter Style . .30
Served with Syrup (or honey) and butter

BAKED CHICKEN PIE . . .75

Tender, flavorful chicken, complemented by potatoes, peas and carrots; served with a buttered toasted roll.

ENTREES
All Meat Orders Served With Buttered Toasted Roll.

Special Spaghetti, Tam o' Shanter Style Allow 12 minutes for cooking Spaghetti. Served with Fresh Mushroom Sauce, Parmesan Cheese and Buttered Toasted Roll.	.50
Special Spaghetti, Tam o'Shanter Style with Meat Balls Allow 12 minutes for cooking Spaghetti. Served with Fresh Mushroom Sauce, Parmesan Cheese and Buttered Toasted Roll.	.70
Hamburger Steak with or without Onions Hash Browned or Mashed Potatoes and Buttered Toasted Roll.	.55
Hamburger Steak with Fresh Vegetable Hash Browned or Mashed Potatoes and Buttered Toasted Roll.	.65
Hamburger Steak with Chili-Beans Hash Browned or Mashed Potatoes and Buttered Toasted Roll.	.65
Chili and Beans, with Crackers	.30
Tamale with Chili Beans	.50
Meat Balls, with Fresh Mushroom Sauce and Buttered Toasted Roll Hash Browned or Mashed Potatoes and Buttered Toasted Roll.	.55
Meat Balls, with Mashed Potatoes, Fresh Vegetable and Buttered Toasted Roll	.70
Little Pig Sausages and Eggs Hash Browned or Mashed Potatoes and Buttered Toasted Roll.	.65

WE RESERVE THE RIGHT TO REFUSE SERVICE TO ANYONE   NOT RESPONSIBLE FOR LOST ARTICLES

OPEN DAILY 11:30 A. M., CLOSE DAILY 9 P. M.; SATURDAYS, 10 P. M.
CLOSED TUESDAYS

All prices listed are ceiling prices—which means the highest prices prevailing from April 4 to 10.

11-20-44

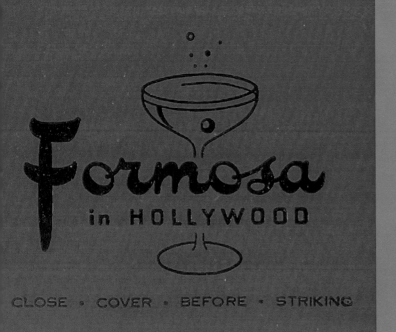

Formosa Café

OPEN: 1925–2016

LOCATION: 7156 Santa Monica Boulevard
Los Angeles, CA 90046

ORIGINAL PHONE: HO 2-9992

CURRENT PHONE: (323) 850-9050

CUISINE: California and Chinese

BUILDING STYLE: Train Car

IN 1919, MARY PICKFORD AND DOUGLAS FAIRBANKS BOUGHT A STUDIO ON EIGHTEEN ACRES OF LAND IN THE LOS ANGELES SUBURBS FROM SILENT FILMMAKER JESSE DURHAM HAMPTON. Pickford-Fairbanks Studios, as they called it, was located at 7200 Santa Monica Boulevard. Later, the studio evolved into the United Artists Studio, and then Warner Hollywood Studios. Today, it's known simply as The Lot.

Across the street from this studio, a tiny eatery called the Red Post Café sat for a number of years, serving breakfast and lunch in its cramped space. In 1925, New York prizefighter Jimmy Bernstein bought the little restaurant and named it the Formosa Café. In order to add more space and serve more people, Bernstein affixed a red train car to one side of the building.

Because of its proximity to the studio, the Formosa saw its share of movie and television stars. Its walls were lined with over a thousand 8 x 10 glossies of every star known to man, from the iconic (John Wayne) to the more recently iconic (Johnny Depp). The café's two slogans were also posted on an inside wall: "Meet Me at the Formosa" and "Where the Stars Dine." The Formosa itself appeared in many films, including *L.A. Confidential*, *Swingers*, and *The Majestic*.

In 1945, Bernstein brought on Hong Kong-born chef Lem Quon as his partner. It was a perfect business relationship, with Quon running the kitchen and Bernstein at the front of the restaurant, greeting customers and running the staff. The partnership lasted thirty-one years.

Over the years, the Formosa changed its menu from bistro-style meals, to Asian cuisine, to California-style fare. If your grandparents had dined at the Formosa in their day, they would have eaten steaks and slow-cooked, braised meats; your parents, on the other hand, would have seen the introduction of Asian cuisine at the café, such as noodle bowls and raw fish dishes. In its later years, fresh farm-to-table ingredients were used in the Formosa's kitchen.

The Formosa saw its fair share of controversy. On October 23, 1944, with the war still going strong, the café was closed down for the night when sisters Francis

Opposite: **The Formosa Café on Santa Monica Boulevard, 1999.**

and Betty Malson were arrested for selling "set-ups" after hours. On April 4, 1950, about an hour prior to opening, a "baby-faced" gunman (as Bernstein described him) came in through the café's back door and demanded about $1,500 in cash and checks (the equivalent of about $14,000 today). For years, Los Angeles gangster Johnny Stompanato and his lover, actress Lana Turner, frequented the Formosa for their "back room" meetings with Johnny's boss, mobster Mickey Cohen. In 1952, Cohen's arrest for tax evasion put an end to those meetings.

When Bernstein died in 1976, Quon became the sole owner of the café. In the last years of Quon's life, he arrived at the café every morning at around 5:00 AM to have coffee and breakfast, and worked until 9:00 PM, managing the kitchen and staff from his favorite corner booth (which also happened to have been Ava Gardner's favorite). In December of 1993, Quon passed away from chronic heart failure. Before its closure, the café was run by Quon's grandson, Vince Jung.

The Formosa fought two major threats in its near-century of existence. In 1991, the Friends of the Formosa preservation group was formed to fight Warner Bros., which owned the property the café sat on at the time and wanted to turn it into a parking lot. Actors and other frequenters of the café got involved, and the Formosa was saved; the parking lot was constructed a few blocks down from the eatery instead. In 2001, another fight to save the Formosa ensued when the West Hollywood Gateway Center—a two-story shopping center that would take up a full city block—was proposed. Although the Formosa was left alone, it was suddenly in the middle of West Hollywood's largest shopping complex.

Lacking customers, the Formosa paired up with the Red Medicine Restaurant team in early 2014 to revamp its menu, calling it "Red Med at the Formosa." Although the café's new offerings were well-received, the partnership lasted only three months. The Formosa then brought in sixth-place *Top Chef* winner Brian Huskey, who added eclectic dishes to the menu like Korean brisket with Asian slaw and fried chicken sliders with sweet potato and sambal aioli. They also put *On the Rocks* winner Joseph Brooke behind the bar, where he whipped up tasty, Asian-themed concoctions like the Canton Iced Tea (which contained jasmine and black teas mixed with vodka, lemon, mint, and soda). This team lasted a few years.

In July 2015, the inside of the Formosa went through a complete transformation. All of the 8 x 10 glossies were taken down, the red interior was painted a battleship gray, and a rooftop garden bar was added. The menu changed drastically, featuring new items like microbrew beers and toasted cheese sandwiches. In the last months of 2016, the restaurant quietly closed its doors. Rumors of its imminent reopening, however, continue to make news in the Los Angeles restaurant world.

Many thought of the Formosa as just a dive bar, while others appreciated its historical value. Lem Quon felt that the Formosa's success was due to the fact that everyone who came into the restaurant was treated like a star. "I never looked down on people," he told the *Los Angeles Times*. "Here at the Formosa, we always make small people feel like big stars. We are all the same." ✕

Below and opposite: Outside the Formosa, 2006.

Mai Tai

It's been said that Don the Beachcomber made very first mai tai, but this version is unique to the Formosa.

Serves 1

1 large, tall glass filled with crushed ice
3 oz. 151 rum
1 oz. amaretto liqueur
½ medium lime
½ medium orange, juiced
1 splash pineapple juice

1. Pour the rum and amaretto into a tall glass filled with ice. Mix in the orange juice and squeeze the lime juice on top. Pour in the pineapple juice, and stir.
2. Decorate with citrus wedges.

The dark red interior of the Formosa, lined with 8 x 10 glossies, 1991.

House Rules:

1. ✿ Means Hot and Spicy. Yet, We do cater to your taste, in terms of spicyness. Please ask your server for special request.

2. Most dishes are designed and served as is. Special request may be charged minute amount in addition to the original price. Please feel free to do so.

3. We'll have house speciality on sale periodically. Please ask your server for information.

4. We'll prepare special items for you with advance ordering for ex. Peking duck, live sea food ..... etc. You would not want us to kill a tyrannsaurus for a mere 10 oz Dino steak in two minutes. Would you?

5. We do not add M.S.G. in our food while cooking. So, Relax and enjoy your food.

6. The house do not responsible for personal belongings Please look after them while you're in "Formosa" Thats including kids, However, we'll do our best to keep them in good shape while in our custody.

7. We aim to please, if we do step on a toe, Please let us know! We can either transplant from J.F.K. or cut it off for you. Suggestions and Recommondations will be greatly appreciated!

The Brown Derby

OPEN: 1926–1985

LOCATION: 3427 Wilshire Boulevard
Los Angeles, CA 90010

ORIGINAL PHONE: OX-5151

CUISINE: American

DESIGN: Carl Jules Weyl

BUILDING STYLE: Roadside Vernacular

CURRENTLY: Equitable Life Building

THE FIRST BROWN DERBY RESTAURANT OPENED IN 1926, ACROSS THE STREET FROM THE AMBASSADOR HOTEL ON WILSHIRE BOULEVARD. Designed by Carl Jules Weyl, the art director for such films as *Casablanca* and *The Big Sleep*, the eatery was shaped like an enormous derby hat. In an era when it was common for establishments to be built in the shape of what they were selling, many thought that the Brown Derby was a haberdashery at first.

The Derby did well in its first couple of years and opened a second location at 1628 Vine Street in 1929, on Valentine's Day. While the first location was famous for its hat-like shape, the second Brown Derby, which was close to Paramount Studios, Sunset Gower Studios, and Hollywood Center Studios, was known for its celebrity clientele. The restaurant was a tempting alternative to the studio commissaries. The booths along the north wall were reserved for A-listers. At lunchtime, it was not surprising to see Tyrone Power eating boiled brisket of beef, Janet Gaynor devouring her favorite turkey burger, Claudette Colbert savoring chicken hash, Eddie Cantor finishing off a hamburger steak, or Al Jolson eating chicken chow mein.

Jack Berry and Mary Livingston, who broadcast their radio show close by, often came into the Derby for lunch. They collected a lot of their material from the stars and other patrons at the restaurant, and even wrote radio scripts there. Gossip columnists Louella Parsons and Hedda Hopper were also common fixtures at the restaurant, holding court close to the Hollywood action. Every Wednesday at noon, you could find the Hollywood Women's Press Club, an informal group of female reporters and writers, gathering at the Derby to get the latest scoop on Hollywood society. As Joan Crawford said about the Derby in the 1945 film *Mildred Pierce*, "People have to drink somewhere. Why not here?"

The Brown Derby was the birthplace of the Cobb salad, named after the restaurant's owner, Robert Cobb. The story goes that, in the early 1930s, Sid Grauman, the owner of Grauman's Chinese Theater on Hollywood Boulevard, came into the Derby late one night (the restaurant stayed opened until 4:00 AM), asking for something to eat. Robert Cobb threw together leftovers out of the icebox: a salad of lettuce, watercress, chicory, and romaine, topped with diced turkey, bacon, blue cheese, hard-boiled eggs, sliced tomatoes, and avocados. He drenched it in French dressing and tossed everything in a bowl.

The Cobb salad was a hit. It put the Brown Derby on the map, and stars began coming to the restaurant

Above: Postcard featuring the original Brown Derby on Wilshire Boulevard, late 1940s. ▪ *Opposite:* Desi Arnaz and Lucille Ball at the Brown Derby, 1952.

by the busload. Every day, the Derby's awning-covered entry was packed with fans, as if it were the venue of a red carpet event.

"It is not only a place to meet and talk over contracts and plan divorces and further romance under the bronze derby-hatted lights," a 1932 article in *Star Gazer* magazine read, "it is also a place to eat. It is famous both as the spot where Jim Tully battled Jack Gilbert and the spot where you can get Special Hamburger brought sizzling to the table, in copper frying pans. It is a place where the stars gather at lunch time and after premieres to be seen—and to relish some caviar."

In 1937, the original Brown Derby moved a block down the street to make way for new construction, settling in at 3377 Wilshire Boulevard. Although the Derby opened other locations in Los Feliz (4500 Los Feliz Boulevard) and Beverly Hills (9537 Wilshire Boulevard), the original restaurant was the only one built in the shape of a derby hat.

The restaurant served a broad and varied menu. Sunday was paprika chicken. Tuesday was declared Meatless Tuesday by the mayor of Los Angeles on behalf of the war effort. Cobb salad was always on the menu, with lobster thermidor and filet mignon becoming regular items. Waiters tossed the Derby's chef's salad, caliente salad, and about six others at the diners' tables.

The Hollywood Brown Derby was definitely the place to see and be seen. Prior to mobile phones, the maître d' would announce phone calls for celebrities, so everyone would know which stars were there. The Derby was Clark Gable's favorite restaurant; he proposed to Carole Lombard in booth number 54. In 1941, Lombard threw him a surprise party for his fortieth birthday catered by the Brown Derby. Gable's

Above left: **The Marx Brothers—Zeppo (*left*) and Chico, 1932.** ▪ *Above right:* **Clark Gable and Carole Lombard, 1938.** ▪ *Below left:* **Charles Laughton and Carole Lombard, 1940.** ▪ *Below right:* **Zel, one of the Derby's caricature artists, with Cary Grant and Mrs. Ray Milland, 1939.**

favorite items were served, including corned beef hash, pot roast, baked beans, sour cream biscuits, and orange chiffon cake.

Like Sardi's in the theater district of New York, the Brown Derby's walls were lined with 8 x 10-inch framed caricatures of the stars that frequented the restaurant. It has been said that a young man with a complicated last name—nicknamed "Vitch" for short—made the first drawings in exchange for hot coffee and soup. After that, several artists took on the task of creating caricatures for the Derby's walls, including master caricaturist Jack Lane. The caricatures had a cameo in the 1955 *I Love Lucy* episode "Hollywood at Last," when Lucy, Ethel, and Fred paid a visit to the Derby to rub elbows with the stars. In the episode, Lucy pointed out Eve Arden's sketch and Jimmy Durante's double-framed sketch—one for his face, and the other for his nose.

The original Brown Derby on Wilshire Boulevard was sold in 1975 and replaced by a strip mall named the Brown Derby Plaza. The iconic "hat" dome was hoisted onto the third floor of the complex. The Hollywood Brown Derby closed after a fire destroyed most of the structure in 1989. The site is now occupied by an apartment complex. The Beverly Hills Brown Derby closed in 1981, and then was demolished in 1983. The Los Feliz Brown Derby closed in the 1990s; the building, now housing another restaurant, still stands.

In 1987, the Original Brown Derby LLC began a licensing program that would replicate the Hollywood Brown Derby location, complete with the dishes from the original menu and the star caricatures that lined the walls. The Walt Disney Company was the first to license the Derby as part of Hollywood Studios in Orlando, Florida. ✕

Above left: The Brown Derby on Vine Street, 1948. ▪ *Above right:* Jimmy Durante with his Derby caricature, drawn by artist "Vitch," 1936. ▪ *Below left:* Ozzie and Harriet Nelson at the Derby with their sons, Ricky and David, 1948. ▪ *Below right:* New York ex-governor Al Smith with his wife, Catherine, and Hedda Hopper (*far right*), 1939.

Cobb Salad

The original Cobb salad was first created at the Hollywood Brown Derby on Vine Street. It arrived at your table on a platter with the ingredients arranged in separate rows. The waiter would then place the ingredients in a large bowl and mix them tableside, before topping the finished salad with French dressing.

Serves 4 to 6

½ head iceberg lettuce
½ bunch watercress
1 small bunch chicory
½ head romaine lettuce
2 medium tomatoes, peeled, seeded, and diced
2 large chicken breasts, skinned, cooked, and diced
6 strips applewood-smoked bacon, crumbled into pieces
1 large avocado, diced
3 large eggs, hard-boiled and diced
2 tsp. chopped chives
6 oz. Roquefort cheese, crumbled
1 cup French Dressing (recipe follows)

1. Finely chop the lettuce, watercress, chicory, and romaine, toss in a bowl, and mound on a serving platter.
2. Arrange the tomatoes, chicken, bacon, avocado, and eggs in rows on top of the salad greens. Sprinkle with chives and Roquefort cheese.
3. Present the salad, then place the ingredients in a salad bowl with the French Dressing and toss. Serve on salad plates.

Opposite: **Loretta Young outside the Brown Derby on Vine Street, 1931.**

French Dressing

Makes 3 cups

¾ cup red wine vinegar
¼ cup water
1 tbsp. Worcestershire sauce
2 tsp. freshly squeezed lemon juice
1 tsp. granulated sugar
1 tsp. freshly ground black pepper
1 tsp. Dijon mustard
¾ tsp. sea salt
1 clove garlic, cut in half
1 cup extra virgin olive oil
1 cup canola oil

1. Add vinegar, water, Worcestershire sauce, lemon juice, sugar, pepper, mustard, salt, and garlic to a food processor work bowl fitted with metal blade. Purée for 15 seconds. With the motor running, drizzle olive oil and canola oil through the feed tube until emulsified, about 1 minute.
2. Use immediately or cover tightly and store in the refrigerator until ready to use, for up to 2 weeks. Shake before using.

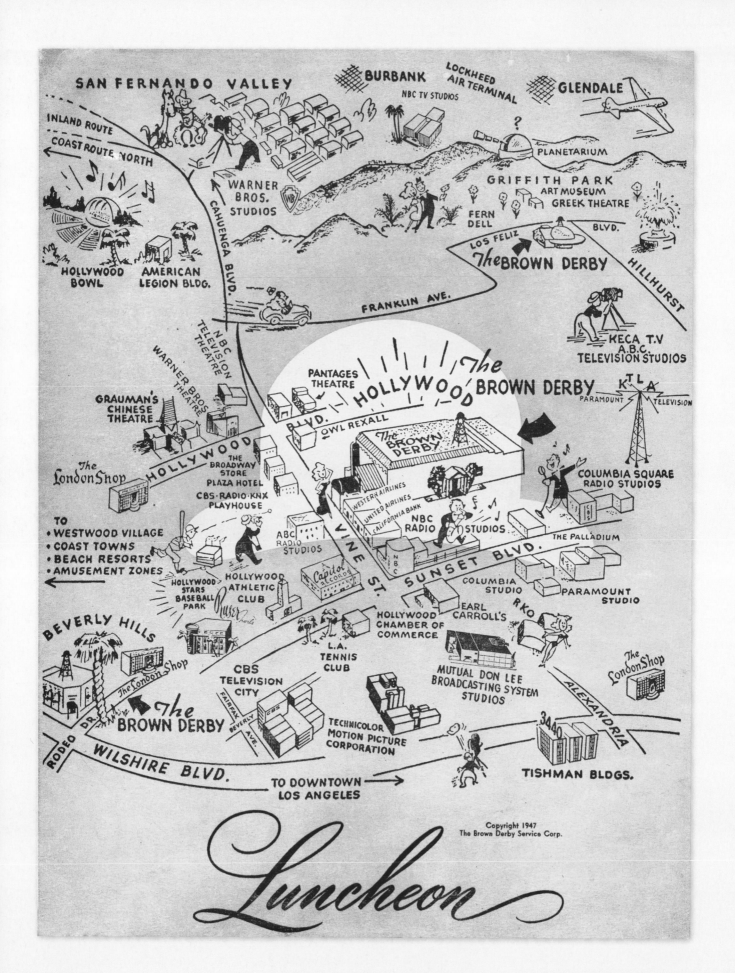

Paprika Chicken

This dish, which was always served as a specialty on the Derby's Sunday dinner menu, originally used a broiler chicken. This update calls for chicken breasts instead.

Serves 4

¼ cup all-purpose flour
salt
ground pepper
4 medium chicken breasts
3 tbsp. unsalted butter
1 tbsp. finely chopped onion
1 tsp. sweet paprika
1 cup heavy cream
1 cup chicken stock
¼ tsp. celery salt

1. In a shallow dish, combine the flour, salt, and pepper. Dredge the chicken through the mixture to coat both sides.
2. Heat the butter in a heavy skillet and sauté the chicken for 3 minutes on each side until golden brown. Add the onion and sauté for a few more minutes. Add the paprika and blend well, then add the cream, broth, and celery salt. Cover and let simmer for about 18 minutes over low heat, or until the chicken is no longer pink in the center.
3. Remove the chicken from the sauce with a slotted spoon and reserve on warmed plates. Turn the heat up under the skillet and reduce the sauce to the desired consistency. (If the sauce is already thick, skip this step and thin it out with a little more broth, if desired.)
4. Serve on a bed of rice or thick pasta noodles.

The Brown Derby "hat," 1926.

Top: Inside the Brown Derby dome. ▪ *Above left:* Errol Flynn with Nora Eddington Flynn at the Derby, 1945. ▪ *Above right:* Judy Garland, Mickey Rooney, and Louise Ranson, 1941. ▪ *Right:* Charlie Chaplin with wife Paulette Goddard, 1942.

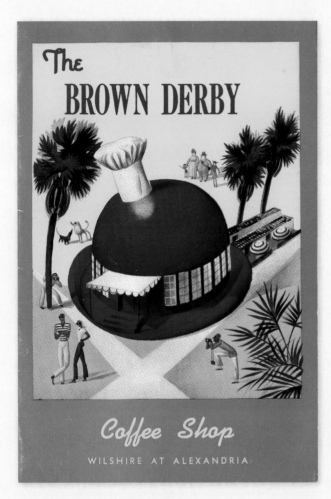

Sour Cream Biscuits

These biscuits were Clark Gable's favorite. They were served at his fortieth birthday party, which was catered by the Brown Derby.

Makes 24 biscuits

4 cups all-purpose flour
1 tsp. cream of tartar
1 tsp. baking powder
½ tsp. baking soda
pinch sea salt
¼ cup vegetable shortening
1 cup raisins
1 cup sour cream
1 cup whole milk

1. Preheat the oven to 450°F. Line a baking sheet with parchment paper.
2. In a large bowl, whisk together the flour, cream of tartar, baking powder, baking soda, and salt. Using a pastry blender, incorporate the shortening until well-blended. Add the raisins, sour cream, and milk. Add more flour or milk until the mixture forms a soft dough.
3. Turn the dough out onto a floured surface, pat it into a round, and roll it out evenly. Cut with a 2-inch biscuit cutter. Place close together on the prepared baking sheet and bake until golden brown, about 12 to 15 minutes.
4. Serve hot with butter.

Pig 'n Whistle

OPEN: 1927–1949; 2001–present

LOCATION: 6714 Hollywood Boulevard
Los Angeles, CA 90028

ORIGINAL PHONE: TRinity 3151

CURRENT PHONE: (323) 463-0000

CUISINE: American

DESIGN: Morgan, Walls & Clements

BUILDING STYLE: Art Deco with Gothic Features

IN THE 1920S, WHEN MOVIE PALACES WERE SHOWING "TALKIES," CINEMAS DIDN'T HAVE CONCESSION STANDS. Enjoying popcorn or candy while watching a movie was unheard of. Instead, moviegoers would enjoy a bite to eat either before or after the film.

In 1927, the Egyptian Theatre, which had been open for a few years, decided to fill this need by opening a Pig 'n Whistle restaurant in its grand courtyard on Hollywood Boulevard. A chain of eateries and candy stores with over forty locations operating on the West Coast from 1908 to 1968, the Pig 'n Whistle began as a soda fountain next to City Hall in downtown Los Angeles. The Egyptian Theatre location featured a soda fountain, a dining room in the back, and a candy shop that sold confections made in a downtown candy factory on Wall Street. The soda fountain offered goodies like the Chop Suey Sundae (vanilla ice cream with chow mein noodles, raisins, dates, and coconut flakes), the Billy Sundae (orange ice cream, vanilla ice cream, strawberries, peaches, pineapple, and whipped cream), and egg creams. Salads, soups, and sandwiches, served in the dining room, rounded out the menu.

The year after it opened, the Pig 'n Whistle was featured in *Architectural Digest.* The elegant eatery, designed by the same architectural firm that had created the beautiful El Capitan Theatre, featured dark, ornate furnishings, including hand-carved Gothic beams, a wood-paneled ceiling, and stained glass windows. Walking through the front entrance of the elegant eatery, guests would pass a mechanical organ playing music. The front of the restaurant looked like another Hollywood movie palace, complete with a marquee over the entrance.

The Pig 'n Whistle soon became a Hollywood landmark. Movie stars young and old loved the place, and Judy Garland, Shirley Temple, Loretta Young, and Howard Hughes were part of the regular clientele. Despite its popularity during Hollywood's Golden Age, the late 1940s were not good to the establishment. In 1949, the restaurant shut its doors, and its contents went up for auction. Restaurateurs Carmen and Sylvia Miceli collected some of the auctioned items for their new Sicilian family restaurant, Miceli's, located a few blocks away at 1646 N. Las Palmas Avenue (see page 181). In

Above: **The candy shop at the Pig 'n Whistle.**

SEASON'S GREETINGS
Melody Lane

addition to some equipment, the Micelis purchased the entire lot of the Pig 'n Whistle's dark wooden booths, complete with carved wooden pigs. The booths are still at Miceli's today.

After the Pig 'n Whistle closed, decay set in. The Egyptian Theatre also closed and was boarded up. Many small shops and fast-food eateries opened in places that had once housed beautiful stores and restaurants. Luckily, false walls were built over the Pig 'n Whistle's ornate wooden interior, preserving the history underneath.

Almost fifty years later, restaurateurs Chris Breed and Alan Hajjar began a $1.5 million renovation project to bring the Pig 'n Whistle back to its former glory. Many of the theater palaces, including the Egyptian, the El Capitan, the Pantages, and the Chinese, have also been restored. Today, the restaurant is up and running again. Entering the front doors is just like walking back into 1927. Although the soda fountain, candy counter, and mechanical organ never returned, the ceiling's beautiful carved wooden beams are still intact, and the restaurant is filled with cases of its original memorabilia, including candy boxes and menus. Of the original forty-plus locations, this is the last remaining Pig 'n Whistle still standing. ✕

Below: **The Pig 'n Whistle's fountain counter, 1928.** ▪ *Opposite:* **The ornate entrance to the Pig 'n Whistle, 1946.**

Lentil Soup with Bacon

This hearty broth was the Pig 'n Whistle's signature soup, selling for just five cents a bowl. Lentils were inexpensive, and the bacon added a lot of flavor without the high cost.

Serves 8

8 strips applewood-smoked bacon,
  cut into ½-inch pieces
1 large onion, chopped
4 medium carrots, thinly sliced
4 cloves garlic, minced
3 tbsp. tomato paste
2 cups lentils, picked over and rinsed

¾ tsp. dried thyme
46 oz. chicken stock or broth
2 cups water
1½ tbsp. red wine vinegar
salt
freshly ground black pepper

1. In a Dutch oven (or other 5-quart pot with a tight-fitting lid), cook the bacon over medium-low heat until browned and crisp, 8 to 10 minutes. Pour off all but 1 tbsp. of the fat.
2. Add the onion and carrots and cook until softened, about 5 minutes. Stir in the garlic and cook until fragrant, about 30 seconds. Stir in the tomato paste and cook for 1 minute.
3. Add the lentils, thyme, broth, and water. Bring to a boil, then reduce to a simmer. Cover and cook until the lentils are tender, 30 to 45 minutes, adding more water if needed.
4. Stir in the vinegar, salt, and pepper. Serve immediately.

𝔖𝔢𝔳𝔢𝔫 𝔄𝔯𝔦𝔰𝔱𝔬𝔠𝔯𝔞𝔱𝔦𝔠 𝔖𝔱𝔬𝔯𝔢𝔰 𝔦𝔫 ℭ𝔞𝔩𝔦𝔣𝔬𝔯𝔫𝔦𝔞		Candies packed and shipped to all parts of the world

Ice Cream, Ices, Etc.

Chocolate Ice Cream 15c	Neapolitan 25c
Strawberry Ice Cream 15c	Pineapple Ice 15c
Vanilla Ice Cream 15c	Orange Ice 15c

Pig'n Whistle Special Orange Ice Cream 20c

Fancy Mixed Drinks 15c

Creme de Chocolate	Frosted Coffee	Loganberry Freeze
Grape Cobbler	Frosted Chocolate	Grenadine Punch
Grape Float	Pineapple Smash	Fruit Punch
Ideal Punch	Mint Freeze	Mint Smash

Fancy Sundaes

Pig'n Whistle Special 30c
One Nabisco Wafer, Orange Ice Cream, Pineapple Ice, Crushed Peaches, Whipped Cream, Cherry

Meringue Glacé 25c
Two Meringue Shells, Vanilla Ice Cream, Whipped Cream and Cherry

Creme de Violet Sundae 25c
Vanilla Ice Cream, Violet Syrup, Whipped Cream, Cherry and Crystallized Violets

Society Sundaes, all flavors, 20c
Vanilla Ice Cream, your choice of flavor, Whipped Cream and Cherry

Billy Sundae 30c
Orange Ice Cream, Vanilla Ice Cream, Strawberries, Peaches, Pineapple Fruit, Whipped Cream, Favor

Fruit Melba 30c
Sliced Pineapple, Peaches, Vanilla Ice Cream, Crushed Pineapple, Ground Nuts, Whipped Cream and Cherry

Banana Special 30c
One Banana cut in halves, Orange Ice, Vanilla Ice Cream, Crushed Raspberry, Ground Nuts, Whipped Cream and Cherry

Pineapple Special 30c
One slice Pineapple, Vanilla Ice Cream, Pineapple Ice, Crushed Pineapple, Ground Nuts, Whipped Cream and Cherry

Automobile Special 30c
One Nabisco Wafer, Vanilla Ice Cream, Orange Ice, Crushed Pineapple, Mint Wafers, Whipped Cream, Favor

Cerise Punch 25c
Grenadine Syrup, Pineapple Ice, Soda, Grape Juice floated on top

Marshmallow 25c	Club 40c	Chop Suey 25c
Peter Pan 25c	Peach Melba 30c	Caramel Sundae 25c
Floradora 25c	Lovers' Delight 25c	Tutti Frutti 25c
	Maraschino Cherry 25c	

Special Milk Chocolate Sundae 20c

Nut Sundaes

Fruit or Nut Sundaes, all flavors, 20c

Parfaits

Parfaits, all flavors, 25c

Patrons are requested not to take dogs into the parlor. We are not responsible for lost articles. Single orders served to one person only.

Pig'n Whistle Candies Excelled by None

Egg Drinks

Egg Coffee, hot, 25c   Egg Malted Milk, cold, 25c
Egg Coffee, cold, 25c   Egg Phosphate 25c
Egg Chocolate, hot, 25c   Egg Cream 30c
Egg Chocolate, cold, 25c   Egg Flip 25c
Egg Malted Milk, hot, 25c   Egg Caramel 25c

Egg Drinks, all milk, 25c

Lemonades

Plain 15c   Grape 20c
Soda 15c   Egg Lemonade 25c
Shasta 15c   Orangeade 15c
Fruit 20c   White Rock 25c
Limeade 15c   Jackson's Napa Soda 25c
Raspberry 20c   Seltzer 15c
Grape Floated 20c   Loganberry 20c

Phosphates

Phosphates, all flavors, 10c

Standard Drinks

Root Beer 10c   Bromo Seltzer 10c
Root Beer, Creamed 15c   Milk 15c
Sierra Club Ginger Ale 20c   Milk and Cream 25c
Ginger Ale, Domestic, 10c   Sweet Apple Cider 15c
Clicquot Club Ginger Ale 30c   Creamed Buttermilk 15c
White Rock Ginger Ale 20c   Buttermilk 10c
Grape Juice 15c   Pineapple Juice 15c
Coca Cola 10c   Plain Malted Milk 20c
Carbonated Water 10c   Milk Shake 15c
Loganberry Juice 15c

Frappes

Frappes, all flavors, 25c
One Egg, Sweet Cream, Ice Cream, your choice of flavors

Ice Cream Sodas

Plain Ice Cream Sodas, all flavors, 15c
Sodas with Assorted Ground Nuts 20c

Mineral Waters

Shasta 10c   Red Raven Splits 15c
Imported French Vichy 25c   Bartlett Water 15c
White Rock Splits 20c   Napa Soda 15c

Hot Drinks

Pig'n Whistle Special Coffee 10c
Tomato Bouillon 10c   Cocoa 15c
Tomato and Beef Bouillon 10c   Special Beef Bouillon 10c
Hot Lemonade 15c   Hot Malted Milk 20c
French Chocolate 15c   Hot Chocolate Malted Milk 20c
Hot Ginger Cordial 10c

Teas

Ridgeway's Special Tea, Per Pot, 15c
English Breakfast   Five o'Clock (mixed)
Green Ceylon   Her Majesty's Blend (mixed)
Orange Pekoe

Ice Cream and Ices to take home, packed in special cartons, will remain hard an hour or more

Special Hot Lunches, Tea and Evening Dinners

Les Frères TAIX

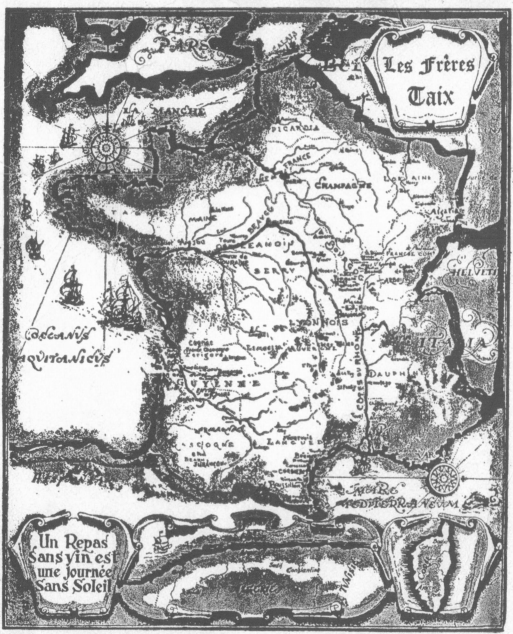

1911 SUNSET BOULEVARD   **LOS ANGELES, CALIF.**

Phone: 484-1265

Taix French Restaurant

OPEN: 1927–present

LOCATION: 1911 W. Sunset Boulevard
Los Angeles, CA 90026

ORIGINAL PHONE: MUtual 2574

CURRENT PHONE: (213) 484-1265

CUISINE: French Country

BUILDING STYLE: Provincial French

WHEN THE TAIX (PRONOUNCED "TEX") FAMILIES EMIGRATED FROM THE HAUTES-ALPES REGION OF FRANCE TO LOS ANGELES IN 1870, MARIUS TAIX SETTLED IN A PART OF DOWNTOWN L.A. CALLED THE FRENCH QUARTER, ABOUT THREE BLOCKS AWAY FROM CITY HALL. Marius opened the Champ d'Or Hotel at 319 E. Commercial Street in 1912 and debuted Taix French Restaurant inside the hotel with his sons, Marius Jr. and Louis Larquier, in 1927. They remained partners until 1964.

Taix was very successful in downtown, being located not too far from the government buildings and Bunker Hill mansions. Offering hearty French country fare for a fair price and serving their meals at long tables, family style, Taix became an institution. Lines down Commercial Street on weekends were not uncommon. French food was unique for the city, and Taix's excellent cuisine, great service, and fair prices (they were famous for their fifty-cent chicken dinners) made it a destination for any special event or dinner.

In 1934, two years after the successful X Olympiad, many French cafés sprang up around downtown's French Quarter, but Taix was the first of the lot and the most well-established. Its menu included such plates as pot-au-feu, Pigs Feet Paysanne, roasted leg of lamb, navy beans bretonne, and baba au rhum. In 1938, the restaurant began to offer lunch and dinner at different price points: lunch for forty cents and dinner for fifty cents, both served at long tables as communal meals. If you wanted a private booth, it cost fifty percent more. In 1940, Taix celebrated the Fourth of July with a fried chicken dinner for only sixty cents. The restaurant sold over 650 meals that day, from 2:00 PM to closing at 8:30 PM.

Louis and Marius Jr. opened Les Frères Taix on Sunset Boulevard in 1962. Two years later, after thirty-seven years of running the restaurants with his brother, Louis died in his office at the downtown location. Three months later, hard times fell on the family and their restaurants. Taix was going out of business, and the city was taking over the property to make room

Above: **Taix on Sunset Boulevard.** ▪ *Right:* **The Champ d'Or Hotel.**

for a six-level parking structure for the new Federal Building. The family moved its operations to the Sunset Boulevard location and shortened the newer restaurant's name to Taix.

Marius Jr.'s sons, Raymond and Pierre, worked with two other relatives to manage the new Sunset location for a number of years before Raymond took over the entire operation. He built up the restaurant's wine collection to hundreds of bottles. Marius Jr. had also been a pharmacist and, during Prohibition, had purchased wine for "medicinal purposes" that was served quietly to high-profile patrons at the restaurant. These rare wines became quite valuable later on. In 1980, when Raymond's son, Michael, came on board to help manage Taix, he inventoried the collection, sold some of the prized vintages at auction, and used the cash to boost their collection for the restaurant. Today, the subterranean wine cellar (which is carefully kept at 58°F) houses one of the top collections of French and Californian wines in Los Angeles, with a whopping 700 different vintages.

In the 1970s, it was not uncommon for a restaurant to host cooking classes and shows in the Southern California Gas Company Kitchens. In 1971, Taix's executive chef, Hurbert Balland, packed his knives and stills and set off to teach a series of classes sponsored by the Assistance League of San Pedro. He named the series "The Secrets of Gourmet Cooking." Besides French dishes, Chef Balland taught special cooking techniques and the history of French countryside foods.

In 2010, Raymond Taix passed away at age eighty-five. He continued to work at the restaurant until two weeks before his death. His son, Michael, is now in charge of operations—the fourth generation to run the famous French restaurant. ✕

Above: The dining room at Taix, 1960s. ▪ *Right:* Marius Taix (*left*) at the original Taix location, late 1930s. ▪ *Opposite:* The French Navy paying a visit to Taix, 1940s.

Coq Au Vin

In 1969, Chef Louis Sangouard created this dish at Taix. Today, it remains one of the most popular items on the menu.

Serves 6

1 roasting chicken (2½ lbs.)
bacon fat
1 cup small white onions, chopped
3 cups burgundy wine
1 cup chicken stock
salt

pepper
2 cloves garlic, minced
1 small bay leaf
8 oz. mushrooms
2 tbsp. butter
1 tbsp. all-purpose flour

1. Preheat the oven to 375°F.
2. Cut chicken into serving pieces, then set aside. Melt enough bacon fat to cover the bottom of a casserole dish. Add the peeled small onions and brown lightly. Remove the onions, add the chicken, and brown on all sides. Add the wine, chicken stock, salt, pepper, and bay leaf. When the liquid begins to simmer, return the onions to the chicken and add a few whole mushrooms.
3. Place the casserole dish in the preheated oven. Cover and simmer for 45 minutes or until chicken is tender.
4. Remove and discard the bay leaf. Make a roux with the butter and flour and add to the casserole dish. Cook until slightly thickened.
5. Serve on a bed of rice or pasta noodles.

Left: Pierre Taix (*left*) and bartender Jean-Claude Etchegaray, 1960s. ▪ *Right:* Postcard featuring the original Taix location in downtown L.A.

L.A.'s Legendary Restaurants

Fillet of Sea Bass

To change up the flavor of this dish, you can also try squeezing lemon or lime over the fish. Sea bass is an easy fish to overcook, so watch the pan carefully.

Serves 4

¼ cup canola oil
1 lb. sea bass fillets
salt
freshly ground black pepper

⅓ cup all-purpose flour
2 tbsp. butter
juice from ½ medium lemon
lemon slices

1. Heat the oil in a frying pan over medium heat.
2. While the oil is heating, dry the fillets between paper towels and sprinkle with salt and pepper. Dredge through the flour, shaking off excess. Place the fillets in the heated oil and cook until light brown on both sides (about 4 minutes on each side) or until fish begins to flake.
3. Keeping the fish in the pan, pour off the excess oil from the pan. Add butter and cook until golden in color. Add lemon juice. Remove from heat and place on a platter.
4. Pour the hot butter over the fish and garnish with lemon slices.

1976 House Dressing

In 1976, the *Los Angeles Times* ran a story on the best dressings at the top-notch restaurants in the city. This was Taix's contribution.

Makes 1 pint

1 tbsp. dry English mustard
1 tsp. coarsely ground black pepper
½ tsp. salt
pinch dry tarragon

pinch dry oregano
water
⅔ cup red wine vinegar
2 cups canola oil

1. In a large bowl, whisk together the mustard, pepper, salt, tarragon, and oregano. Add warm water to make a slurry. While whisking, add the vinegar and then the oil.
2. Place in a covered jar and shake prior to use. Keeps for up to 2 weeks.

Note: This recipe originally included MSG in its list of ingredients. Prior to the '80s, MSG was used in a variety of recipes to enhance the flavor. However, it has been found to cause headaches and other problems. The menus at Taix state that they currently do not use MSG in any of their dishes.

Bullocks Wilshire
Tea Room

OPEN: 1929–1993

LOCATION: 3050 Wilshire Boulevard
5th Floor
Los Angeles, CA 90010

ORIGINAL PHONE: DUnkirk 2-6161

CUISINE: Teatime Fare

DESIGN: John Parkinson

BUILDING STYLE: Art Deco

CURRENTLY: Southwestern Law School

DUBBED THE "CATHEDRAL OF COMMERCE," BULLOCKS WILSHIRE WAS THE SHOWPIECE OF THE BULLOCKS DEPARTMENT STORE CHAIN. The green-and-copper, cathedral-inspired store on the Miracle Mile offered *the* premier shopping experience to stars and the elite for nearly sixty-four years, beginning in 1929.

Located close to the wealthy neighborhood of Hancock Park, the "blue bloods" of Los Angeles arrived at Bullocks Wilshire in chauffeured cars. To cater to the new automobile culture, architect John Parkinson designed the store's back entrance as a beautiful, gated porte cochère. There, valets were lined up and ready to open your door, whisk your car away, and return it later with your purchases stacked neatly inside. Along with its upscale neighborhood patrons, the store's star clientele included Mae West, Greta Garbo, John Wayne, ZaSu Pitts, Walt Disney, Alfred Hitchcock, Marlene Dietrich, and Clark Gable. The store was also staffed with many celebrities in the making: Angela Lansbury, June Lockheart, and future First Lady Patricia Nixon were once sales clerks there.

Bullocks Wilshire designed its in-store experience with the whole family in mind. There was a nursery where mothers could drop off their little ones before shopping, and a private wood-paneled salon where husbands could enjoy a cigar and brandy while being shown the latest men's apparel.

The department store's interior was unsurpassed in elegance. Handcrafted Lalique glass fixtures lined the showroom. Live models showed off the latest fashions throughout the store on weekends. The management at Bullocks Wilshire felt that its clientele were more likely to buy garments worn properly by stylish models rather than by stiff, uninspired mannequins. The most impressive department was the marble "Hall of Perfume" on the ground floor that spanned the entire length of the lobby.

The Bullocks Wilshire customers who worked up an appetite while shopping paid a visit to the store's Tea Room on the fifth floor. The epitome of graceful afternoon dining, the large green-and-pink space featured Art Deco designs and offered private dining rooms. Famous for its Cantonese chicken salad and coconut cream pie, the Tea Room menu also offered small finger sandwiches, salads, soups, popovers, cheese plates, fresh fruits, and tea breads, as well as cheesecake, strawberry shortcake, and lemon pie for dessert. There was also a "streamline menu"—a platter of healthy veggies for customers who were watching their figures. On Tuesdays, patrons were treated to a fashion show luncheon in the

Above: The Bullocks Wilshire building, late 1930s.

TEA ROOM BRUNCH

Tea Room for $1.25. As the models passed by, they presented little cards to each table with information about their outfits and where they could be purchased.

In 1968, the Bullocks Wilshire building was named a Los Angeles Historic-Cultural Monument, and was listed in the National Register of Historic Places in 1978. In the late 1980s, however, Bullocks Wilshire's sparkle started to fade as the surrounding neighborhood declined and shoppers began turning to malls in the suburbs. Even a visit by the Duke and Duchess of York in March of 1988 could not revive the store. The Tea Room's posh appeal fell out of fashion as well, only retaining its elderly clientele.

In 1992, L.A. rioters broke into the department store and shattered every glass case and fixture on the main floor. The rioters set fires and tried to burn the building down. Luckily, the employees shut off the power so the elevators couldn't run, preventing the looters from accessing the higher floors. Parkinson's decision to use elevators instead of escalators may have saved the landmark.

Above: The Bullocks Wilshire Tea Room, 1929. ▪ *Opposite:* The bar at the Bullocks Wilshire Tea Room, 1980.

After the riots, Bullocks Wilshire reopened for about six months, and then was boarded up. In 1988, after many corporate takeovers and buyouts, the Bullocks and Bullocks Wilshire brands had been purchased by R. H. Macy's, making the legendary Wilshire store part of the equally legendary I. Magnin chain of specialty stores. Eventually, R. H. Macy's declared bankruptcy, and Federated Department Stores, Inc. took over all the stores. Sentimentality lost out to the bottom line, and Bullocks, Bullocks Wilshire, and I. Magnin all became part of retail history. The Los Angeles Conservancy led a successful yearlong effort to retrieve the historical elements from Bullocks Wilshire that had been lost in the messy transition. More than 166 items were returned to the original location.

In 1994, Southwestern Law School bought the Bullocks Wilshire building and began restoration of the site for their campus and law library. The Tea Room is now used as a study hall and can be rented out for private functions. ✗

Above: **The Bullocks Wilshire's porte cochère featured a ceiling fresco named "Spirit of Transportation," late 1930s.** ▪
Opposite: **The Hall of Perfume, 1930s.**

Cantonese Chicken Salad

This salad, considered exotic at the time, was served in the Bullocks Wilshire Tea Room on delicate glass plates.

Serves 4 to 6

1 head iceberg lettuce, chopped
canola oil for frying
6 oz. wonton wrappers, sliced into sticks
3 cups diced cooked chicken
6 tbsp. sliced almonds, toasted
Mustard Mayonnaise Dressing
(recipe follows)

1. Place the lettuce in a bowl. Set aside.
2. Heat about 1 inch of the oil in a deep-bottomed pot to 370°F on a deep-fry thermometer. Add the wonton wrappers and fry until golden brown and puffy, 1 to 2 minutes. Remove with a slotted spoon and drain on paper towels.
3. Add the wonton wrappers, chicken, and almonds to the lettuce. Add the dressing to taste and toss gently. Serve immediately.

Mustard Mayonnaise Dressing

Makes 2 cups

2 cups mayonnaise
4 tsp. prepared mustard
2 tsp. soy sauce
2 tsp. canola oil
1½ tsp. Worcestershire sauce
¼ tsp. freshly squeezed lemon juice

1. In a bowl, whisk together the mayonnaise, mustard, soy sauce, canola oil, Worcestershire sauce, and lemon juice until smooth. Store leftover dressing in an airtight container for up to 2 weeks in the refrigerator.

Appetizers and Light Snacks

Crab Meat Cocktail Supreme 4.25
Seafood Sauce Maison

Wilshire Fruit Bowl 2.95
A Compote of Fresh Fruit with Choice of
Cottage Cheese, Sherbet or Frozen Yogurt

Salad Chandler 3.95
Mixed Greens, Chopped Hard-Cooked Eggs,
Bacon Crumbles and a Sprinkle of Bleu Cheese

Princess Salad 4.25
Combination of Lettuce, Watercress,
Fresh Mushrooms, Artichoke Hearts,
Tomato Wedge and Vinaigrette Dressing

Tiny Bay Shrimp Cocktail 3.75
Seafood Sauce Maison

English Cold Soups 4.25
Served with Cucumber and Watercress Sandwich

Soups

Cup of Soup du Jour 1.50

Onion Soup au Gratin 2.75
Crowned with Pastry Shell and a Dash of Sherry

*Served with Assorted Cracker and
Bread Basket and Sweet Butter*

Cold Salad Service
Served with Fresh Baked Breads

Spinach Salad Oriental 5.75
Fresh Pulled Spinach Mingled with
Chunks of Chicken, Water Chestnuts,
Mushrooms and Diced Cooked Eggs, Tossed
at Your Table with a Special Dressing
With Seafood ...... 2.75 Additional

Alfie's Luscious Fruit Salad 5.50
Topped with a Swan of Cream Cheese
and Served with Our Own Poppyseed
Dressing and Date Nut Bread

Wilshire Trio Salad 6.95
An Arrangement of Tender Chicken Salad,
Crab and Shrimp Salad and a Lettuce
Basket of Fresh Fruits in Season

*Salad du Bombay 7.25
A Mixture of Crab Meat, Bay Shrimp, Artichoke
Hearts, Avocado, Tomato Aspic and Garni

Poulet Maison Blanc 5.95
Tender Chunks of Chicken Tossed with Toasted
Pecans, Diced Celery in Mayonnaise Dressing and
Fresh Seasonal Fruits to Tempt M Lady Wilshire

The Trimmer 4.75
Our Lady Wilshire Cold Plate. Alaskan Red
Salmon Heaped on a Bed of Lettuce and Served
with an Array of Lemon Wedges or Herb Dressing

My Lady Gilmore Tomato 4.75
With Tuna or Chicken Salad

*Denotes House Specialty

From The Sandwich Board

*Wilshire Tower 'Five' Sandwich 4.25
Featuring Breast of Turkey, Ham, Swiss Cheese,
Avocado and Sliced Eggs Layered Between Wafer
Thin Bread and Topped with Russian Style
Dressing, Presented with Frozen Fruit Salad

Garden and Seafood Sandwich 4.50
A Combination of Crab Meat and Shrimp
Salad Crowned with Avocado and Water
Chestnuts, Served Open Face on
Pinwheel Rye with Sliced Tomato

Breast of Chicken Sandwich 4.25
Served Open Face on Thick Egg Bread
and Accompanied by a Peach Filled
with Nutty Cranberry Salad

Individual Petite Sandwiches 4.25
An Assortment of Five Sandwiches Served with
Compote of Avocado and Grapefruit Segments

A.B.T. 4.25
Tiered with Bacon and Avocado on Toasted
Cheese Bread, Garnished with Slices
of Tomato, Lettuce and Tasty Treats

Tuna Boat 4.50
All White Meat Tuna Salad Heaped
in a Boat of Cantaloupe (In Season),
Served with a Toasted English Muffin

> **Soup and Sandwiches** 3.95
> The Trio Consists of Chicken, Tuna
> and Egg Salad Served on Open Face
> Rolls to Enhance the Soup du Jour

From the Grill

Au Fromage Tante Marie 4.25
A House Specialty. Turkey, Avocado and
Chopped Black Olives Capped with
Cheddar Cheese Sauce and Garni

Grilled Dutch Diplomat 4.25
Breast of Turkey, Baked Ham and Swiss Cheese
and Special Pinwheel Rye, Accompanied by Crisp
Salad and Served with Fine Imported Mustard

Beverages

*Silver Service of Our Favorite Blend
Coffee or Decaffeinated Coffee
Bullock's Wilshire Darjeeling Tea
All Milk Varieties*
.50

Irish Coffee, Always a Favorite 2.00
*Caffe Cappuccino 2.00
A Blend of Four Liqueurs, Hot
Coffee — Hmmm! Hot or Frosty

Traditional Dessert Favorites

Our Very Own Orange Roll 1.00
Laced with Delicate Orange Sauce

Strawberries California (In Season) 1.75
A Dash of Cointreau and Strawberries, Served
with Our Special Sour Cream Walnut Shortcake

*Fresh Coconut Cream Pie 1.50
Baked Daily with Rich Cream Filling, Topped
with Whipped Cream and Flaked Coconut

Old-Fashioned Apple Pie 1.50
Topped with Hot Apricot Sauce
A la Mode 1.95

Date Nut Custard 1.00
With a Special Brandy Sauce

Floating Snow Pudding 1.00
With a Bavarian Style Cream Sauce

**Frozen Fruit Sherbets, Yogurt
or Ice Cream Selections** 1.00

Gourmet Cake Selection .....1.50 to 2.50

Mocha Frosted Tall 1.50
Made with Coffee Ice Cream and Rich Coffee,
Thick and Cool Enough for an Eskimo

OUR OWN ENGLISH TRIFLE ...1.75

A Sundae to Remember

"Dessert to Share or Your Very Own"

Strawberry Sundae 1.75
Served with All the Sundae Trimmings

Yogurt Sundae 1.75
Think Healthy and Refreshing.
Topped with Fresh Fruits in Season

Pecan Crunch Ice Cream Ball 1.75
Topped with Thick Hot Fudge

Cappuccino Royale Sundae 1.75
A Cappuccino Blend of Espresso Coffee
and Chocolate Fudge, Layered with Vanilla
Ice Cream and Lavishly Garnished with
Whipped Cream and Roasted Almonds

Hot Fudge Sundae 1.75

Frosty Orange Freeze 1.75

HIGH TEA SERVED FROM
2:30 to 5:00 p.m.

A Little Hot Snack

Chicken Supreme

Crisp Pastry Shell Laced with Supreme
of Chicken. Garni of Cranberry Salad

4.75

Omelette Selections

4.75

Chef's Omelette du Jour

Chinese Style Omelette
Served Open Face and Filled with Bean
Sprouts, Water Chestnuts and Green Onions

Omelette Harrington
Filled with Chicken Supreme, Eggplant and Garni

Omelette Lorraine
Crisp Bacon, Grated Cheddar Cheese, Diced Fresh Tomato

*Served with Vegetable du Jour,
Hot Breads and Sweet Butter*

PLATA DU JOUR

It's the Chef's Suggestion

*Minimum Service 1.50 per Person
11:30 a.m. to 2:30 p.m.*

Sales Tax Will Be Added to Retail Price of All Taxable Items
9/79

Popovers

These light-as-air puffs were one of the most popular items on the Bullocks Wilshire Tea Room menu.

Makes 8 popovers

6 large eggs
2 cups whole milk
2 cups all-purpose flour

¾ tsp. sea salt
6 tbsp. unsalted butter, softened

1. In a large bowl, whisk eggs and milk together. Set aside.
2. In another bowl, combine flour, salt, and butter until blended well. Add into egg/milk mixture, blending well.
3. Prepare 8 custard cups by coating the inside with butter. Divide mixture evenly among the cups and place cups on a baking sheet. Place in preheated 400°F oven and bake until golden brown, about 22 minutes.

Heavenly Lemon Pie

The Bullocks Wilshire Tea Room was known for its pastries, and especially its pies. This one is indeed heavenly—light and fluffy, with a meringue crust.

Serves 6

Meringue Crust:
4 large egg whites
  (reserve the yolks for the filling)
1 cup granulated sugar
1 tsp. freshly squeezed lemon juice

Filling:
4 large egg yolks
½ cup granulated sugar
1 medium lemon, juice and zest
2 cups heavy cream, whipped
1 tbsp. powdered sugar

1. Preheat the oven to 200°F. Butter a 10-inch pie pan and set aside.
2. To make the meringue, whip the egg whites on medium-high speed in a mixing bowl fitted with the whip attachment, until soft peaks form. Gradually add the sugar, 1 tablespoon at a time. Add the lemon juice and whip to blend.
3. Spoon the meringue into the pie pan, pulling the mixture up the sides to create a crust. Bake until firm to the touch, about 2 hours. Transfer to a cooling rack and let cool completely.
4. To make the filling, whisk the egg yolks, granulated sugar, lemon zest, and lemon juice in a large bowl until light and fluffy. Place over a double boiler with simmering water underneath. Cook, whisking constantly, until thickened, about 5 minutes. Remove from heat and let cool completely.
5. Fold about half of the whipped cream into the egg yolk mixture. Scrape into the meringue crust, smoothing with an offset spatula. Chill for 30 minutes.
6. Fold the powdered sugar into the remaining whipped cream and spread on top of the pie.

Coconut Cream Pie

Like all of the pies served at the Bullocks Wilshire Tea Room, this popular pie was known for its exceptionally light and flaky crust.

Serves 6

Pie Crust:
1¼ cups all-purpose flour
½ tsp. granulated sugar
½ tsp. sea salt
⅓ cup unsalted butter, cut into small pieces
¼ cup vegetable shortening
ice water

Filling:
1 cup evaporated milk
1 cup heavy cream
½ cup granulated sugar
6 large egg yolks
1 tbsp. cornstarch
1 tbsp. unsalted butter, softened
3 tbsp. cream of coconut
¼ tsp. pure vanilla extract
¼ tsp. coconut extract

Topping:
2 cups heavy cream
¼ cup granulated sugar
1 tsp. pure vanilla extract
1 cup shredded coconut, toasted and sweetened

1. Preheat the oven to 325°F. Have a 10-inch pie plate ready.
2. To make the crust, combine the flour, sugar, and salt in a large bowl. With a pastry blender (or two forks), blend the butter and shortening into the flour until pea-sized pieces of shortening and butter appear in the flour. Sprinkle a few tablespoons of ice water onto the dough, blending until the dough starts to come together. Repeat with more ice water as needed. Press the dough into a disk shape and wrap with plastic wrap. Chill for 1 hour.
3. Roll out the dough on a floured surface large enough so that, when placed on top of it, the pie plate has a nice overhang of at least 1 inch.
4. Place the dough into the pan and poke the bottom and sides with a fork. Bake until golden brown, about 25 minutes. Remove and let cool.
5. To make the filling, bring the evaporated milk, cream, and sugar to a boil in a medium saucepan over medium-high heat. Remove from the heat and set aside.
6. In a mixing bowl fitted with the whip attachment, whip the egg yolks on high speed until pale and fluffy. Add the cornstarch and butter and blend until fully incorporated. Add the cream of coconut, vanilla, and coconut extract and blend again. On low speed, add the cream mixture, then pour the liquid into the saucepan and cook over low heat for 10 minutes, whisking constantly. Pour into the baked and cooled pie shell and bake until set, about 35 minutes. Cool completely.
7. To make the topping, beat the cream, sugar, and vanilla on medium speed in a mixing bowl fitted with the whip attachment, until firm peaks form, about 4 minutes. Dollop on top of the cooled pie.
8. Dust the pie with the shredded coconut and serve.

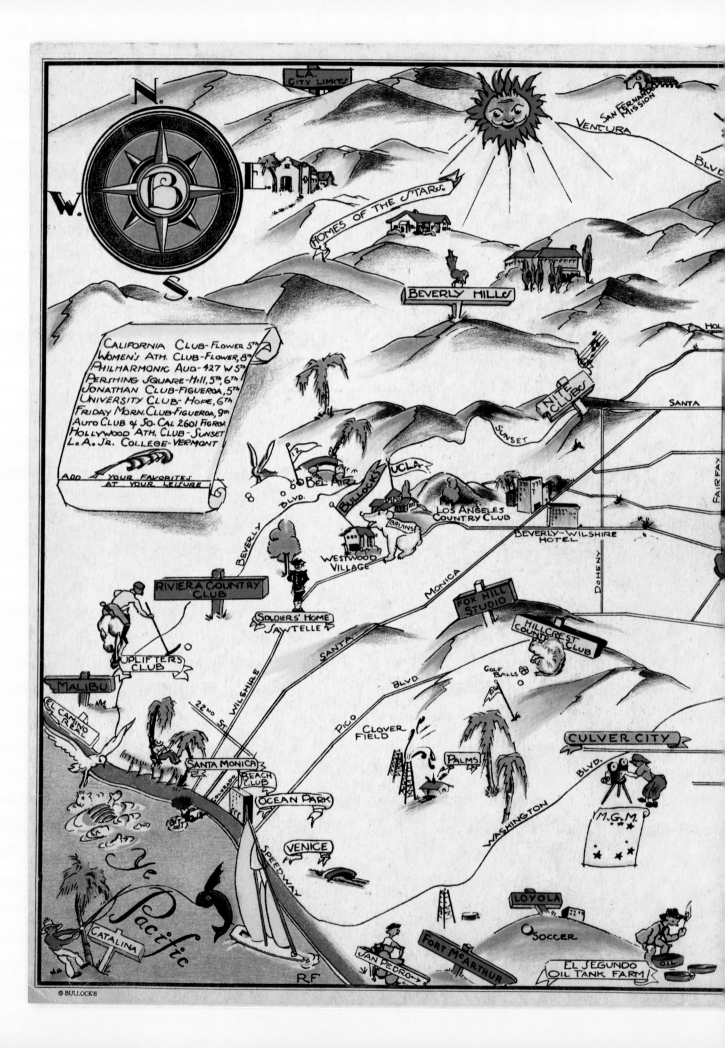

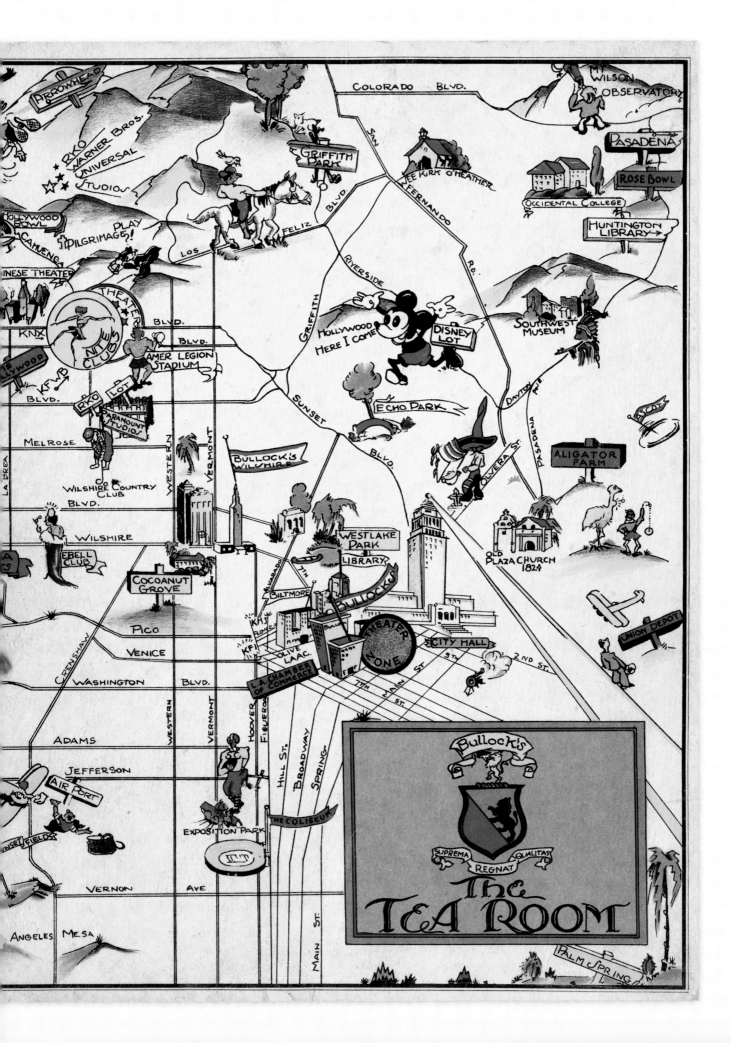

Zebra Room at the Town House of Lafayette Park

OPEN: 1929–1993

LOCATION: 2961 Wilshire Boulevard
Los Angeles, CA 90010

ORIGINAL PHONE: DU 2-7171

CUISINE: American

DESIGN: Norman W. Alpaugh (Town House Building);
Wayne McAllister (Zebra Room)

BUILDING STYLE: Beaux Arts Classicism

CURRENTLY: Filming Location

IN 1929, OIL MAGNATE EDWARD DOHENY OPENED THE TOWN HOUSE, A LUXURY APARTMENT BUILDING BILLED AS "SOUTHERN CALIFORNIA'S MOST DISTINGUISHED ADDRESS." Located across the street from Lafayette Park Place on Wilshire Boulevard, the Town House served as the backdrop for the Charlie Chaplin film *City Lights* in 1931.

In 1937, the Town House was renovated and re-launched as a luxury hotel. As a smaller boutique establishment, it offered a different kind of experience than the 1,200-room Ambassador (see page 35) down the street. While the Town House didn't have the space to provide the amenities found at the Ambassador, it did have the Zebra Room, a swanky supper club that became one of the most glamorous nightclubs in the city. Designed by Wayne McAllister, the Zebra Room interior was true to its name, featuring zebra-striped dinnerware, chairs upholstered with zebra-print fabric, a mural of an African safari on one wall, and jungle prints, wooden masks, and spears for decoration.

The Zebra Room attracted slews of celebrities. Bing Crosby, Tallulah Bankhead, Henry Ford, Marilyn Monroe, and Gina Lollobrigida often enjoyed food and drinks at the restaurant before seeing live shows or going dancing at the Cocoanut Grove. With Bullocks Wilshire (see page 81) just across the street, many stars stayed at the hotel and got their shopping fix at the ritzy department store. Howard Hughes rented one of the top floor suites for a while.

In 1942, hotelier Conrad Hilton took over the building and transformed it into the Hilton Town House, one of the most luxurious hotels in Southern California at the time. Overlooking Lafayette Park Place, the top floors provided views of downtown Los Angeles, only ten blocks away. The brick and terra cotta exterior facade featured rich classical detailing. In 1950, Conrad Hilton's son, Nicky, married Elizabeth Taylor in the hotel's lush central gardens.

In 1954, Hilton sold the fourteen-story hotel to the Sheraton Corporation, and the name was changed to the Sheraton West, keeping the Zebra Room intact for a while. Later, they changed the name to the

Opposite: **The busy Wilshire Boulevard outside the Town House of Lafayette Park, 1940.**

Sheraton Town House and erected a large, red neon sign that could be seen from downtown. In the 1970s, the hotel made several appearances on the TV show *Charlie's Angels*.

In the late 1980s, transients and drug dealers took over the nearby MacArthur and Lafayette Parks. Many of the single-family homes in the area were bulldozed and replaced with larger multi-unit dwellings. The L.A. Riots of 1992 took a toll on the area as well. It was the beginning of the end; the Ambassador closed, and then Bullocks Wilshire. The Town House soon followed.

Six months after it closed, the hotel's Tokyo-based owners wanted to level the historical building and turn it into a parking lot, but the Los Angeles City Council blocked the demolition. In 1994, the building was named a Los Angeles Historic-Cultural Monument, and then listed in the National Register of Historic Places two years later. In 2001, the building was converted into low-income housing. The remainder of the building is now used to film movies and television shows, and the Zebra Room and ballrooms can be rented out for parties. ✕

Below: The Zebra Room, 1940. ▪ *Opposite top:* Postcard featuring the Town House pool, 1951. ▪ *Opposite bottom:* The Zebra Room's dining area, 1939.

THE TOWN HOUSE
LOS ANGELES

Creamy Tomato Soup

This was a staple for the "ladies who lunch" crowd on Wilshire Boulevard. It was also a favorite of Conrad Hilton's son, Nicky. They served it at his garden wedding to Elizabeth Taylor.
Serves 4

2 cups whole milk
2½ cups peeled and seeded tomatoes
2 tbsp. all-purpose flour
1 tbsp. granulated sugar
¼ tsp. onion powder
⅛ tsp. ground black pepper
2 tbsp. unsalted butter
1 tsp. salt
dash of garlic salt

1. Heat the milk in a large saucepan over medium heat.
2. Meanwhile, in a blender, add the tomatoes, flour, sugar, onion powder, black pepper, butter, salt, and garlic salt. Cover and process at high speed until smooth.
3. Slowly pour the tomato mixture into the hot milk while whisking. Heat thoroughly. Do not boil. Serve immediately with croutons.

The Town House Special

Over the years, the Zebra Room always served the same special: a turkey-and-blue-cheese open-faced sandwich.

Serves 1

1 slice white bread
mayonnaise
6 oz. fresh turkey breast, sliced
2 oz. blue cheese crumbles

1. Place the bread on a baking sheet. Spread the mayonnaise thinly on top. Pile on the turkey breast and crumble the blue cheese on top.
2. Toast under the broiler for 15 seconds.

  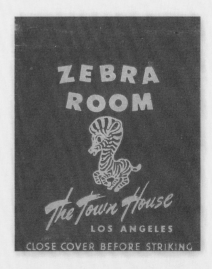

Opposite: The Zebra Room lobby, 1940.

Tick Tock Tea Room
1716 No. Cahuenga Blvd., Hollywood, Cal.

Tick Tock Tea Room

OPEN: 1930–1988

LOCATION: 1716 N. Cahuenga Boulevard
Los Angeles, CA 90028

ORIGINAL PHONE: HE 3-7576

CUISINE: Teatime Fare/American

DESIGN: John W. Pixley

BUILDING STYLE: Colonial

CURRENTLY: Sharky's Woodfired Mexican Grill

IN 1929, THE DEPRESSION WAS IN FULL SWING, WITH THE STOCK MARKET CRASH NOT FAR IN THE PAST. Tea rooms were one way for homeowners to make a few extra dollars, by opening up their houses to the public and serving food there at a low cost with a high turnover. Since it took a lot of customers to make any profit at such low prices, competition was fierce. Many tea rooms around Los Angeles opened, with quaint names such as Pollyanna, Marie Louise's, Carolina Pines, McDonnell's, and Mrs. Mallard's.

That year, Arthur and Helen Johnson loaded up their Model A Ford and drove west, from Minneapolis to the land of sunshine and opportunity, to pursue their dream of opening their own tea room. When they arrived in Los Angeles, they sold their car for $500 and used the profit to help with the tea room. In October of 1930, they bought the Laurel Crest Tea Room at 3906 Beverly Boulevard, a little cottage freshly painted in white and pink hues. The Johnsons renamed it the Tick Tock Tea Room, after a clock they hung in the front room of the little cottage—a family heirloom and one of the few personal belongings they had brought with them on their journey from Minneapolis.

In their first few weeks of operation, the Johnsons only served about thirty meals per day in the tea room. Business was very slow, so they took out an ad that read: "Turkey Dinners with All of the Sides for 65 Cents." The ad was very effective, and their customer count tripled. By the late 1930s, the Tick Tock reportedly served about 2,000 meals per day. To keep up with the pace of business, the Johnsons employed a staff of seventy-five. Helen's serving system—three tables per waitress—was so efficient, one patron reported that he sat down at 8:00 and was back on the road by 8:35. "He Profits Most . . . Who Serves Best" was the motto of the Tick Tock. The saying even appeared on their menu.

A new menu was typed up for the tea room every day. For dinner, you had a choice of a first course, second course, entrée, and dessert. They offered two meal sizes: regular and light, for those watching their calories.

Above: Drawing from a Tick Tock Tea Room promotional piece showing the dining room's large fireplace, which boasted four hearths. ▪ *Opposite:* Postcard of the Tick Tock Tea Room on Cahuenga Boulevard, late 1940s.

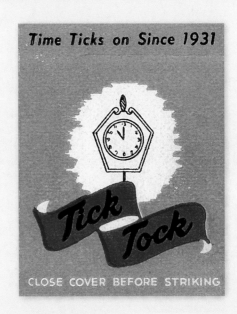

In late 1934, the Johnsons moved the Tick Tock Tea Room to its final location on Cahuenga Boulevard, only a few blocks over from RKO's Pantages Theatre and a few blocks down from the Hollywood Bowl (the tea room created special to-go lunch boxes for Hollywood Bowl patrons). The new location had a large fireplace and hearth in the center of its main dining room, as well as banquet rooms for events, glass chandeliers, heavy furniture, and air conditioning throughout. The dining room could serve 300 people at a time. The Johnsons' heirloom clock, brought all the way from Minneapolis, was installed over the fireplace.

All the food served at the Tick Tock was fresh, rich, and very filling. The meals began with yeast rolls, followed by a salad, then soup, and then the main dishes, which included hearty American fare like chicken pot pie, pounded Swiss steak, and pot roast. The pineapple sheet cake was a favorite for dessert. None of the Tick Tock's ingredients were purchased if they could be homemade in the kitchen.

In the late 1960s, the Johnson children—Michael, Barbara, Buzz, and Jill—took over the tea room's operations, with the help of their five children and thirteen grandchildren. Art passed away in 1980, and Helen a few years later.

In 1987, the Tick Tock hosted a two-day celebration of its fifty-seventh anniversary with a special menu and low prices. The following year, the Johnson children closed the restaurant. Hollywood was on the decline, new competition had emerged, and the heart and soul of the tea room had died out. The area had lost much of the demographic that ate at the Tick Tock, namely families and older clientele. ✕

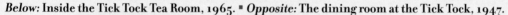

Below: **Inside the Tick Tock Tea Room, 1965.** ▪ *Opposite:* **The dining room at the Tick Tock, 1947.**

Pineapple Sheet Cake

This rich and moist Tick Tock favorite can be made into either a layered cake or shortcakes.

Serves 18

2 cups granulated sugar
2 large eggs
¾ cup canola oil
12 oz. crushed pineapple, not drained

2 cups all-purpose flour
1 tsp. baking soda
1 tsp. salt

1. Preheat the oven to 350°F and butter a 9 x 13-inch baking pan.
2. In a mixing bowl on medium speed, blend the sugar and eggs until incorporated. Add the canola oil and the pineapple.
3. In a medium bowl, combine the flour, baking soda, and salt. Add it to the egg mixture and blend to combine.
4. Pour the batter into the prepared pan and bake for 30 to 40 minutes, or until the center springs back when lightly touched. Serve with icing or whipped cream.

Daily Specials

LUNCH
11:00 to 2:00 — 40c, 50c, 60c

TUESDAY—Individual Chicken Pot Pie
WEDNESDAY—Pot Roast with Homemade Noodles
THURSDAY—Pounded Swiss Steak
FRIDAY—Baked Lamb Chop

✢

DINNER
4:30 to 8:00 — 65c, 75c, 85c

TUESDAY—Smothered Chicken
WEDNESDAY—Fried Rabbit or Virginia Baked Ham
THURSDAY—Individual Chicken Pot Pie
FRIDAY—Baked Fish or Swiss Steak
SATURDAY—Roast Prime Ribs of Beef

✢

SUNDAY DINNER
12:00 to 8:00 — 65c, 75c, 85c

✢

Closed Mondays

The fresh flowers on our tables
are selected and arranged every day by
BESS MENASCO, Florist
OLympia 5957

THURSDAY, SEPTEMBER 8, 1938

Fruit or Shrimp Cocktail   Relishes   Sherbet
SOUP: Vegetable   or   Consomme Noodle
SALAD: Old Fashioned Cole Slaw   or   Fruit Whip Aspic

Roast Turkey; Dressing; Cranberries   85¢
Fried Half Chicken; Home Style   85¢
Broiled New York Cut Steak; French Fries $1.00
Special Filet Mignon; French Fries $1.00

-----DESSERTS-----

Deep Dish Apple Pie; Cheese or Whip Cream
Apricot Pie   Iced Watermelon
Blueberry Pie   Special Ice Cream
Graham Cracker Chocolate Pie   Sherbet
Grapenut Custard Pudding   Chocolate Sundae
Butterscotch Sundae   Chocolate Parfait
Butterscotch Parfait
Marshmallow Spice Layer Cake with Whipped **Cream** or Ala Mode
Fudge Layer Cake with Whip Cream or Ala Mode

Fruit or Shrimp Cocktail   or   Choice of Soup
Choice of Salad   Sherbet

Roast Turkey; Dressing; Cranberries   75¢
Broiled Lamb Chops; French Fries   75¢
Sliced Cold Turkey; Potato Salad   75¢
Special T-Bone Steak; French Fries   85¢
                              CHOICE OF DESSERTS

CHOICE OF: Tomato Juice Fruit Cocktail Consomme Noodle
                or Vegetable Soup
SALAD: Old Fashioned Cole Slaw   or   Fruit Whip Aspic

INDIVIDUAL CHICKEN POT PIE   65¢
Sliced Cold Cuts; Potato Salad   65¢
Home Made Sausage; Apple Sauce   65¢
Roast Prime Ribs of Beef Au Jus   65¢
Roast Leg of Lamb; Brown Gravy   65¢
Baked Turkey Hash   65¢
Fresh Vegetable Plate; Poached Egg   65¢
Baked Halibut; Tartar Sauce   65¢
                              CHOICE OF DESSERTS

CHILDRENS PORTION, 10 YRS. OR UNDER, 45¢ 55¢ 65¢

In addition to the above quoted prices there is a charge of
3% sales tax.

A LA CARTE

Bowl of Soup	15c
Combination Vegetable Salad, with Rolls	45c
Mixed Fruit Salad with Rolls	45c
Sliced Lamb Sandwich	25c
Baked Ham Sandwich	25c
Sliced Turkey Sandwich	35c
Hot Turkey Sandwich with Potato and Gravy	45c
Hot Lamb Sandwich with Potato and Gravy	35c
Pot of Tea	15c
Hot Chocolate	20c
Postum, per cup	10c
Pot of Coffee	15c
Coffee, per cup	10c
Iced Tea	10c
Pie, with Whipped Cream or Cheese	15c
Pie a la Mode	20c
Cake, per cut	15c
Cake a la Mode	20c
Sundaes, Any Flavor	15c
Pudding	10c
Parfaits	20c

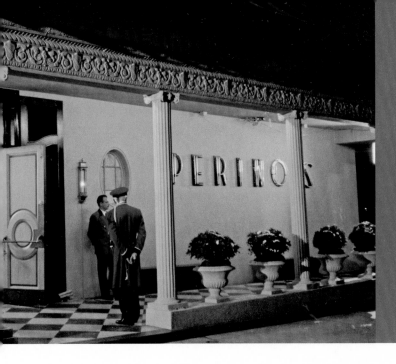

Perino's

OPEN: 1932–1986

LOCATION: 4101 Wilshire Boulevard
Los Angeles, CA 90010

ORIGINAL PHONE: FEderal-1221 and DU 3-1221

CUISINE: French-Italian

DESIGN: Paul Revere Williams

BUILDING STYLE: Vogue Regency

CURRENTLY: Perino's Luxury Apartments

ALEXANDER PERINO, THE YOUNGEST OF TWELVE CHILDREN, WAS BORN IN THE PIEDMONT REGION OF ITALY IN 1895. He idolized his father, a winemaker, who died when Perino was only thirteen.

When Perino's mother sent him to apprentice at a pastry shop on the Italian Riviera, it was the beginning of a love for food that would eventually lead him to become a famous restaurateur. Two years later, Perino's mother passed away, and he boarded a ship headed for New York City.

For the next two decades, Perino worked his way westward through a variety of establishments in the U.S., from Delmonico's in New York City, to the Plaza, to Chicago's Congress Hotel, to Cleveland's Hotel Deshler. His English became so good that his voice lost every trace of his original Italian accent. By 1925, he had reached Los Angeles, where he worked briefly at the newly opened Biltmore Hotel but was fired after dropping a tray of tea and crumpets. After becoming head waiter at the posh Victor Hugo's, he realized that he could do better. So, with a $2,000 loan, he opened Perino's in 1932, in the midst of the Great Depression. A few days after opening, he hired chef Attilio Balzano, beginning a thirty-seven-year culinary relationship.

In 1934, a grease fire in the Perino's kitchen sent its patrons running for safety, escorted by Perino himself. By 1935, the kitchen had been rebuilt and was up and running again. The restaurant expanded even more in the early 1950s when it moved to its new location at 4101 Wilshire Boulevard, designed by Paul Revere Williams. The main dining room and two private dining rooms could seat 360 people at a time.

The restaurant suffered another fire in 1954, this one reportedly started by a lit cigarette that landed on an upholstered chair. In February 1955, the resilient Perino's reopened once again. For the twenty years that followed, high society luncheons, pre-theater and pre-sporting event dinners, and elegant birthday and engagement parties were held at the restaurant. Perino's was known for its wealthy patrons. Dorothy Chandler even visited the restaurant with hopes that diners would give donations for the construction of the Music Center.

Above: The entrance to Perino's. ▪ *Opposite:* Alexander Perino arriving at his restaurant, 1952.

The restaurant's very large menu included more than 150 entrées and 270 wines. Perino had very high standards for the food served in his restaurant. "Food, service, cleanliness, and no cheating" was his motto. He also believed that "the best service is that which is never seen." He never served food that had been frozen and discouraged excessive seasoning, preferring natural flavors and simplicity. "A salad," he said, "should be like a beautiful woman in a plain dress."

Perino's standards were just as exacting for everything from the bar, to the tableware, to the music. Ice for the drinks was taken directly from the freezer to the bartender, so it would not inadvertently absorb flavors or scents from the kitchen. Serving from glass dishes was forbidden; Perino felt that glass was not as appealing to the eye, and could break easily. Every detail was carefully considered, from the silver-plated serving dishes, to the solid silver pastry cart, to the pink Irish linen napkins and tablecloths. Every table was decorated with a vase containing a single pink rose.

The restaurant's location, close to the Brown Derby and the Ambassador Hotel, drew Hollywood celebrities and the "blue blood" elite from the neighboring Hancock Park, where the city's old money lived at the time. Stars like Frank Sinatra, who played the Steinway at the bar, provided entertainment

In all the world of commerce, there are a few products for which there are no acceptable substitutes. And among these, most certainly, must be counted the great Cadillac car. For in beauty and elegance . . . in luxury and comfort . . . in value and practicality . . . in everything that contributes to making a motor car supreme—Cadillac is in a realm all its own. To see it and to drive it is to discover a new measure of fulfillment in modern motoring. Your Cadillac dealer will be most happy to demonstrate this fact to you at any time—and to explain why Cadillac is now such an unusually sound investment for such a surprisingly wide group of motorists. We hope you will accord him the opportunity—*soon.*

CADILLAC MOTOR CAR DIVISION • GENERAL MOTORS CORPORATION
EVERY WINDOW OF EVERY CADILLAC IS SAFETY PLATE GLASS

In a realm all its own... *Cadillac*

from time to time. One table was permanently reserved for Bette Davis. Mae West, who lived close by at the Ravenswood Apartments, ate at Perino's with her manager every Sunday. Bugsy Siegel was a regular and had a booth in the back of the restaurant, where he could see everyone and still not draw much attention. Cary Grant liked to sit close to the bar. Cole Porter reportedly wrote a song on the back of a Perino's menu. Perino himself once taught Ronald Coleman how to make salad dressing. Other regulars included Joan Crawford, Spencer Tracy, ZaSu Pitts, Eleanor Roosevelt, Elizabeth Taylor, Irene Dunne, Howard Hughes, Fred Astaire, Cary Grant, and Gary Cooper.

The restaurant was sold to Frank Esgro, Inc. in 1969, with the understanding that Perino would remain in charge. This agreement didn't last, and Perino left, taking Chef Balzano with him. Esgro ran the restaurant until 1983. In 1985, he tried to open a downtown Los Angeles Perino's location, but it failed to the tune of $7.5 million.

Perino died on New Year's Day in 1982, at the age of eighty-six. The restaurant closed soon after, in 1986. For nine years after it closed, the restaurant served as a filming location for more than 200 productions. The dining room was perfect for filming because it was large enough to accommodate cameras and lighting equipment, and the room's soft colors provided a flattering background. The restaurant was also used as a private banquet hall for events after its neighbor, the Ambassador, closed down.

In 2005, an auction took place for all of the items left at the restaurant, including the Steinway that Sinatra had played, Tyrone Power's favorite booth, and all of the silver platters that celebrities had eaten their meals off of. Before the auction, real estate developer Tom Carey and his partner, Tef Kutay, bought the building and its contents for $4 million. They spent $20 million to construct a forty-seven-unit luxury apartment building named Perino's Condominiums (later to become Perino's Luxury Apartments). The foyer, name, logo, and distinctive entryway awning were incorporated into the complex. ✗

Top left: Alexander Perino with architect Paul Revere Williams (*right*), 1949. ▪ *Top right:* George Burns with Gracie Allen (*right*) and a friend, 1959. ▪ *Left:* Barbara Nichols and Dana Andrews, 1956. ▪ *Opposite top:* The elegant dining room at Perino's, 1980s. ▪ *Opposite middle:* Perino's sugar cubes. ▪ *Opposite bottom:* Cadillac advertisement featuring Perino's, 1959.

Pumpernickel Toasts

Perino's pumpernickel toast strips were usually brought to the table tucked in crisp cloth napkins for guests to nibble on before their orders were taken. You can make your own pumpernickel bread for this recipe if you like, but a high-quality, store-bought variety will also work—it did for Perino's.

Makes 30 toasts

1 lb. pumpernickel bread loaf, unsliced and frozen

½ cup unsalted butter, softened

2 cloves garlic, crushed

½ cup grated Parmesan cheese

1. Preheat the oven to 275°F.
2. Slice the bread paper-thin with a serrated knife; you should get about 30 slices.
3. Melt the butter in a saucepan over low heat. Add the garlic and cheese, and stir to blend well. Brush on one side of each bread slice.
4. Place the pieces on a baking sheet in a single layer. Bake until crisp, about 15 to 20 minutes. The bread may curl slightly at edges.
5. Let cool, then store in an airtight container until ready to use. Serve as an appetizer or with soups and salads.

Below: Joe DiMaggio, General William Dean, Bob Hope, and Marilyn Monroe, 1953. ▪ *Opposite:* The Perino's entrance on Wilshire Boulevard, *circa* 1960s.

Spaghetti Bolognese

This dish was a favorite of the stars! You can really taste the fresh vegetables in the Bolognese sauce.

Serves 6

¼ cup plus 1½ tsp. unsalted butter, softened
1 cup chopped onion
1 cup chopped carrot
1 cup chopped celery
1 lb. top sirloin, ground and very lean
1 cup Burgundy wine

4 cups beef stock
2 cups tomato purée
1 lb. dry spaghetti
sea salt
grated Parmesan cheese

1. In a Dutch oven over medium heat, melt ¼ cup of the butter and add the onion, carrot, and celery. Stirring occasionally, cook until softened, about 4 to 5 minutes. Add the beef and sauté for a few minutes until no longer pink. Add the wine, lower the heat, and simmer for 10 to 15 minutes.
2. Add the beef stock and 1 cup of the tomato purée and simmer uncovered for 1½ hours, until thickened.
3. Meanwhile, in a large skillet, melt the remaining 1½ tsp. butter and the remaining 1 cup tomato purée. Heat thoroughly.
4. Bring a large pot of salted water to a boil over medium-high heat. Add the spaghetti and cook according to the package directions, until al dente. Drain.
5. Add the spaghetti to the skillet with the butter and tomato purée and turn to coat the pasta. Then add the sauce to the pasta and turn again to coat.
6. Serve on a platter, topped with the grated Parmesan cheese.

Whitefish Italienne

Out of more than 150 entrées on the Perino's menu, this was one of the most popular dishes with the Hollywood crowd. In fact, it was such a hit that when Perino took it off the menu on a Thursday, it was back by Saturday.

Serves 6

1 tbsp. clarified unsalted butter
2 tsp. dried shallots
4 lbs. whole white fish, filleted and skinned
4 oz. button mushroom caps, sliced
1 tsp. freshly squeezed lemon juice

dash of sea salt
½ cup dry white wine
Sauce Italienne (recipe follows)
chopped parsley

1. In a skillet over medium heat, melt the butter, then add the shallots and fish. Lay the mushrooms over the fish and add the lemon juice, salt, and wine. Cover and cook slowly for 10 minutes.
2. Remove the fish and mushrooms from the pan with a spatula and place on a serving dish.
3. Place the skillet back over medium heat and reduce the liquid that is left in the pan by a fourth. Add the Sauce Italienne to the pan liquid and cook for 2 to 3 minutes.
4. Pour the sauce over the fish, sprinkle with parsley, and serve.

Sauce Italienne

Makes about 2 cups

⅓ cup clarified unsalted butter
½ cup diced onion
4 large tomatoes, peeled, halved, and diced, with the juice squeezed out
2 tbsp. tomato paste
¼ tsp. freshly ground black pepper
2 tsp. granulated sugar
1 tsp. sea salt
¼ tsp. nutmeg

1. In a skillet over medium heat, melt the butter and add the onion. Cook until softened but not brown, 2 to 3 minutes.
2. Add the tomatoes and tomato paste and stir to combine. Add the pepper, sugar, salt, and nutmeg. Simmer for 15 minutes, or until it starts to bubble up the sides of the pan. Serve or store in an airtight container in the refrigerator for up to 2 weeks.

PERINO'S

LUNCHEON

Saturday, February 21, 1942

COCKTAILS

Crab Cocktail .70   Crab Legs .90
Shrimp Cocktail .70   with Avocado .85
Lobster .90   Blue Points .90
Crab Legs with Avocado .90
Oyster Rockefeller 1.30   Fresh Fruit Supreme .60

Cotuits 1.00
Crab Louie 1.25
Cherry Stone Clams .90
Tomato Juice .30

Olympia Oyster Cocktail .90
Clam Juice Cocktail .45
Half Cracked Crab, Mustard Sauce 1.00
Half Avocado .65   Sauerkraut Juice .30
Avocado Cocktail, 1000 Island Dressing .80

HORS D'OEUVRES

Nova Scotia Salmon 1.10
Mackerel in White Wine .80
Smoked Sturgeon .90
Marinated Herring .75
Filets of Tuna Fish .75
Imported Russian Fresh Caviar, p.p. 2.90

Assorted Hors d'Oeuvres 1.00
Prosciutto 1.00
Stuffed Celery au Roquefort .65
Celery Victor .65
Celery en Branche .40   Green Olives .40   Colossal Ripe Olives .40; Stuffed w. Anchovie .70
Au Blinis 3.25   Canape 2.50

Tarrine Pate de Foie Gras 1.20
Boneless French Sardines 1.15
Antipasto .90   Salami .60
Crab Meat Ravigott 1.00

Canape Lorenzo 1.20

SOUPS   Puree of Lentil Conty .35

Consomme .30   Chicken Broth .30
Tomato Bouillon .30
Clam Broth .40   Consomme Bellevue .45

Onion Soup Gratin .55
Petite Marmite .50
Green Turtle au Sherry .75

Vermicelli a l'Uovo .55
Cream of Fresh Tomato .50
Cream of Fresh Peas .55

COLD: Vichysoisse .50   Cream Senegales .55   Madrilene .35   Consomme .35

EGGS

Eggs Benedict .95   Perinos 1.10
Omelette with Chicken Livers 1.25

Eggs Florentine 1.15
Spanish Omelette 1.20

Eggs with Bacon or Ham .90
Eggs Mornay 1.15

FISH

Whitefish Saute Meuniere 1.50
Frog Legs Saute Fines Herbes 1.40
Fried Eastern Scallops 1.15
Filet of Sole Florentine 1.20
Lobster Thermidor 1.60

Filet of Sole Bonne Femme 1.20

Brook Trout Saute Meuniere 1.20
Filet of Sole Colbert 1.25
Lobster Americaine 1.85

Crab Legs a la Turque 1.60
Filet of Sole Marguery 1.30
Fried Filet of Sole, Tartar Sauce 1.15
Crab Leg with Marrow Bordelaise 1.50
Lobster a la Newburg $1.60

PLATS DU JOUR

Veal Saute Marengo .95
Calf's Brains and Artichoke Doree 1.15
Lamb Kidney Saute Chippolata Spinach 1.20
Grenadine of Beef Tenderloin Bernaise, String Beans 1.15
Chicken a la King en Casserolette Peas   1.50

Home Made Mexican Enchiladas .90
Fresh Mushrooms Saute Colbert 1.15
Deviled Sliced Turkey Virginia 1.50
Chicken Curry a l'Indienne 1.75
Genuine Calf's Liver Saute, Bacon Spinach 1.15

FROM THE GRILL

French Lamb Chop 1.25; with Bacon 1.40
Brochette Chicken Livers Colbert 1.30
Half Milk Fed Chicken 1.30
Jumbo Squab 1.40

½ Baby Squab Turkey, Colbert Sauce (for 2) 3.50
English Mixed Grill 1.40
Mushrooms on Toast 1.15
Breast of Capon, Sauce Diable Virginienne 1.60
Sauce Bernaise .35

Filet Mignon 1.90; w. Fresh Mushrooms 2.25
Eastern Corn Fed Beef Sirloin (for 1) 2.10
Special Corn Fed Steer Sirloin (for 1) 3.25
Steak Minute 1.60; with Bordelaise Sauce 1.90
Mushroom Sauce .50

TO ORDER

Breast of Chicken under Glass Queen Sheba 1.50
Breast of Guinea Hen under Glass Lucullus 1.75
Chicken en Casserole Paysanne (for 2) 3.75
Chicken Jerusalem 1.60   A la King 1.40
Chicken Saute Sec Perino's 1.60
Chicken Cacciatora 1.60
Squab en Casserole Paysanne 1.75

Gnoicchi Piedmontaise .85
Spaghetti Bolognaise .95
Spaghetti Tetrazzini 1.25
Ravioli Genovese .95
Tagliarini Bolognaise 1.10
Risotto Milanaise 1.00
Piedmontaise 1.25

Lamb Kidney Saute au Madere with Mushrooms 1.30
Veal Scallopine Marsala .95   Scallopine Perinos 1.30
Veal Escallop Bon Femme 1.15
Sweetbreads Saute Sec with Mushrooms 1.30
Sweetbreads Saute Financiere 1.40   Sweetbreads Eugenie 1.40
Rack or Saddle of Lamb en Casserole Paysanne (for 2) 3.50
Tournedos of Beef Medici 2.00   Tournedos Hawaiian 2.25

SALADS

Lettuce .30-.50   Romaine .35-.55   Sliced Tomatoes .40-.60
Mixed Greens .30-.50   Escarole .35-.55   Sliced Cucumber .60-.90
Heart Romaine with Grapefruit or Avocado .60   Endive .60-.90

Chiffonade .45-.70
Combination .45-.80
Roquefort Cheese Dressing .25 p.p.   Lorenzo Dressing .20

Watercress .40-.65
Celery Root .35-.50

SPECIALS

Chef Special .95
Lorenzo 1.15   Avocado Salad .75
Lobster Salad 1.35

Perinos 1.00   Fresh Fruit .85
Pineapple and Cottage Cheese .85   Fresh Vegetable .85
Stuffed Tomato Surprise with Chicken 1.15   With Crab 1.10
Chicken Salad Parisienne 1.40   Crab Salad 1.30

Heart of Palmes, 1000 Isl. Dressing 1.00
Colossal Asparagus, Mustard Sauce 1.00

Shrimp Salad 1.25

Breast of Chicken: Isabelle 1.30   Jeanette 1.65   Cold Roast Beef, Potato Salad 1.30   Half Cold Roast Chicken 1.30
Sliced Chicken or Turkey 1.25   With Virginia Ham 1.40   Assorted Cold Cuts 1.00   With Chicken 1.25

VEGETABLES

Garden Peas .35-.60   Paysanne .40-.65
String Beans .35-.60   Au Gratin .45-.70
English Spinach .30-.50   Creamed .40-.65   Cauliflower, Hollandaise or Au Gratin .40-.65
Spinach a la Provencale .50
Broccoli Hollandaise .50
Heart of Palms .90   Artichoke .45
Corn Saute .35-.50   Au Gratin .45-.70

Lima Beans .45-.65   Carrots Vichy .25-.40
Zucchini Florentine .40-.65   Provencale .40-.65
Egg Plant Fried .40-.60   Portugaise .40-.60
French Fried Onions .50-.75

Artichokes Doree .50-.75

POTATOES

Baked Potato .30
Au Gratin .40-.60   Hashed in Cream .35-.50

Hashed Brown .35-.50
Cottage Fried .40-.70   Souffle .50-.75
Grilled Sweet .40-.65   Candied Sweet .45-.70

Lyonnaise .40-.60   Minute .30-.45
French Fried, Long Branch or Julienne .30-.50

CHEESE TRAY .45 per person   FRESH FRUIT in Season .40

DESSERTS

Coupe au Marrons .70
Coupe St. Jacques .50
Roman Punch .65
French Pastry .25

Meringue Glace .50
Crepe Suzette 1.50
Cherry Jubilee 1.10
Pie .25

Strawberry Romanoff 1.35
Baked Alaska .80
Zabaglione .75
Spumoni .50

French Pancake .75
Compote of Fruit .50
Peach Melba .65
Wild Strawberries .75
Chocolate or Vanilla Souffle (for 2) 2.20

Parfaits: Cafe .50   Strawberry .50   Marron .60
Ice Creams: French Vanilla .30   Chocolate .35   Coffee .35   English Toffee .35
Sherbets: Lemon .30   Pineapple .30   Orange .30   Raspberry .30

BEVERAGES

Pot of Coffee with Cream .25   Demi Tasse .15
Cafe Diablo 1.25   Orange Pekoe, Green, Oolong, Black Tea .25

Chocolate or Cocoa .30
Milk .15

Kaffee Hag .30
Buttermilk .15

Sanka or Postum .30
Peppermint Tea .30

Continental Lunch Served Daily Except Sunday $1.25, Including Beverage
In Addition to the Quoted Prices There Is a Charge of 3% Sales Tax   Minimum Charge, 50c

Schwab's Pharmacy

OPEN: 1932–1983

LOCATION: 8024 Sunset Boulevard
Los Angeles, CA 90046

ORIGINAL PHONE: HO 4-3141

CUISINE: Soda Fountain

DESIGN: Alvin Nordstrom and Milton Anderson

BUILDING STYLE: Renaissance

CURRENTLY: Shopping Complex

THE WORLD'S MOST FAMOUS PHARMACY, SCHWAB'S, WAS THE SCENE OF MANY HOLLYWOOD TALES, BOTH TALL AND TRUE. The pharmacy was owned and run by brothers Bernard, Jack, Leon, and Martin Schwab, who discovered the failing drugstore and decided to cash in on its location, which was close to all the movie studios.

Besides filling prescriptions, the brothers also ran a soda and lunch counter, where their Hot Fudge Brownie Sundae was a big seller. According to Hollywood lore, Lana Turner was discovered while drinking a milkshake at the Schwab's counter. Writer F. Scott Fitzgerald reportedly had a heart attack at Schwab's while purchasing a pack of cigarettes. It is said that composer Harold Arlen wrote "Over the Rainbow" for *The Wizard of Oz* on a Schwab's napkin. Once, Humphrey Bogart reportedly asked Leon Schwab for a hangover cure. Schwab told him to stop drinking. Bogart was not pleased with Schwab's retort and replied that he was not looking for a lecture.

Whether these events actually happened or not, stories like these drove aspiring actors and actresses to the pharmacy in hopes of rubbing elbows with the stars. On weekend evenings in the 1950s, the sidewalk in front of the pharmacy was filled with customers six deep, standing around with a soda or a malt. Schwab's had an impressive Rolodex of actors who referred to it as "headquarters." In the early days, you could run into Orson Welles, Mickey Rooney, Judy Garland, the Marx Brothers, Marilyn Monroe, and Ronald Reagan there. Hollywood columnist Sidney Skolsky set up an office in one of the booths on the premises to stay close to the action. If the newspapers wanted some new gossip, they would send a reporter to Schwab's to get the scoop. Articles described the celebrity-filled atmosphere as "Schwabadero," a name inspired by the old Trocadero.

For Billy Wilder's 1950s noir classic *Sunset Boulevard*, an exact replica of the pharmacy was created on the Paramount Studios backlot. In the film, when screenwriter Joe Gillis (played by William Holden) finds himself down on his luck after being rejected by Paramount, he explains: "Schwab's was kind of a combination office, coffee klatch, and waiting room. Waiting, waiting, waiting for the gravy train."

Over the years, Schwab's became a popular local mini-chain, with locations at 6255 Hollywood Boulevard, 430 N. Roxbury Boulevard, and 401 N. Bedford Drive. The Bedford Drive location, which had a special department and phone number reserved for the famous, was where Marilyn Monroe filled her

Above: The premiere party for *The Jolson Story* at Schwab's, 1949. ▪ *Opposite:* The soda fountain counter at Schwab's, 1949.

prescriptions. One of her prescription bottles sold for $3,200 in 2014.

In the 1970s and early '80s, a new set of celebrities began gracing the fountain with their presence, including Eric Estrada, Al Pacino, Sylvester Stallone, Goldie Hawn, and Jerry Brown. In 1980, Jack Schwab passed away at age seventy-five, and after five decades of service, the Schwab's on Sunset Boulevard closed down. Leon Schwab stated that the closure was due to family reasons, but the truth was that the company was in financial distress. In 1983, everything that was not bolted down, from the stools and counters to the pharmacy's famous Rolodex, was auctioned off to the highest bidder. The large red-and-blue neon sign that hung over the front door sold for $650; a leather payroll bank bag with the Schwab's name sold for $300. An investment banker from Beverly Hills paid $500 for the Rolodex.

The pharmacy's closure hit the staff hard. Waitress Margy Handley, who had worked for the Schwab

Above left: **Hurd Hatfield and Angela Lansbury at Schwab's after attending the premiere of** *The Picture of Dorian Gray,* **1945.** ▪ *Above right:* **The pharmacy at Schwab's, 1939.** ▪ *Below left:* **Leon, Jack, and Bernard Schwab behind the counter, 1948.** ▪ *Below right:* **Evelyn Keyes selling cigarettes and cigars at Schwab's, 1949.**

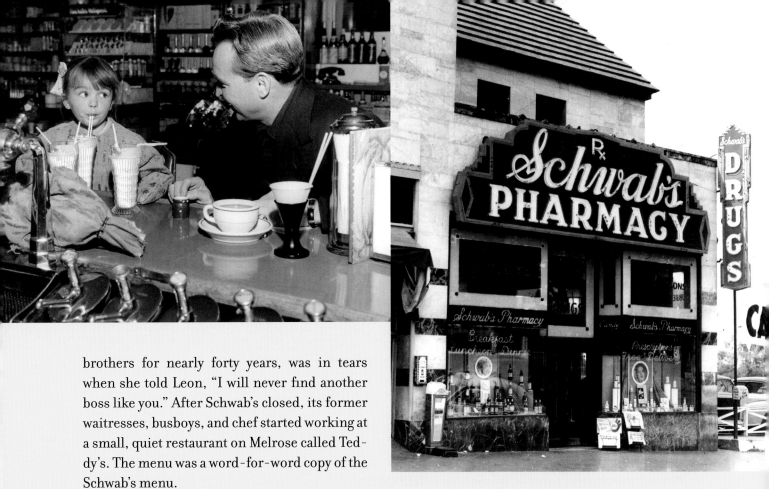

brothers for nearly forty years, was in tears when she told Leon, "I will never find another boss like you." After Schwab's closed, its former waitresses, busboys, and chef started working at a small, quiet restaurant on Melrose called Teddy's. The menu was a word-for-word copy of the Schwab's menu.

About six months after Schwab's closed, the location was transformed into a themed dance venue named the L.A. Heartbreakers, owned by Jerry Preston. Booths from the defunct Tiny Naylor's (see page 169) were also incorporated into the setup. In October 1988, a new $40 million complex was planned for the location, including a glamorized Schwab's with an underground parking lot, an atrium, a movie theater, a grocery store, a branch of the Carnegie Deli from New York, and other retail stores. Unfortunately, the plans fell through and never came to fruition.

Thanks to all the Hollywood stories associated with the place, the Schwab's legend lives on. And so does the recipe for its most famous sundae, a treat that's worth replicating. ✕

Above left: **Customers enjoying desserts at the fountain counter, 1952.** ▪ *Above right:* **A rare quiet moment outside Schwab's, 1949.** ▪ *Below left:* **Janet Blair with Sidney Skolsky (***right***), 1949.** ▪ *Below right:* **Sidney Skolsky in his telephone booth "office," 1948.**

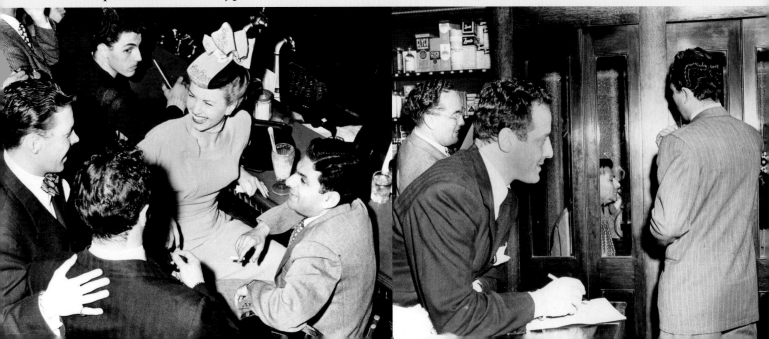

Holiday Hot Fudge Brownie Sundae

Even though the Hollywood starlets who came to Schwab's were constantly watching their waistlines, the Hot Fudge Brownie Sundae was the most popular sundae on the pharmacy's menu. Here is a special version of the sundae, served during the holidays.

Serves 1

1 Holiday Fudge Brownie (recipe follows)
1 scoop vanilla bean ice cream
4 oz. Hot Fudge Sauce (recipe follows)
whipped cream
1 tsp. chopped pecans
1 maraschino cherry

1. Place the brownie in the bottom of an ice cream dish and add the ice cream on top.
2. Drizzle with the hot fudge sauce, then top with the whipped cream, sprinkle with the pecans, and place the cherry on top.

Holiday Fudge Brownies

With a load of candy canes left over from the holidays one year, Schwab's decided to chop them into their brownie batter and create a new dessert. After they used up the candy canes, they switched to hard candy mints, which were available year-round.

Makes 24 brownies

1¼ cups granulated sugar
¾ cup unsalted butter, at room temperature
½ cup unsweetened cocoa powder
2 large eggs
1 tsp. pure vanilla extract
1½ cups all-purpose flour

1 tsp. baking powder
¼ tsp. baking soda
1 cup whole milk
1 cup chopped candy canes or hard candy mints

1. Preheat the oven to 350°F. Line a 9 x 12-inch baking pan with foil and spray the foil with nonstick cooking spray.
2. In a 2-quart saucepan over medium heat, heat the sugar, butter, and cocoa powder until the butter melts, stirring constantly. Remove from the heat. Whisk in the eggs and vanilla. Beat lightly until just combined. Set aside.
3. In a large bowl, whisk together the flour, baking powder, and baking soda. Add the dry ingredients, alternating with the milk, to the chocolate mixture in a few batches. Beat after each addition. Stir in the candy canes. Pour into the prepared baking pan.
4. Bake for about 20 minutes, or until a tester comes out with small crumbs attached. Cool in the pan on a wire rack before cutting into squares.

Hot Fudge Sauce

Makes 2 cups

1 cup heavy cream
6 tbsp. unsalted butter
⅔ cup granulated sugar
⅔ cup firmly packed dark brown sugar
pinch of sea salt
1 cup Dutch-process cocoa powder, sifted
¼ cup dark corn syrup

1. In a heavy-bottomed saucepan over medium heat, bring the cream and butter to a low boil. Add the granulated and brown sugars, stir to dissolve, and heat for about 3 minutes.
2. Lower the heat, add the salt and cocoa powder, and whisk until smooth.
3. Add the corn syrup and stir for 2 minutes over medium heat, being careful not to boil over.
4. Serve warm. If the sauce cools down, you can place it in a jar and reheat in a saucepan of hot water.

Behind the counter at Schwab's, 1945.

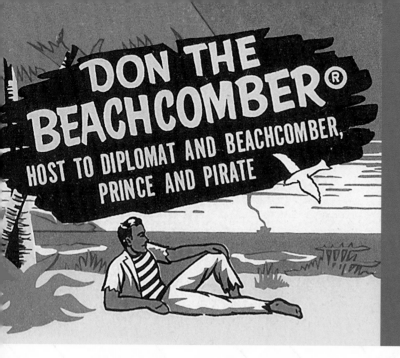

Don the Beachcomber

OPEN: 1934–1985

LOCATION: 1727 N. McCadden Place
Los Angeles, CA 90028

ORIGINAL PHONE: HO 9-3968

CUISINE: South Pacific

BUILDING STYLE: Polynesian

CURRENTLY: Apartment Building

"DONN BEACH" WAS BORN ERNEST RAYMOND BEAUMONT GANTT IN TEXAS IN 1907. After traveling in the South Pacific and the Caribbean, he landed in Hollywood and worked as an illegal bootlegger, making moonshine during Prohibition for a number of years.

After Prohibition was repealed in 1933, Donn opened Don the Beachcomber, a small café and bar in the corner of a small hotel bar at 1722 N. McCadden Place, where he concocted powerful rum drinks for his customers. With his business growing in popularity, Donn had his eye on a larger space across the street, at 1727 N. McCadden. He and his girlfriend, Cora Irene "Sunny" Sund, raised the money together to move into the new location three years later.

Inspired by his travels, Donn filled the new place with Polynesian flair, including a bamboo bar with matching barstools, fishing nets draped on the walls, large glass fishing weights in every shade of blue and green imaginable, and the now-ubiquitous cocktail umbrellas adorning his drinks. Thus, Donn Beach became the founding father of the Polynesian "tiki" bar. Donn could also rightly claim that he was the first cross-marketing restaurateur, with a rum shop, gift store, and Chinese grocery just inside his bar's front door.

A shrewd businessman, Donn installed a sprinkler system on top of the bar's tin roof so customers would think it was raining and stay for another drink. The food Donn served paired

Don the Beachcomber, 1938.

perfectly with the drinks he developed. His dishes were mainly hyped-up Chinese fare, with pineapple and coconut flavors and island flair in the presentation.

Donn was, above all, a creative bartender. His cocktails were mostly rum-based; rum was the drink of the islands, and it was very accessible. Many say that Donn created the mai tai in 1934 (Trader Vic's of San Francisco claims that they were the drink's original creators, but not until the 1940s). Also first shaken, stirred, and blended by Donn were the PiYi (served in a miniature pineapple), the Missionary's Downfall,

the Vicious Virgin, the Never Say Die, the Cobra's Fang, the Zombie, the Tahitian Rum Punch, and the Navy Grog (said to be Frank Sinatra's favorite drink at the Don the Beachcomber Palm Springs location). Donn created a total of eighty-four different cocktails.

Donn served in the U.S. Army during World War II, leaving his beloved tiki bar under Sunny's management. She helped expand the place into sixteen locations from coast to coast. Upon his return, Donn and Sunny filed for divorce, and she gained full control of the business.

Under the terms of his divorce from Sunny, Donn was not allowed to open a Don the Beachcomber in the United States. Since Hawaii was not a state at the time, Donn moved to Waikiki, where he opened a Don the Beachcomber location on Waikiki Beach and fully immersed himself in tiki paradise. He also built the open-air International Market Place in the center of Honolulu's tourist area, where his offices were located above an enormous banyan tree. (The International Market Place was closed in 2014 to make way for a Saks Fifth Avenue.)

In 1958, the Don the Beachcomber franchise was sold to Joe Drown, owner of the Hotel Bel-Air. At the time, the area had become a haven for tiki bars, such as the Zamboanga South Seas Club, the Pirate's Den, the Tonga Hut, Tiki Ti, and many others, all frequented by celebrities.

Donn died of liver cancer in Hawaii in 1989, at the age of eighty-one. Today, only three locations still carry the name Don the Beachcomber. In 2001, Disney's California Adventure in Anaheim, California, opened a small Don the Beachcomber that served food without the rum drinks; it closed a few years later. Today, Marisol, LLC, owns the rights to the bar and its name. They opened two locations in Hawaii in 2005 and struck a licensing deal with Huntington Beach's Sam's Seafood in 2009 for the use of Don the Beachcomber signage and many of the original recipes. ✕

F. Hugh Herbert and Mark Robson, producers of MGM's *The Little Hut*, at Don the Beachcomber for a press party, 1957.

Malihinis . . . .

IN ORDER to serve our Cantonese cuisine in the finest way possible, we cook all our dishes to order. This policy permits us to serve a large variety of Beachcomber dishes —in fact, more than forty. However, we suggest that until you become familiar with our menu, it is better to consult with your waiter who will recommend not only entrees that complement each other, but also quantities that will assure a satisfying dinner for you and your guests. This is only a suggestion, of course, but a great majority of our old-time Beachcombers prefer this procedure, and we thought you would like to know about it.

BEACHCOMBER APPETIZERS

FRIED SHRIMP (Cantonese) Cooked in Peanut Oil............. 1.75
Half Order .90

CHINESE BARBECUED TENDERLOIN OF PORK............ 1.60

EGG ROLL Stuffed with minced Crab Meat, Pork, Bamboo Shoots and Water Chestnuts................................ 1.35

RUMAKI Spiced Chicken Liver, Water Chestnuts wrapped in crisp Bacon 1.35

HAWAIIAN-CHINESE BARBECUED SPARERIBS 1.75

BARBECUED CHICKEN (Canton Style) Disjointed and served with Seaweed Salt.................................... 2.25

BABY SQUAB (Canton Style) Disjointed and served with Seaweed Salt........ 2.25

CANTONESE SOUPS

(All prepared with Chicken Broth)

CHINESE WONTON .... .70

HEART OF CHINESE GREENS............................. .60

CHINESE EGG NOODLES with Pork and Chinese Greens........ .85

MINCED BREAST OF CHICKEN WITH RICE................. .85

EGG FLOWER WITH SHERRY............................... .75

CHINESE EGG NOODLES with Breast of Chicken and Chinese Greens .... .85

ENTREES

MANDARIN DUCK Boned, molded, crisped in Peanut Oil and served with Wild Plum Sauce................................... 2.50
Half Order 1.30

BEACHCOMBER CHICKEN Strips of Chicken cooked with whole Soya Beans, Ginger, Garlic and other Spices............... 2.50

BEACHCOMBER LOBSTER Prepared Cantonese style with Black Bean sauce, Eggs, and Chinese spices.................... 2.75

CHICKEN ALMOND Tender Chicken cooked with Mushrooms, Bamboo Shoots, Celery and Water Chestnuts.............. 2.10

CHICKEN MUSHROOM Thinly-sliced Chicken cooked with whole, Black Chinese Mushrooms 2.10

CHICKEN PINEAPPLE Chicken sauted with Pineapple and Green Peppers 2.10

CHICKEN MANUU Strips of Breast of Chicken with fine cut Chinese Vegetables and Mushrooms....................... 2.10

CANTONESE CHICKEN Thinly sliced Chicken rolled in Egg Batter and sauted with Pineapple and Green Peppers............ 2.10

CHICKEN SOYO Tender Chicken cooked in Soyo Sauce with Water Chestnuts, Onions, and Bamboo Shoots.................... 2.10

CHICKEN TOMATO Tender Chicken cooked with fresh Tomatoes. 2.10

BEEF SOYO Tenderloin of Beef sauted in Soyo Sauce with Water Chestnuts, Onions, and Bamboo Shoots.................. 2.00

BEEF TOMATO Beef Tenderloin cubes cooked with fresh Tomatoes. 1.90

BEEF VEGETABLE Fine cut Filet of Beef with sliced Chinese Vegetables 1.90

INDIVIDUAL NOODLES Fried Crisp in Peanut Oil............. .50

CHINESE PEA PODS Young tender Chinese Pea Pods cooked with Celery and Pork 1.75

CHINESE GREENS Hearts of Chinese Greens cooked with Pork.. 1.75

MIXED GREENS Pea Pods, Chinese Greens, Onions, Water Chestnuts, Celery, Bean Sprouts, Green Peppers and Pork........ 1.75

WATER CHESTNUTS Imported Chinese Water Chestnuts sliced and cooked with Pork.................................... 2.00

CHOW DUN Chinese Water Chestnuts, Green Peas, sauted and scrambled with eggs.
With Pork. 1.60   With Shrimp. 1.60   With Chicken. 1.75

SEA BASS BEACHCOMBER Pacific Sea Bass browned, then cooked with sliced Vegetables and Chinese Spices............... 2.25

SHRIMP CANTONESE Fresh Shrimps rolled in Egg Batter then sauted with Pineapple and Green Peppers................. 2.00

SHRIMP VEGETABLE Fresh Shrimps cooked with hearts of Chinese Greens, Onions and Celery...................... 2.00

CHUNGKING SHRIMP Shredded Shrimps cooked with Pork, Water Chestnuts, Eggs and Green Onions...................... 2.25
Half Order 1.25

LOBSTER CHUNGKING New Zealand Lobster tails cooked in a Chungking sauce with Water Chestnuts, Eggs, and Green Onions 2.50

FRIED WONTON Crisped and served with sauce of fresh Tomatoes, Green Peppers, Onions and Barbecued Pork............. 1.25

CANTONESE PORK Thinly sliced Tenderloin of Pork rolled in batter and sauted with Pineapple and Green Peppers........ 2.00

PORK SOYO Pork Tenderloin sauted in Soyo Sauce with Water Chestnuts, Onions and Bamboo Shoots.................... 2.00

PEAS & CHESTNUTS Pea Pods, sliced Pork cooked with Imported Chinese Black Mushrooms and Water Chestnuts........... 2.00

CHINESE FRIED RICE

RICE with minced Roast Pork, Water Chestnuts and Green Onions .35

(Also served with either Chicken or Shrimp)

(Above prices are for individual servings)

DESSERTS

FRESH HAWAIIAN SUGAR LOAF PINEAPPLE............... 1.50
Half Order .85

JALAPA TREE RIPENED MANGOES (individual serving)...... .50

ASSORTED FRUITS IN SEASON served on snow ice........... 1.50
Half Order .85

ALMOND COOKIES ....each .10

Roasted Tenderloin of Pork

Donn created this recipe to work with any of his signature drinks, for a perfect balance of flavors.

Serves 4

½ cup granulated sugar
1½ tsp. sea salt
⅛ tsp. garlic powder
⅛ tsp. white pepper
¼ cup ketchup
¼ cup soy sauce
1 tbsp. brandy
3 lb. pork tenderloin

1. In a bowl, combine the sugar, salt, garlic powder, white pepper, ketchup, soy sauce, and brandy. Set aside.
2. Place the meat in a shallow dish and pour the mixture on top to coat. Turn the meat over to make sure both sides are coated. Cover and marinate in the refrigerator for 3 hours.
3. Preheat the oven to 400°F.
4. Line a shallow pan with foil, remove the tenderloin from the marinade, place in the pan, and roast for 35 minutes, or until no longer pink inside.
5. Slice the tenderloins thin and serve with spicy mustard.

Servers at Don the Beachcomber, 1947.

Above: The entrance to Don the Beachcomber, 1957. ▪ *Below:* The restaurant was filled with Polynesian-themed decor, 1947.

Navy Grog

Donn Beach created a number of tropical drinks, and this one—Frank Sinatra's favorite—was copied in most tiki bars nationwide.

Serves 1

1 oz. white rum
1 oz. demerara rum
1 oz. dark rum
¾ oz. freshly squeezed lime juice
¾ oz. white grapefruit juice
1 oz. honey
club soda
1 orange slice
1 cherry

1. In a cocktail shaker filled with ice, blend the three rums with the lime juice, white grapefruit juice, and honey. Shake well.
2. Fill a collins glass with ice. Strain the drink into the glass. Top with club soda. Garnish with the orange slice and cherry.

Donn Beach taking a call at the restaurant, 1947.

DON THE BEACHCOMBER ORIGINAL RUM DRINKS

BEACHCOMBER'S PUNCH

COCONUT RUM

Q. B. COOLER

DON BEACH

ZOMBIE

TEST PILOT

Barbados Punch	. . . . . .	$1.10
Barbados Swizzle	. . . .	.95
Beachcomber's Gold	. . . . .	.95
Beachcomber's Punch	. . .	1.10
Beachcomber's Rum Barrel, *serves 2* . .	2.25
Beachcomber's Sangaree	. . . . .	.95
Beachcomber's Silver	. . . .	.95
Caribbean Punch	. . . . . .	1.10
Cobra's Fang	. . . .	1.25
Coconut Rum	. . . .	2.00

Myrtle Bank Punch	. . . . . .	$ .95
Mystery Gardenia	. . . . .	.95
Navy Grog, *limit of 3*	. . . . .	1.60
Nelson's Blood	. . . .	.95
Never Say Die	. . . . . .	1.10
Nui Nui, *limit of 3*	. . . . . .	1.60
Panama Daiquiri	. . . . .	.95
Pearl Diver	. . . . . .	1.10
Penang Afrididi No. 1	. . . . .	1.60
Penang Afrididi No. 2	. . . . .	.95

DR. FUNK

SHARK'S TOOTH

QUEEN'S ROAD COCKTAIL

MONTEGO BAY

PLANTER'S RUM PUNCH

COLONIAL GROG

DON'S PEARL

SUMATRA KULA

Colonial Grog	. . . . . .	$ .95
Cuban Daiquiri	. . . . . .	.95
Demerara Cocktail	. . . . .	.95
Demerara Dry Float	. . . . .	1.10
Don Beach	. . . .	.95
Donga Punch	. . . . . .	.95
Don's Own Planters, *limit of 2 per person* . .	1.75
Don's Pearl	. . . .	.95
Dr. Funk	. . . .	.95
Pi Yi	. . . .	2.00

Planter's Rum Punch	. . . . . .	$1.10
Puka Punch, *limit of 2*	. . . .	1.60
Q. B. Cooler, *limit of 2*	. . . .	1.60
Queen's Road Cocktail	. . . .	.95
Rum Cow	. . . .	.95
Rum, Gum and Lime	. . . .	.95
Rum Julep	. . . .	1.10
Shark's Tooth	. . . . . .	1.10
Skull & Bones	. . . . . .	1.10
Don's Reserve Rum Daiquiri	. . . .	1.10

BEACHCOMBER'S GOLD

DEMERARA DRY FLOAT

COBRA'S FANG

NEVER SAY DIE

PI YI

COFFEE GROG

VICIOUS VIRGIN

CUBAN DAIQUIRI

NAVY GROG

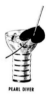

PEARL DIVER

General Pico	. . . . . .	$ .95
Governor General	. . . . .	.95
Hot Buttered Rum	. . . . .	.95
Hot Rum Grog	. . . . . .	.95
Kona Coffee Grog	. . . . .	1.20
Martinique Cocktail	. . . . .	.95
Martinique Milk Punch	. . . .	.95
Missionary's Downfall	. . . .	.95
Mona Punch	. . . . . .	2.00
Montego Bay	. . . . . .	.95

Sugar Loaf Punch	. . . . . .	$ .95
Sumatra Kula	. . . . . .	.95
Sunakora	. . . .	1.10
151° Swizzle, *limit of 3*	. . . .	1.60
Tahitian Rum Punch	. . . . .	1.00
Test Pilot, *limit of 2*	. . . .	1.80
Three Dots and a Dash (• • • — V)	1.10
Vicious Virgin	. . . . . .	.95
West Indian Punch	. . . . .	.95
Zombie, *limit of 2*	. . . . .	2.00

MISSIONARY'S DOWNFALL

THREE DOTS AND A DASH

TAHITIAN RUM PUNCH

MYSTERY GARDENIA

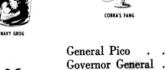

The bamboo bar at Don the Beachcomber, 1947.

The Zombie

Donn Beach reportedly created this drink as a cure for a friend's hangover. It didn't help.

Serves 1

½ oz. white rum
1 oz. dark rum
1½ oz. golden rum
1 oz. freshly squeezed lime juice
1 tsp. pineapple juice
1 tsp. papaya juice
½ oz. 151-proof rum
1 cherry

1. In a cocktail shaker filled with ice, blend the white, dark, and golden rums with the lime, pineapple, and papaya juices. Shake well.
2. Fill a collins glass with ice. Strain the drink into the glass. Top with the 151-proof rum. Garnish with a cherry. You can also light this drink on fire for a dramatic effect.

Clifton's Brookdale Cafeteria

OPEN: 1935–2011; 2015–present

LOCATION: 648 S. Broadway
Los Angeles, CA 90014

ORIGINAL PHONE: MA7-1673

CURRENT PHONE: (213) 627-1673

CUISINE: Cafeteria

DESIGN: Charles F. Plummer

BUILDING STYLE: Woodland Kitsch

CLIFTON'S BROOKDALE CAFETERIA, ONCE PART OF A CHAIN OF CLIFTON'S RESTAURANTS, IS THE OLDEST SURVIVING CAFETERIA-STYLE RESTAURANT IN LOS ANGELES. The name Clifton's is a combination of the first and last names of its founder, Clifford Clinton.

Each Clifton's location had its own theme and look. The first Clifton's, which opened in 1931 at 618 S. Olive Street, had a Pacific Seas theme, with waterfalls and tropical plants and flowers. The location on Broadway in downtown L.A., which opened four years later in the former Boos Brothers Cafeteria, was named Clifton's Brookdale and redecorated to resemble a nature lodge Clinton had visited in the Santa Cruz Mountains. Artist Einar C. Petersen created a life-size forest on canvas to cover one wall, and rock sculptor Francois Scotti created a twenty-foot waterfall for the cafeteria that cascaded into a stream flowing past faux redwood trees. Between the trees, you could also find a taxidermied raccoon, a fishing bear, and a moose head.

The three-story eatery offered seating for 600 people. Known as the largest public cafeteria in operation, the Brookdale location—one of seven Clifton's restaurants in the city—remained open for seventy-six years.

Most of the food produced in the mass kitchen is homemade, without the use of mixes or packaged products. The dishes are sold on a pay-per-item basis, and the selection is immense. The menu includes comfort food like creamy mac and cheese, fried chicken with buttermilk biscuits, oxtail stew, turkey and dressing, whipped and fried potatoes, cranberry jewel gelatin, and grilled cheese sandwiches cooked crisp and pressed flat as a pancake.

Above: A postcard of Clifton's Brookdale Cafeteria. ▪ *Left:* Clifford Clinton, 1945. ▪ *Opposite:* The forest-themed Clifton's Brookdale Cafeteria, 1950.

(MPM) MULTI-PURPOSE MEAL. Clifton's COMPLETELY BALANCED, NUTRITIONALLY ADEQUATE FIVE-CENT MEAL (no charge to those without funds).

When it originally opened, Clifton's maintained a precedent known as Clifton's Golden Rule, which was "Dine Free Unless Delighted." Determined to make an impact on world hunger, Clifford Clinton worked with the California Institute of Technology to develop what they called "Multi-Purpose Meals"—high-protein, nutritious meals that could be sold at Clifton's for just a nickel per serving. During the war years, the cafeteria served upwards of 10,000 customers, with lines wrapping around the block. The restaurant never turned anyone away hungry. During one ninety-day period, Clifton's served 10,000 free meals, and then decided to open up an emergency "Penny Cafeteria" a few blocks away from the Broadway location, with the help of vendors and generous suppliers. By 1940, the cafeterias were serving up to 25,000 meals a day.

One notable patron of the Brookdale cafeteria was science fiction writer Ray Bradbury. The author spent his afternoons writing at the Los Angeles Central Library, and then would walk the few blocks down to Clifton's for lunch. Many times, he would take advantage of the Clifton's policy that anyone who couldn't afford to pay didn't have to. In the 1930s, Bradbury visited Clifton's to attend meetings of the Los Angeles Science Fiction Society, which met on the third floor for years. Bradbury also celebrated his eighty-ninth birthday at Clifton's in 2009.

Aloha— Clifton's "Pacific Seas" 618 So. Olive St., Los Angeles

Above: The Clifton's Brookdale facade, 1940. ▪ *Opposite top:* Pictorial showing a woman eating Clifton's Multi-Purpose Food, 1950. ▪ *Opposite bottom:* Postcard showing the Clifton's Pacific Seas location.

In 1935, L.A. County Supervisor John Anson Ford inadvertently inserted Clifford Clinton into the political arena by asking him to investigate food operations at the County General Hospital. After Clinton submitted his report that patients were being served food that was low-quality at best and rancid at worst, Clifton's was suddenly inundated with health inspections and complaints about food poisoning. Clinton did not take these attacks lying down. He formed a committee to investigate vice in the city, exposing bribery and other illegal activity taking place at City Hall. Clinton remained involved in politics for the rest of his life—despite literal death threats, such as the bomb that exploded in his basement in 1937.

In 1946, Clinton and his wife, Nelda, sold the cafeteria interest to their three children and retired to devote their attention to their nonprofit charitable organization, "Meals for Millions," which they had founded in the middle of World War II. The organization distributed food to millions of hungry and malnourished people throughout the world.

Clinton died peacefully in his Los Angeles home in 1969, at the age of sixty-nine. He was buried at Forest Lawn Cemetery in Glendale. After his death, Clinton's cafeterias closed one by one, until finally only the Clifton's location on Broadway remained.

In 2006, Robert Clinton took final steps to purchase the Clifton's Brookdale building that he had been leasing for seventy-one years. In 2010, Andrew Meieran, owner of the Edison nightclub in downtown L.A., bought Clifton's Brookdale and renovated the place with the aim of preserving the food and history of the establishment, including some of its original recipes from the 1950s. The renovated Clifton's, which opened in 2015, retains many of its original design features, including the forest theme, taxidermied animals, and the woodland mural on the wall. ✗

Buttermilk Biscuits

In the morning, Clifton's pairs these biscuits with gravy for breakfast; for lunch, they're served as a side with fried chicken.

Makes 16 biscuits

1½ cups all-purpose flour
1½ cups cake flour
4¼ tsp. baking powder
1½ tsp. sea salt
½ cup vegetable shortening
⅛ tsp. baking soda
1 cup plus 2 tbsp. buttermilk
¼ cup all-purpose flour
1 large egg white, beaten

1. Preheat oven to 375°F.
2. Using a mixer with a paddle attachment, mix together the flours, baking powder and salt. Add the shortening and mix at low speed until the shortening is broken up well.
3. In a cup, combine the baking soda and buttermilk. Add to the flour mixture. Mix until all ingredients are well-blended.
4. Place dough on a floured surface and roll out to about ¾-inch thick. Cut with a 2-inch biscuit cutter dipped in flour. Place cut biscuits on a parchment-lined baking sheet, close enough that they are touching each other.
5. Brush tops with a little beaten egg white.
6. Bake in preheated oven until golden brown, about 15 to 18 minutes.

Zucchini Monterey

Clifton's serves this dish mainly on the weekends.

SOUVENIR TICKET
CLIFTON'S   Nº 85596
COURTESY CITY TOUR
Seeing down town Los Angeles, Exposition Park, Wilshire Blvd., General McArthur Park, Plaza and Civic Center.
PRICE 15c
Starting Point Clifton's Cafeteria, 618 So. Olive.

Serves 4 to 6

1½ lbs. zucchini, diced
4 large eggs, beaten
½ cup whole milk
1 tsp. sea salt
dash of red pepper flakes
2 tsp. baking powder
3 tbsp. all-purpose flour
¼ cup chopped parsley
4 oz. diced green chiles
2 tbsp. diced pimiento
1 lb. Monterey Jack cheese, shredded
1½ tsp. canola oil
⅓ cup breadcrumbs
1 tbsp. unsalted butter, softened

1. Preheat oven to 350°F
2. Steam zucchini over boiling salted water, until tender yet still crisp. Set aside.
3. In a bowl, combine eggs, milk, salt, red pepper flakes, baking powder, flour, and parsley. Whisk well to remove lumps. Add chiles, pimiento, and cheese. Mix very well. Add steamed zucchini.
4. Butter a 2-quart casserole dish and dust with breadcrumbs. Place zucchini mixture in the dish, top with the remaining breadcrumbs, and dot with butter. Bake for 50 to 55 minutes, or until browned on top. Serve hot.

Rice Custard

This rice custard—along with the jewel gelatin—is a favorite at Clifton's.

Serves 8

4 large eggs, beaten
½ cup granulated sugar
⅔ tsp. ground mace
¼ tsp. sea salt
3 cups whole milk, room temperature
1 tsp. pure vanilla extract
1⅓ cups cooked rice

1. Preheat oven to 400°F
2. In a bowl, blend the eggs, sugar, mace, and salt. Add the milk and mix well.
3. Place the cooked rice into prepared 8-inch square pan. Pour milk mixture over the rice, filling the pan to within ½ an inch from the top.
4. Place the rice pan into a larger pan. Pour hot water into the larger pan, until it comes about halfway up the side of the rice pan.
5. Bake until a knife inserted in the center comes out clean, about 35 to 40 minutes.
6. Cut into servings.

Above: The woodsy, life-size wall mural and faux redwood trees at Clifton's Brookdale. ▪ *Opposite left and right:* A 1950 Clifton's pictorial showed the entrance to the Clifton's Brookdale service room, which featured an old mill wheel, and a Clifton's photographer who would capture "your photograph, in beautiful surroundings while you dine."

Zucchini Cake

This moist, delicious cake is topped with cream cheese icing for a tasty treat.

Serves 10 to 12

2 cups granulated sugar
1 cup canola oil
3 large eggs
2 cups all-purpose flour
1 tsp. baking soda
1 tsp. sea salt
1 tbsp. ground cinnamon
2 cups zucchini, shredded and packed
1 cup finely chopped pecans
1 tbsp. pure vanilla extract
Cream Cheese Icing (recipe follows)

1. Preheat oven to 350°F.
2. Using a mixer with a paddle attachment, blend the sugar, oil, and eggs at medium speed for 4 minutes. Set aside.
3. In a large bowl, whisk the flour, soda, salt, and cinnamon and set aside. Fold the zucchini and pecans into the egg mixture. Fold the egg mixture into the flour mixture and add the vanilla, blending thoroughly.
4. Pour into prepared 10-inch tube pan. Bake until a toothpick inserted into the center comes out clean, about 60 to 65 minutes.
5. Cool cake in the pan for 15 minutes. Invert onto a cooling rack.
6. Top with Cream Cheese Icing.

Cream Cheese Icing

Makes about 3 cups

3 cups powdered sugar
6 oz. cream cheese, softened
5 tbsp. unsalted butter, softened
1 tsp. freshly squeezed lemon juice

1. Using a mixer with a paddle attachment, blend the sugar, cream cheese, butter, and lemon juice. Whip at a higher speed to make fluffy. Refrigerate until needed.

Pumpkin Cake with Cream Cheese Frosting

This cake is a crowd favorite in autumn.

Serves 12 to 18 (one 9 x 13-inch cake)

3 cups granulated sugar
3 cups all-purpose flour
1 tbsp. baking powder
1 tbsp. baking soda
1 tbsp. ground cinnamon
¾ tsp. sea salt
1½ cups canola oil
3¼ cups canned pumpkin purée
4 large eggs, beaten
Cream Cheese Frosting (recipe follows)

1. Preheat oven to 325°F.
2. Using a mixer with a paddle attachment on medium speed, blend the sugar, flour, baking powder, baking soda, cinnamon, and sea salt until well-mixed. With the mixer running, add the oil and beat until completely moistened. With mixer still running, add the pumpkin and eggs and blend 1 minute.
3. Pour into prepared 9 x 13-inch baking pan, sprayed with a non-stick spray and lined with parchment on the bottom. Smooth out the batter.
4. Place in preheated oven for 38 to 40 minutes, or until a toothpick inserted into center comes out clean. Cool in the pan for 10 minutes, then invert on a wire rack and cool completely.
5. Top with Cream Cheese Frosting.

Cream Cheese Frosting

Makes about 3 cups

1 lb. powdered sugar
8 oz. cream cheese, softened
½ cup unsalted butter, softened
2 tsp. pure vanilla extract
½ cup chopped raisins

1. Using a mixer with a paddle attachment on medium speed, mix the sugar, cream cheese, butter, and vanilla until well-blended. Add raisins. Refrigerate until needed.

Chasen's

OPEN: 1936–1995

LOCATION: 9039 Beverly Boulevard
Los Angeles, CA 90048

ORIGINAL PHONE: CR 1-2168

CUISINE: American

DESIGN: Paul Revere Williams

BUILDING STYLE: Vogue Regency

CURRENTLY: Bristol Farms Grocery Store

ORIGINALLY NAMED CHASEN'S SOUTHERN BARBECUE PIT, CHASEN'S WAS DESTINED TO BECOME HOLLYWOOD'S MOST FAMOUS EATERY. After receiving a $3,500 advance from *New Yorker* magazine founder and editor Harold Ross to help fund the restaurant, Dave Chasen and his partner, Joe Cook, opened Chasen's on Beverly Boulevard in 1936, a few weeks before Christmas.

Chasen's was small, with only six tables, a six-stool bar, and an eight-stool counter. The menu was limited and offered Southern fare like chili and ribs. The price of spareribs was thirty-five cents, a bowl of chili was twenty-five cents, and a call drink (a tipple containing the customer's choice of liquor) was thirty-five cents. In the entire history of Chasen's, the restaurant never accepted checks or credit cards—only cash.

With Ross's help, news of the restaurant spread and celebrities started coming to the barbecue pit. Ross talked Dave Chasen into giving Dorothy Parker one free drink a night, because her presence at the restaurant drew publicity. The restaurant's list of famous regulars grew, including Frank Sinatra, Buddy Ebsen, Groucho Marx, W. C. Fields, Jimmy Cagney, Charlie Chaplin, Ray Bolger, Joan Bennett, Joe DiMaggio, William Powell, Joan Blondell, Nunnally Johnson, James Thurber, Robert Benchley, and Alexander Woollcott.

Within a year, the place expanded from a small rib parlor to a restaurant, with more than thirty-five items on the menu served by full-service, uniformed waiters. As the space, clientele, and menu expanded, the name was shortened to "Chasen's." Every night, when the venue opened for dinner, Dave Chasen, who was always impeccably dressed, welcomed guests at the door wearing a suit lined in red silk and a bowtie.

Bill Grady, Hollywood's number-one casting director in the 1930s, loved the restaurant's steak and garlic bread and had his own table at the venue. Grady thought of his table as his own private office. "I did more business there, and I signed more actors there, than anywhere else," he recalled. Grady ate at the restaurant with his favorite client, Jimmy Stewart, about four times a week, as well as other clients such as Mickey Rooney and Clark Gable. Jimmy Stewart even wined and dined his future wife, Gloria McLean, at Chasen's. In 1949, Grady rented out the entire restaurant for Stewart's bachelor party,

Above: Dave Chasen, Jimmy Stewart, Bill Grady, and Spencer Tracy at Chasen's, 1949. ▪ *Opposite:* Dave Chasen outside his restaurant.

Above: Jimmy Stewart and his wife, Gloria McLean (*left*) were regulars at Chasen's, 1955. ▪ *Opposite:* Child stars Freddie Bartholomew, Peggy Ryan, Mickey Rooney, Deanna Durbin, Judy Garland, and Jackie Cooper at Chasen's, 1936.

attended by Spencer Tracy, Gary Cooper, Frank Morgan, George Murphy, Jack Benny, Lew Wasserman, and David Niven. Stewart's booth from Chasen's is now on display at the Jimmy Stewart Museum in his hometown of Indiana, Pennsylvania.

Other celebrities had their "special" tables at the restaurant as well, including Cary Grant, Ronald Colman, and Leslie Howard. Humphrey Bogart, Alfred Hitchcock, Frank Sinatra, and Ronald Reagan had their own permanent booths. Reagan proposed to actress Nancy Davis at Chasen's in 1952; his booth from the restaurant is on permanent display at the Ronald Reagan Presidential Library in Simi Valley, California.

Of all the restaurant's star patrons, Orson Welles reportedly had the biggest appetite; according to Hollywood lore, he ordered two of everything. Frank Sinatra was the smallest eater, reportedly only consuming half of what was served or ordering half portions, if it was allowed. And it's said that Howard Hughes had the simplest palate, ordering tomato juice, butterflied steak, and salad.

Chasen's became famous for its delicious cheese toast appetizer, colossal seafood platter, Caesar salad prepared tableside, and buffet that offered Beluga caviar. Regulars requested off-the-menu items like the renowned Hobo Steak, a thick New York cut that was roasted very rare in a crust of salt before being sliced and finished in butter in a copper sauté pan at the table. The chili at Chasen's was its biggest culinary draw; customers ordered it even after it was taken off the menu. Dave Chasen reportedly kept the recipe a secret, and came in every Sunday to make up a batch for the week. Today, the Bristol Farms grocery store, built on the site of the former restaurant, takes special orders for Chasen's chili in its catering department.

In 1939, newlyweds Clark Gable and Carole Lombard took Alfred Hitchcock to Chasen's soon after he arrived in Hollywood to direct *Rebecca*. From then on, Hitch had a standing dinner reservation in booth number 2 on Thursday nights for more than forty years. Hitchcock routinely fell asleep at the table. A picture of Hitch's daughter, Patricia, hung on the wall behind the booth.

When Howard Hughes bought Transcontinental and Western Air in 1939, he asked Dave Chasen to help him become the first airline to serve passengers hot food on good china and linens instead of the usual boxed sandwiches that Bill Marriott and his "Hot Shoppes" were serving on the East Coast. Hughes selected Chasen's to cater the party for the launch of the Spruce Goose for its one and only flight on November 2, 1947.

During the war years, it was difficult to get a seat at Chasen's. The Hollywood hot spot had strict rules that forbade autograph hounds and photographers from disturbing its celebrity diners. Because of this, stars felt that they could let their hair down at the restaurant. At one time, the building even included a barbershop, steam room, and shower area so stars traveling from the East Coast could go straight to the restaurant and freshen up before their meal.

Tommy Gallagher, one of the captains of the restaurant's prestigious "Station 8" front room, worked at Chasen's for over forty-six years. Gallagher often greeted the famous at the front door by their first name, and occasionally with a cunning remark. One time, he said to then-Vice President George Bush, "George, you know what your main problem is? You need a new tailor." Only Gallagher could get away with making a comment like that.

The Chestnut Room

RIEN SUPERIEUR

The Magnolia Room

Despite his lighthearted demeanor, Gallagher took his job seriously. When Nancy Reagan was in the hospital giving birth, he showed up with bags of Chasen's food for her. Such behavior was not considered outrageous; taking care of the Chasen's regulars was a staple of the house. When Lana Turner was expecting, Dave Chasen sawed off part of a table at the restaurant to accommodate her. He even shipped Chasen's special chili to Elizabeth Taylor when she was in Europe filming *Cleopatra* in the early 1960s. It came to be known as the most expensive chili on earth.

Chasen's was also the birthplace of a hit song. During a Grammy Awards celebration at the restaurant, singer Donna Summer went into the ladies room and noticed that the bathroom attendant had fallen asleep while watching a small portable television between visitors. This inspired Summer to write the song "She Works Hard for the Money."

After Dave Chasen's death in 1973, his wife and business partner, Maude, controlled the restaurant's operations for twenty-two years. By 1995, she was ready to retire. When Chasen's closed in April of that year, it had become a virtual time capsule of Old Hollywood, and many veteran stars turned out to bid it a fond farewell. An auction event was held in one of the restaurant's banquet rooms to sell off nearly sixty years' worth of memorabilia. On the auction list were sketches by Toulouse-Lautrec, drawings by humorist James Thurber, a picture of ballerinas signed "Degas" (no one was sure whether it was genuine), and a sketch by W. C. Fields of himself and John Barrymore. An enormous pressure cooker, four pianos, and 396 margarita glasses were also auctioned off.

In 1996, Chasen's reopened briefly for a very private catered event. Hollywood luminaries joined some of politics' biggest names to celebrate the eighty-fifth birthday of President Ronald Reagan. The president did not attend his own event, but dined quietly at his home in Bel-Air; former First Lady Nancy Reagan preferred that her husband avoid large gatherings after he was stricken with Alzheimer's disease.

Chasen's will be in my mind forever. In 1982, while working at a bakery called the Cake Walk, I delivered special chocolate cakes for a private party at Chasen's. The code on the order form read "RR." I can imagine who the cakes were for. When I entered the back door with the cakes in tow, Maude Chasen herself was there to greet me. That was my last view of Chasen's. ✕

The Chasen's entrance, 1951.

Hobo Steak

Dave Chasen developed this unusual treatment for New York steak, which produces a rich, tender, and memorable dish.

Serves 2

1 large New York steak, cut 3 inches thick
freshly ground black pepper
3 pieces applewood-smoked bacon
1 cup sea salt

2 tbsp. water
½ cup unsalted butter, softened
1 lb. loaf sourdough French bread,
    sliced ¼ inch thick and toasted

1. Season the steak with pepper. Wrap the sides with the bacon and secure with kitchen string. Place in a baking pan.
2. In a bowl, combine the salt and water to make a paste. Mound about three-fourths of the mixture on top of the steak, covering the meat completely. Place the steak under the broiler for 8 to 10 minutes.
3. Carefully remove the salt crust; try to keep it in one piece. Turn the steak over and place the crust on top. (If the crust breaks, mend it with the remaining one-fourth of the salt mixture.) Broil the steak again for another 8 to 10 minutes; the salt crust will become dark and dry-looking.
4. Discard the bacon and the salt crust. Let the meat stand for 15 minutes, then slice on the diagonal.
5. In a large skillet, melt the butter until foamy and lightly browned. Place a few pieces of the meat in the butter and cook to the desired doneness, about 1 minute on each side. Place each slice of meat on a piece of toast and spoon some of the hot butter over it.

Inside Chasen's, where countless celebrities dined for nearly six decades.

Maude Salad

This salad was created for and named after the Chasen's matriarch, Maude Chasen.

Serves 6

Salad:
8 cups shredded iceberg, romaine, and
chicory lettuces
4 large plum tomatoes, seeded and diced
4 large hard-boiled eggs, diced
2 bunches chives, chopped

Dressing:
1 cup mayonnaise
¾ cup sour cream
2 cloves garlic, minced
½ cup chili sauce
¼ cup red wine vinegar
10 oz. Roquefort cheese, crumbled
sea salt
freshly ground black pepper

1. In a large salad bowl, combine lettuces, tomatoes, eggs, and chives and toss. Chill.
2. To make the dressing, whisk mayonnaise, sour cream, garlic, chili sauce, and vinegar in a large bowl until well-blended. Stir in Roquefort cheese. Season with salt and pepper. Use desired amount to coat salad well. Sprinkle with Roquefort cheese.

Chasen's on Beverly Boulevard, 1956.

Chasen's

CR 1-2168

Close Cover Before Striking

Carrot Soufflé

Whenever a waiter brought out this dish at Chasen's, it would wow the entire table. It was originally dished out in single servings; this recipe has been modified so it may be served family style.

Serves 8

1½ lbs. carrots, sliced 1 inch thick and
    steamed until tender
⅓ cup unsalted butter, softened
½ medium onion, diced
⅓ cup all-purpose flour
½ tsp. sea salt

¼ tsp. ground nutmeg
1 cup whole milk
2 tbsp. packed light brown sugar
¼ cup apple or orange juice
6 large eggs, separated
¾ tsp. cream of tartar

1. Preheat the oven to 350°F.
2. Butter a 9 x 13-inch baking pan, sprinkle with sugar, and set aside.
3. Purée the carrots in a blender or food processor and set aside.
4. In a saucepan over medium heat, melt the butter, add the onion, and cook until tender, 3 to 4 minutes. Blend in the flour, salt, and nutmeg and cook until the mixture is smooth and bubbly, about 6 to 8 minutes. Whisk in the milk all at once. Add the brown sugar and cook, stirring constantly, until the mixture boils and thickens. Remove from the heat; add the puréed carrots and juice and stir to combine.
5. Using a mixer with a whip attachment, whip the egg whites with the cream of tartar at high speed until stiff, but not too dry. Stir the egg yolks into the carrot mixture. Fold the egg white mixture into the carrot mixture. Pour into the prepared pan and smooth the surface.
6. Bake until puffy and light brown, 40 to 45 minutes. Serve immediately.

Collier's

DECEMBER 6, 1941

© THE CROWELL-COLLIER PUBLISHING COMPANY—PUBLISHERS OF COLLIER'S—THE AMERICAN MAGAZINE—WOMAN'S HOME COMPANION

FIVE CENTS SEVEN CENTS IN CANADA

FLOHERTY JR

THE Cock'n Bull
Hollywood's Hot Spo

Cock 'n Bull

OPEN: 1937–1987

LOCATION: 9170 Sunset Boulevard
West Hollywood, CA 90069

ORIGINAL PHONE: BR 5-1397 and CR 6-7814

CUISINE: British Pub Fare

BUILDING STYLE: Colonial

CURRENTLY: Jaguar Dealership

JACK MORGAN, A FORMER WRITER AT MGM, HAD ALWAYS WANTED TO OWN AN ENGLISH PUB AS A HAPPY REMINDER OF HIS DAYS AS A STUDENT AT OXFORD UNIVERSITY. In the fall of 1937, his dream became a reality, and by 1968, the Cock 'n Bull reigned as the oldest restaurant on the Sunset Strip.

The Cock 'n Bull's cozy interior displayed antiques and art that Morgan had collected during his travels. British Empire etchings and polished brass fixtures hung from the walls; pewter and porcelain sat on the tables. Mementoes of royalty, including a portrait of Queen Victoria, were placed throughout the pub, instead of the typical Hollywood celebrity photographs. A plaque also hung on the wall listing the names of deceased regulars, including actor Jack Webb. On the restaurant's closing day, the plaque was marched down to Scandia (see page 173), which would become its new home.

The Cock 'n Bull was more of a private club than a restaurant. You would see the same people in the same booths on the same nights of the week, year after year. The menu was consistent as well, hardly changing at all over the years. Even the employees seemed to remain there forever. Ralph Olsen was a bartender at the Cock 'n Bull for fourteen years prior to becoming the pub's manager. Chef Vivian Langford held her position for more than twenty-five years.

Errol Flynn, F. Scott Fitzgerald, Sinclair Lewis, and Somerset Maugham were regulars around the bar, along with industry agents and deal-makers of the day. Hollywood gossip columnist Hedda Hopper often came to the Cock 'n Bull to observe its star patrons—what they ate, what they wore, what they said, and, of course, who they dined with. Hopper and her archrival, Louella Parsons, were the only members of the press allowed on the premises. One March night in 1938, Hopper was at the pub entertaining some friends from New York when she spotted a station wagon in front of the Cock 'n Bull packed with everything for a trip, including luggage strapped to the roof. Immediately, she knew exactly who was at the pub, eating dinner before leaving on a hunting trip: Clark Gable and Carole Lombard. Hopper commented in her column the next day that the two must have been fighting because Lombard was wearing a crazy hat, knowing full well that Gable hated her in hats like that. Further proof of the brouhaha, according to Hopper, was that Gable was overeating, since he usually watched his diet carefully.

The restaurant's hearty British pub fare was served as a daily buffet: prime rib with Yorkshire

Above: Servers dish out food at the Cock 'n Bull's buffet table, 1941. ▪ *Opposite:* The Cock 'n Bull was featured on the cover of *Collier's Weekly*, 1941.

pudding, beefsteak and kidney pie, roasted ham, curries, and duck. Friday was fish day. The buffet, which also featured salads, house-made pickled beets, and steamed zucchini, cost $2.50 for lunch and $6.00 for dinner. The Sunday brunch buffet also included eggs, ham, sausages, kippers, and bloaters for $3.25. The Cock 'n Bull also had a pastry chef on its staff who produced an assortment of desserts ranging from dark chocolate cake to blueberry pie. The pub's dessert specialties were English trifle and warmed crumpets. From 11:00 PM until closing, the kitchen served Welsh rarebit, and customers were allowed to play darts.

In the 1940s, Jack Morgan created the famous Moscow Mule, a concoction made with ginger beer, vodka, and fresh lime juice poured over ice in a copper mug. Many celebrities had their own copper mugs (with their names engraved on them) that were kept behind the bar.

In 1987, John Morgan Jr., who took over the pub's operations when his father died in 1974, decided to close the fifty-year-old restaurant after receiving an offer he could not

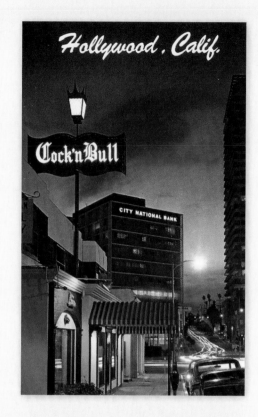

Above: Janet Leigh and Tony Martin at a publicity luncheon at the Cock 'n Bull, 1951. ▪ *Opposite top:* Postcard featuring the Cock 'n Bull. ▪ *Opposite bottom:* The Cock 'n Bull on Sunset Boulevard.

refuse. The Cock 'n Bull was the longest-running restaurant of the Sunset Strip's Golden Era, and one of the last of its establishments to close. Today, a plaque hangs outside the original entrance to the Cock 'n Bull building, which now houses a Beverly Hills Jaguar dealership. The inscription reads:

FORMER SITE OF
THE COCK 'N BULL RESTAURANT
(LICENSED VICTUALER)

FOUNDED DURING THE FIRST YEAR OF
HIS MAJESTY GEORGE VI'S REIGN
&
SITUATED IN THE REGION OF
SUNSET-UPON-THE-STRIP

CLOSE BY THE HAMLET OF HOLLYWOOD

MCMLXXII ✄

Welsh Rarebit

This popular dish was often washed down with a pint of ale at the Cock 'n Bull.

Serves 6

1½ cups whole milk
1 lb. cheddar cheese, grated
¼ cup unsalted butter, softened
½ cup all-purpose flour
1 tsp. dry mustard
dash of cayenne pepper

¼ tsp. sea salt
¾ cup American beer
2 tsp. Worcestershire sauce
2 tsp. steak sauce
2 dashes of hot pepper sauce
6 English muffins

1. In the top of a double boiler with simmering water underneath, heat the milk, add the cheese, and stir until melted.
2. In a large skillet over medium heat, melt the butter, then add the flour, mustard, cayenne, and salt. Stir until it forms a thick paste.
3. Gradually add the milk/cheese mixture and cook for 10 minutes, stirring constantly. Stir in the beer, Worcestershire sauce, steak sauce, and hot pepper sauce. Keep warm until serving time.
4. Split the muffins and toast. Pour the sauce over the muffins and serve.

Moscow Mule

Every drink has its origin story, and the Moscow Mule's begins at the Cock 'n Bull. Invented at the Sunset Boulevard pub in the 1940s, the drink is best served in a copper mug, as the coldness of the metal enhances the flavors.

Serves 1

1 cup ginger beer
1½ oz. vodka
1 tsp. freshly squeezed lime juice
1 lime wedge

1. In a shaker filled with ice, add the ginger beer, vodka, and fresh lime juice. Shake for 10 seconds.
2. Strain into a copper mug that has been filled with fresh ice and garnish with a lime wedge.

Below: Cock 'n Bull owner Jack Morgan mixing a Moscow Mule. ▪ *Opposite:* The dining room at the Cock 'n Bull, 1955.

Florentine Gardens

menu

Built of Concrete and Steel -- IT'S SAFE!

FLORENTINE GARDENS

5955 HOLLYWOOD BLVD.
HOLLYWOOD, CALIF.

Florentine Gardens

OPEN: 1938–present

LOCATION: 5955 Hollywood Boulevard
Los Angeles, CA 90028

ORIGINAL PHONE: HE-4801 and HO-6311

CURRENT PHONE: (323) 464-0706

CUISINE: Italian

DESIGN: Gordon Kaufmann (original design);
Paul Revere Williams (1953 modifications)

BUILDING STYLE: Florentine

RADIO WAS BIG IN THE 1930S AND '40S, WITH STATIONS LINING THE STREETS AROUND HOLLYWOOD AND VINE. They beckoned listeners, dancers, and entertainers to come to Hollywood, an invitation that brought large crowds from the suburbs on the weekends.

In the heyday of the Golden Age, ballrooms packed with big-band sounds filled the Hollywood scene. The opening of Florentine Gardens was not as big as the star-studded Palladium's grand event two years earlier. Even so, when emcee Nils Thor Granlund opened the Gardens, it took off from its first day. Many who could not get into Earl Carroll's nearby would settle for the Gardens, which was large enough to hold more than a thousand guests for dinner.

The nightclub's acts ranged from scantily dressed or partly nude showgirls to the all-American Ozzie Nelson. Other performers included the Mills Brothers jazz group, acclaimed dancer Yvonne De Carlo, Tony Award-winning actress and dancer Gwen Verdon, burlesque dancer Sally Rand, and the comical and risqué Sophie Tucker Revue. Sometimes the acts featured entertainers hanging from the ceiling over the diners on swings.

True to its name, Florentine Gardens was decorated in ancient Florentine style, with faux-paint-

FLORENTINE Gardens

Foremost CABARET RESTAURANT in America

ed columns surrounding the largest spring dance floor on the West Coast at the time. The club served Italian fare, paired with salads and roasted garlic bread. When the Gardens opened, you could have dinner, watch a singing act and dancers, and then dance to live music, all for $1.50. In that era, clubs on Hollywood Boulevard were less expensive than the pricey and elegant Sunset Boulevard clubs.

The servicemen of the 1940s flocked to the Gardens for their entertainment. In 1942, Norma Jeane Baker (Marilyn Monroe) met a defense-plant worker from the Westside named Jim Dougherty, and they later held their wedding reception at the Gardens. Also in the early 1940s, Elizabeth Short (who would later become renowned as the Black Dahlia) rented a room from the Gardens' manager at the time, Mark Hansen, on Carlos and Gower, only a few blocks away.

In 1948, Florentine Gardens went bankrupt. It closed for a short time and then reopened as the Cotton Club, but it struggled as well. The space served briefly as the Korean War-era Hollywood Canteen, but by the mid-1950s, the clientele had changed, as had the neighborhood. The wars were over, and military men were no longer filling the place. The entertainment at the club became seedy, with nude and topless shows. It operated sporadically for two more decades.

In 1982, the Gardens transformed into a popular disco open on Sundays, boasting 8,000 square feet of floating dance space for more than 2,000 people. In an effort to lure tourists, the disco offered free admission for those on vacation.

In 2005, the club, though historic, was threatened with demolition and development when the City of Los Angeles proposed building a new fire station on the site. The proposal suggested incorporating the historic club's exterior into a training facility for the new station. The club's owner, Kenneth MacKenzie, did not want to sell, but the city council voted to acquire the land and building. In the final hour, the Hollywood Heritage organization and then-councilman Eric Garcetti prevailed to save the building. The new firehouse was built around the corner instead.

Today, Florentine Gardens still stands. It is currently a nightclub featuring live groups and DJs, but the kitchen has long since closed. ✕

The Best Meatballs

The secret to Florentine Gardens' moist and flavorful meatballs? Three kinds of ground meat.

Serves 8 to 12

1 lb. ground beef	2 tbsp. finely chopped Italian parsley
8 oz. ground pork	salt
8 oz. ground veal	black pepper
4 cloves garlic, minced	2 cups breadcrumbs
2 large eggs	1½ cups warm water
1 cup freshly grated Romano cheese	1 cup olive oil

1. In a large bowl, combine the beef, pork, and veal. Add the garlic, eggs, cheese, and parsley, and season with salt and pepper.
2. Using a wooden spoon, combine the breadcrumbs into the mixture. Slowly add the water, about ½ a cup at a time. The mixture should be very moist and hold its shape. Using a melon baller, scoop and shape meatballs.
3. Preheat the oven to 300°F and line a baking sheet with foil.
4. Heat the olive oil in a large skillet. Fry the meatballs in batches until light brown and crisp. Remove and drain on paper towels, then transfer to the baking sheet to keep warm in the oven while you fry the next batch.
5. Serve with your favorite tomato sauce and pasta.

Florentine Gardens on Hollywood Boulevard, 1939.

Roasted Garlic Bread

Before Florentine Gardens closed its kitchen, baskets of piping hot roasted garlic bread were brought to every table. During World War II, margarine was used in the recipe instead of butter.

Serves 8

1 bulb garlic
⅓ cup unsalted butter, melted
⅓ cup olive oil
dash of salt

1 cup unsalted butter, at room temperature
2 tbsp. chopped parsley
2 loaves French bread, sliced lengthwise

1. Preheat the oven to 350°F.
2. Cut off the stem of the garlic bulb so that about ⅛ inch of the garlic cloves show. Do not peel the garlic. Place on a piece of foil, drizzle with the melted butter and oil, and sprinkle with salt. Wrap tightly and bake for 45 minutes. Remove from the oven, unfold the foil, and let cool.
3. When the garlic is cool, squeeze the cloves out into a large bowl. Add the softened butter and parsley and blend well.
4. Spread the mixture on top of the bread. Wrap the bread in foil and return to the oven for 15 minutes. Serve warm.

Romanoff's

OPEN: 1939–1962

LOCATION: 140 S. Rodeo Drive
Beverly Hills, CA 90210

ORIGINAL PHONE: CR 4-2105

CUISINE: Country Club

DESIGN: Honnold and Rex, Architects and
Associated Architects

BUILDING STYLE: Modernist Sleek

CURRENTLY: Real Estate Office

ROMANOFF'S, CALLED THE "SUPPER CLUB OF THE STARS" DURING HOLLYWOOD'S GOLDEN AGE, WAS BUILT ON A MOUNTAIN OF LIES. Its owner—originally born Hershel Geguzin before he changed his name to Harry Gerguson and then, finally, the pseudonym Michael Romanoff—was a petty criminal and check forger who used a variety of aliases to pose as a Russian gentleman of Hollywood society. In reality, Mike Romanoff had been a poor peasant boy in his home country of Lithuania who, at ten years old, was sent to live with his cousin in New York City, where he worked odd jobs to survive.

Romanoff was a slick con artist. Scraping together a living as a two-bit actor who ingratiated himself with the real movie stars, he claimed to be the last tsar of Russia, Prince Michael Dimitri Alexandrovich Obolensky-Romanoff (at least one member of the Russian Guard identified him as a fraud for this juicy claim). He spoke in an unplaceable accent, sported a bushy mustache, and dressed impeccably in the latest fashions, complete with spats and a walking stick.

Word got around of Romanoff's tall tales. In 1932, the *New Yorker* ran a series of stories about imposters that traced the peasant/tsar/prince's history from birth and uncovered his past. This only seemed to further endear Romanoff to the stars, though; the press loved his scandalous story, and he became famous as a legendary—but loveable—imposter.

In 1939, Romanoff talked Charlie Chaplin, Humphrey Bogart, and James Cagney into backing him in his restaurant endeavor. Romanoff's opened on Rodeo Drive that same year, back when it was a trendy spot for restaurants, rather than a shopping destination. The menu consisted of rich French fare such as filet mignon, eggs Benedict, crab-stuffed tomatoes, and frog legs. The restaurant was especially famous for its chocolate soufflé and special dessert, Strawberries Romanoff.

Fans often stood outside the establishment, hoping to catch a glimpse of their favorite stars—perhaps Lauren Bacall, Sid Luft, Judy Garland, Frank Sinatra, Katharine Hepburn, or Humphrey Bogart, all of whom were regulars. Despite the restaurant's strict rule that men must wear ties, Bogart insisted on entering without one. In 1942, Myrna Loy and her first husband, producer Arthur Hornblow Jr., celebrated their divorce at Romanoff's (less than a year later, she married John Hertz Jr. of the Hertz car rental family).

Romanoff's had a second location at 140 S. Rodeo Drive, and, in 1951, it moved a few blocks down

Above: The self-styled Prince Michael Dimitri Alexandrovich Obolensky-Romanoff, also known as Hershel Geguzin.

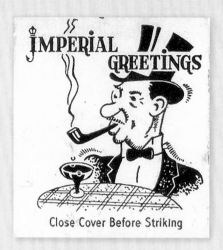

IMPERIAL GREETINGS

Close Cover Before Striking

the street to 240 S. Rodeo, behind the Beverly Wilshire Hotel. The top floor housed a rooftop garden that was perfect for stargazing. The large ballroom could accommodate 125 people, the main dining room offered 24 booths, and a smaller, private dining room was reserved for intimate gatherings. The four booths around the staircase leading up to the rooftop were the most desirable seats in the house; anyone sitting there had a view of the entire dining room and could see who was going up to the rooftop.

Romanoff's did well in the '50s, but with so many great restaurants in town, it was becoming difficult to fill the room. It didn't help that Mike Romanoff was a conservative Republican serving a Democratic community. He often handed out right-wing literature with the menus, and even his most loyal friends and star patrons were offended by his friendship with J. Edgar Hoover. Gangsters tried to buy out Romanoff more than a few times, to no avail. In the end, his political views may have cost him his restaurant and business.

Romanoff's officially closed after a New Year's Eve party in 1962. Romanoff himself—deemed "the most wonderful liar of the twentieth century" by *Life* magazine—spent the rest of his life in retirement and died of a heart attack in 1971, at the age of seventy-eight.

After the restaurant closed, Stouffer's Top of the Rock restaurant in Chicago began serving Romanoff's Noodles. After Stouffer's closed its restaurant division, it focused on its frozen food brands and started packaging Romanoff's Noodles.

The exterior of Romanoff's can be seen in the 1967 film *A Guide for the Married Man*, in which the maître d' is played by Romanoff himself. He appeared in more than twenty films and television shows, either acting in bit roles or playing himself—his specialty. ✕

Below: Romanoff's on Rodeo Drive, 1955. ▪ *Opposite:* Sophia Loren, Jayne Mansfield, and Clifton Webb at Romanoff's, 1957.

Strawberries Romanoff

Originally created by Chef Auguste Escoffier and served at the Carlton Hotel in London as Strawberries Americaine Style, this dessert was "borrowed" by Mike Romanoff, who renamed it after himself. It became the signature dessert at Romanoff's.

Serves 4

2 cups strawberries, rinsed, hulled, and halved
1 tbsp. granulated sugar
2 tsp. orange liqueur
1 tsp. orange zest
1 tbsp. freshly squeezed orange juice
whipped cream

1. In a bowl, combine the strawberries, sugar, liqueur, zest, and orange juice. Let marinate for 2 hours at room temperature. Divide evenly among stemmed glassware.
2. Dollop the whipped cream on top and serve immediately.

The bar at Romanoff's, 1950.

Top left: Elizabeth Taylor and Michael Wilding, 1953. ▪ *Top center:* Jimmy Stewart outside Romanoff's on Rodeo Drive, 1947. ▪ *Top right:* Myrna Loy and Mike Romanoff, 1948. ▪ *Bottom left:* Dave Chasen, Mike Romanoff, and Fred Hayman, 1962. ▪ *Bottom right:* Juliet Prowse, Frank Sinatra, and Judy Garland, 1962.

The Mike Romanoff

Who names a drink after themselves? Prince Mike Romanoff, of course! This drink is similar to an old-fashioned.

Serves 1

2 oz. vodka
1 tsp. orange-flavored liqueur
1 tsp. apricot liqueur
1 oz. freshly squeezed lime juice
2 dashes of bitters
1 orange peel twist

1. In a cocktail shaker filled with ice, combine the vodka, orange-flavored liqueur, apricot liqueur, lime juice, and bitters. Shake.

Menu

HOLLYWOOD
Palladium

Hollywood Palladium

OPEN: 1940–present

LOCATION: 6215 W. Sunset Boulevard
Los Angeles, CA 90028

ORIGINAL PHONE: HO 9-7356

CURRENT PHONE: (323) 962-7600

CUISINE: American

DESIGN: Gordon B. Kaufmann

BUILDING STYLE: Streamline Moderne

IT TOOK ONLY ONE YEAR FOR FILM PRODUCER MAURY M. COHEN TO BUILD THE HOLLYWOOD PALLADIUM ON SUNSET BOULEVARD. After receiving $1.6 million in funding from *Los Angeles Times* publisher Norman Chandler, Cohen began the theater's construction on the original Paramount lot. In the last few weeks prior to its grand opening, decorators and craftspeople worked around the clock to finish the ballroom and accompanying café.

The 1940 opening gala, which featured music by Frank Sinatra and Tommy Dorsey and His Orchestra, had a unique Halloween theme that attracted a lot of attention. The society pages announced that Judy Garland, Tony Martin, John Astor, George Burns, Alfred Hitchcock, Harold Lloyd, Lana Turner, Rudy Vallee, and Mickey Rooney would be in attendance. That same evening, the Cocoanut Grove across town was hosting a jack-o'-lantern ball to aid handicapped children. Unfortunately, it had a small turnout because all the stars wanted to attend the Palladium's opening, which drew over 10,000 revelers.

The theater, decorated in shades of deep coral and silver, featured a unique dome-top cocktail

lounge, a special emerald-colored room serving soft drinks, and a 200-foot-long bar on the balcony overlooking the dance floor. The $10,000 dance floor, which is still in use at the Palladium today, was made of spiral maple planking built on top of springs, to literally put a spring in the step of those dancing. Touted as a technological wonder

Top: Postcard featuring the Hollywood Palladium marquee on Sunset Boulevard.

of its time, the dance floor could accommodate up to 7,500 people, and another 1,000 could be seated for dinner around it. To entertain its diners, the Palladium projected an image on the wall of a misty group of damsels dancing in a cloud of stars. Another visual effect was a color keyboard projected onto the dance floor that was synced to the music and displayed a sparkling spectrum of eighteen hues.

The Palladium also became a venue for movie premieres, beginning with *The Great Dictator*, starring Charlie Chaplin and Jack Oakie. NBC broadcasted the event with a transcontinental hookup for the nation to enjoy "Live from the Palladium." Again, Tommy Dorsey provided the music. Dorsey continued to play at the Palladium for a few weeks after it opened, but the relationship soon soured and he opened a competing ballroom, the Casino Gardens, in 1944.

But nothing could compete with the Palladium. In the 1940s, it was like New Year's Eve there every night, especially when the servicemen were in town. Betty Grable hosted song requests live on radio broadcasts. Bandleader Guy Mitchell was a fixture at the Palladium; in the early 1950s,

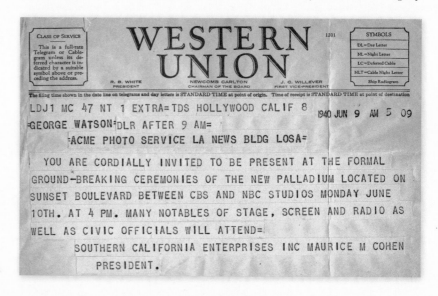

Above: Telegram invitation to the groundbreaking ceremony for the Hollywood Palladium, 1940. ▪ *Below:* The ballroom at the Palladium. ▪ *Opposite:* Lawrence Welk on the Palladium's marquee.

his song "Pittsburg, Pennsylvania" had hit gold. In 1961, the long-running *Lawrence Welk Show* began taping at the Palladium, and in 1971 and 1974, the Grammy Awards were broadcast live from the venue. The ballroom was also used as a stand-in venue for film productions.

The Palladium offered a simple menu to serve its 1,000 diners in a few short hours, including roast turkey, Virginia baked ham, roast prime rib, and a fish special. All dishes came with a "deluxe" green salad, chef's potatoes, and a garden vegetable. The menu remained the same throughout the years, but in 1963, the exterior of the Palladium was updated. Most of the building's two-story entry marquees and Streamline Moderne details were removed, as was its distinctive neon sign featuring two dancing figures. In 2008, a renovation restored the facade to its original 1940 splendor, making it the perfect place for former President Bill Clinton to hold his sixty-fifth birthday celebration gala in 2011.

Today, the Palladium hosts live concerts without food service. Adele played there in 2011, and Guns N' Roses in 2012. Prince popped up for two shows in 2014. Many political and media groups have used the venue for celebration victories. Now, almost seventy-five years later, the Palladium has evolved from an all-inclusive club and dinner establishment to a standing-room-only venue, but it is still going strong. ✂

Virginia Baked Ham with Cherry Sauce

Out of the few main dishes served at the Palladium, this was the most popular option.

Serves 12 to 16

7 lbs. fully cooked, spiral Virginia ham
    on the bone
8 cloves garlic
4 oz. mango chutney
¼ cup Dijon mustard
½ cup packed light brown sugar
1 medium orange, zest and juice
Cherry Sauce (recipe follows)

1. Preheat the oven to 350°F. Place the ham in a roasting pan and set aside.
2. In food processor fitted with a metal blade, process the garlic, chutney, mustard, sugar, and orange zest and juice until smooth.
3. Spread the mixture on the ham. Bake for sixty minutes, or until the glaze is golden brown. Serve with Cherry Sauce.

The most exciting announcement of the year...the new Palladium Ballroom-Cafe, truly an indescribable spectacle of glamour, beauty and romance, proudly announces the ...World Premiere Opening...

THURSDAY EVENING
OCTOBER 31, 1940

Plan now to attend.

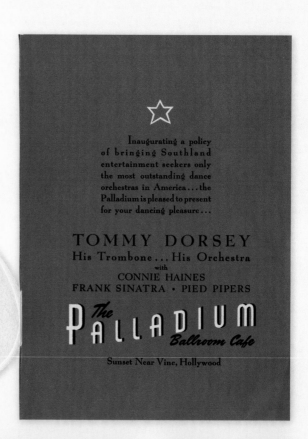

Inaugurating a policy of bringing Southland entertainment seekers only the most outstanding dance orchestras in America...the Palladium is pleased to present for your dancing pleasure...

TOMMY DORSEY
His Trombone...His Orchestra
with
CONNIE HAINES
FRANK SINATRA • PIED PIPERS

The **PALLADIUM** *Ballroom Cafe*

Sunset Near Vine, Hollywood

Excellent Food
no cover · no minimum
Dine and Dance at the World Famous
HOLLYWOOD Palladium
SUNSET near VINE

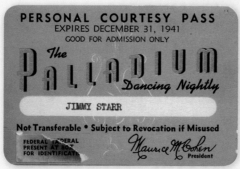

PERSONAL COURTESY PASS
EXPIRES DECEMBER 31, 1941
GOOD FOR ADMISSION ONLY
The **PALLADIUM** *Dancing Nightly*
JIMMY STARR
Not Transferable • Subject to Revocation if Misused
FEDERAL FEDERAL PRESENT AT BOX FOR IDENTIFICAT.
Maurice M Cohen President

HAVE YOUR NEXT...
Private Party Banquet or Benefit
at the
HOLLYWOOD Palladium
call HO. 9-7356 for information
THE OHIO MATCH CO., WADSWORTH, OHIO

Cherry Sauce

¾ cup granulated sugar
2 tbsp. cornstarch
16 oz. tart canned pie cherries, undrained
⅓ cup orange juice
1 tbsp. freshly squeezed lemon juice
1 tsp. ground cinnamon
dash of salt

1. In a medium saucepan, whisk together the sugar and cornstarch. Add the cherries, orange juice, lemon juice, cinnamon, and salt.
2. Cook over medium heat, stirring, until thickened and bubbly, about 4 minutes. Serve warm.

NO CROWD TOO LARGE!—Our spacious, hardwood, circularly-laminated dance floor is the finest in the entire world. Here is a typical Friday-Saturday scene of happy patrons.

TRANSFORMATION. From Dinner-Dancing to Trade and/or Consumer Product Show in only a few hours—to display your company's products in a jewel-like setting!

PRIVATE PARTIES are especially handled in our new Small-Banquet Room for dinners, luncheons and breakfasts. We invite your query.

213-466-4311

BE SAFE-CLOSE COVER BEFORE STRIKING

"Where The Important Events Happen"

World-Famous HOLLYWOOD
PALLADIUM
HOLLYWOOD, CALIFORNIA

An evening at Ciro's is an evening of excitement and enjoyment

H. D. HOVER

Ciro's

OPEN: 1940–1957

LOCATION: 8433 Sunset Boulevard
West Hollywood, CA 90069

ORIGINAL PHONE: HI 7171 and HO 2-721

CUISINE: American

DESIGN: Douglas Honnold

BUILDING STYLE: Mid-Century

CURRENTLY: The Comedy Store

IN 1940, THE UNITED STATES HAD NOT YET JOINED THE WAR, AND IT WAS AN EXCITING TIME IN HOLLYWOOD. When entrepreneur Billy Wilkerson opened Ciro's on Sunset Boulevard, films were being made close by and the stars were in need of evening excitement. The Hollywood Palladium had not opened yet, and the hotel ballrooms were always filled on the weekends.

Wilkerson, who had founded the *Hollywood Reporter* a decade earlier, felt that owning a nightclub for the rich and famous would help his publication. Nine months after Ciro's opened, Wilkerson expanded its dance floor and its kitchen with a more extensive menu. He added French favorites and also a cheese course with imported European cheeses.

A classy, high-end French restaurant and dance venue, Ciro's was nothing like Florentine Gardens on the other side of Hollywood. It was the place to be seen, located directly in the middle of the Sunset Strip and only blocks away from Beverly Hills. Everyone from Peggy Lee to Duke Ellington to Sammy Davis Jr. performed onstage at the venue.

In 1942, Wilkerson sold the club to Herman Hover, a producer for the Earl Carroll Broadway and Hollywood Theatres. Hover spent a great deal of money on publicity to lure talent to the Ciro's stage. That same year, he added a second floor to the building, with a partial third floor for offices and dressing rooms. Knowing that the country was fixated on television at the time, Hover turned one of the upstairs rooms into a TV salon—just in time for the upcoming presidential election.

Fistfights were not uncommon at the club. A few days before Valentine's Day in 1954, film producers Bert Friedlob and Milton Pickman started boxing in the front area of Ciro's, with the dining room packed with patrons. Later that night, John Donovan, a watch manufacturer's representative, clashed with clothing manufacturer Sy Devore and dressmaker Arthur Edelman. The three men began the second fistfight of the evening before Hover came along to break it up.

Ciro's closed its doors on May 26, 1956. Hover claimed that he was forced to close the venue "due to the pressures of two entertainment agencies." In the 1960s, Ciro's transformed into It's Boss, a rock club like so many of the other venues on the street. In 1972, the Comedy Store took over the location and is still in operation today. ✕

Opposite: Gary and Veronica Cooper with Jack Benny at Ciro's, 1947.

Crabmeat Cocktail

This was Ciro's number-one hors d'oeuvre, served in an iced glass pedestal dish.

Serves 6

24 oz. crabmeat, free of bones
2 stalks celery, diced
½ medium onion, diced
4 stalks green onion, chopped
2 tbsp. pickle relish
¼ cup mayonnaise
1 tsp. prepared mustard
3 drops hot pepper sauce

1. In a large bowl, combine crabmeat, celery, onion, green onion, relish, mayonnaise, mustard, and hot pepper sauce.
2. Place into a dish or arrange on a bed of lettuce for a first course.

Below: The Ciro's dining area, next to the dance floor. ▪ *Opposite top:* Betty Grable, Lucille Ball, Darryl F. Zanuck, Marilyn Monroe, Jimmy McHugh, Walter Winchell, and Louella Parsons at a Ciro's party for the film *Let's Make Love*, 1960. ▪ *Opposite left:* Frances Robinson and Anitole Litvak dancing at Ciro's. ▪ *Opposite right:* Phyllis Winger and Rock Hudson.

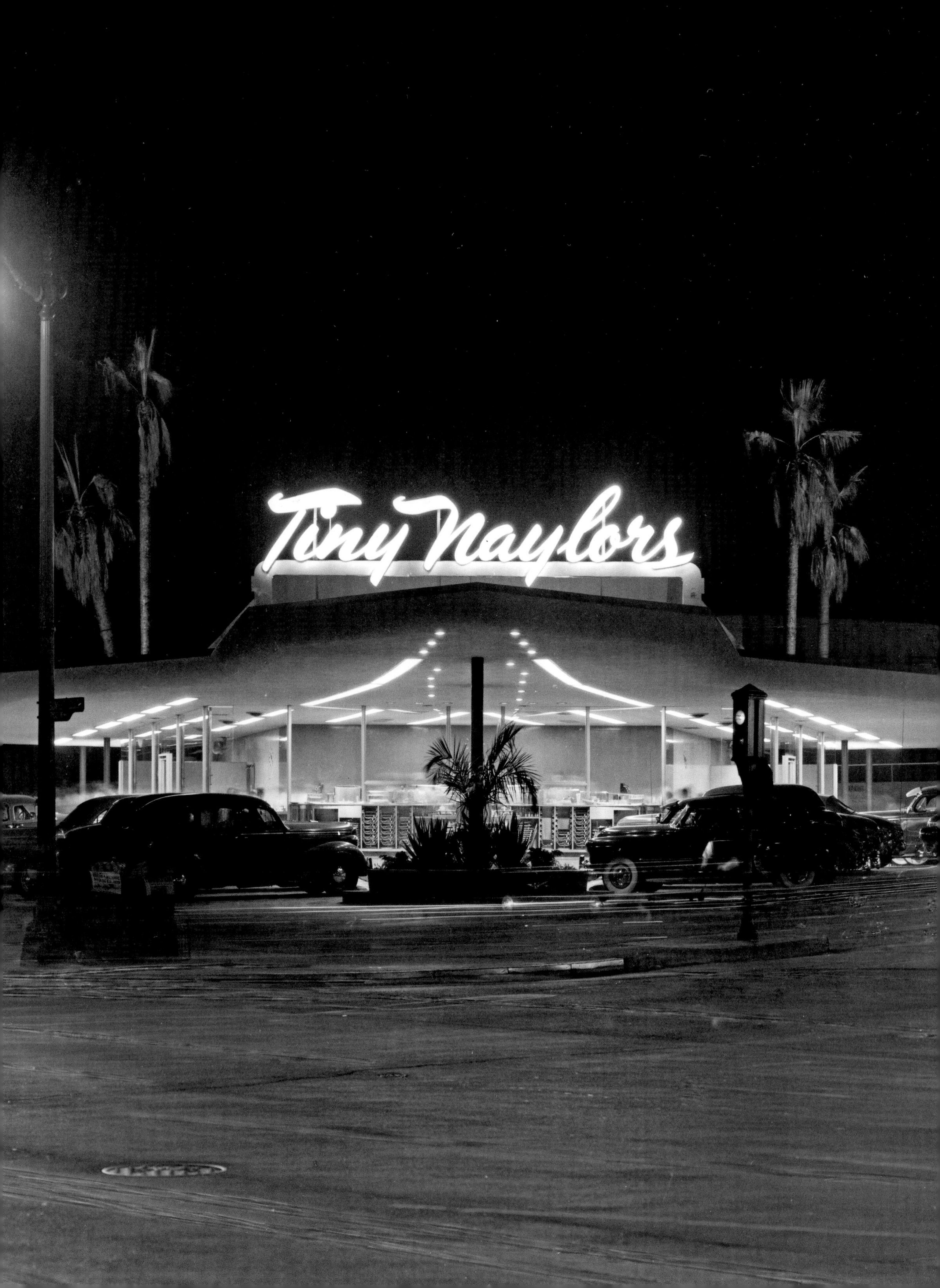
Tiny Naylors

Tiny Naylor's

OPEN: 1949–1980

LOCATION: 7101 Sunset Boulevard
Los Angeles, CA 90046

ORIGINAL PHONE: HO 9-3135

CUISINE: Diner

DESIGN: Douglas Honnold

BUILDING STYLE: Googie

CURRENTLY: El Pollo Loco

SUNSET BOULEVARD HAS SEEN ITS SHARE OF DRIVE-INS OVER THE YEARS, BEGINNING WITH CARPENTER DRIVE-IN, THE VERY FIRST ONE ON THE STRIP IN THE 1930S. Tiny Naylor's soon followed and became one of the most popular drive-ins during the Golden Age of Hollywood, as well as one of the few twenty-four-hour establishments in the area. The eatery was owned by W. W. "Tiny" Naylor, whose six-foot-four, 300-pound frame earned him his ironic nickname.

Movie stars, who loved being able to sit in their cars and go virtually unnoticed by the other patrons, flocked to the Googie-style Tiny Naylor's. On weekday afternoons, the drive-in was packed with students from Hollywood High, which was across the street.

Besides burgers and shakes, the menu at Tiny Naylor's also included corn on the cob, ribs, steak, and baked potatoes—all of which were unheard of for a drive-in. Everything served at the restaurant was made from fresh ingredients, never frozen.

On August 17, 1977, when the UPI wire service reported that Elvis Presley had just died at Baptist Hospital in Memphis, it was 2:30 in the afternoon and Tiny's was mobbed with people mourning the passing of the King. The carhops and waitresses had a difficult time working during that painful afternoon.

In 1980, Tiny Naylor's closed down, and everything from the tables and chairs to the speakers from the drive-in was auctioned off. Despite the restaurant's demise, the Naylor family continues to thrive in the restaurant business. Tiny's son, Biff, opened the Du-Par's chain, which is still in operation today, with five locations in two states. One of the last Hamburger Hamlets (see page 185) was recently converted into a Du-Par's, and Jennifer Naylor (Tiny's granddaughter) is currently a consultant there. ✂

Above: **Tiny Naylor's on Sunset Boulevard, 1965.** ▪
Opposite: **Tiny Naylor's, 1949.**

DRAWN BY GEORGE McMANUS
CREATOR OF MAGGIE 'N JIGGS

Patty Melt

This sandwich was a staple in most diners, but only Tiny Naylor's used ground round instead of ground beef.

Serves 2

the original
Tiny
Naylors
T N

2 tbsp. unsalted butter, softened
4 slices rye bread
1 tbsp. olive oil
1 small red onion, sliced into rings
12 oz. ground round, shaped into patties
   about 2 inches thick

sea salt
freshly ground pepper
2 slices Swiss cheese

1. Preheat the oven to 200°F.
2. Butter both sides of the bread slices. Heat a cast-iron skillet over medium heat. Add the buttered bread and cook until dark brown, about 2 minutes on each side. Transfer to an oven-safe plate, holding in the preheated oven.
3. Add the oil to the same skillet over medium-high heat. Add the onion and cook until very dark and softened, about 10 minutes. Transfer to a small plate and set aside.
4. Season the patties with salt and pepper. Cook in the same skillet over medium-high heat on one side until well-browned, about 2 minutes. Turn the burgers; place a slice of Swiss cheese on each. Cover and cook until the cheese melts and the burgers are medium-rare, about 2 minutes longer.
5. To assemble the Patty Melts, place each cheeseburger on one slice of toast on each plate and cover with half of the onions, then set the remaining slice of toast on each.

Chocolate Malt

This creamy all-American classic pairs perfectly with a burger.

Serves 1

2 large scoops chocolate ice cream
2 tsp. chocolate powdered drink
½ cup whole milk
1 tsp. malt powder
whipped cream
1 maraschino cherry

1. Place the chocolate ice cream, powdered drink, milk, and malt powder in a blender. Blend until creamy, about 30 seconds.
2. Pour into a tall, chilled glass.
3. Top with the whipped cream and cherry.

Below left: The busy drive-in at night, 1973. ▪ *Below right:* Bobby Driscoll and Natalie Wood at Tiny Naylor's, 1953. ▪
Below bottom: The restaurant's Googie-style angled roof, 1952. ▪ *Opposite:* Inside Tiny Naylor's, circa 1967.

Scandia

Scandia

OPEN: 1948–1989

LOCATION: 9040 Sunset Boulevard
West Hollywood, CA 90069

ORIGINAL PHONE: (213) 272-9521

CUISINE: Scandinavian

DESIGN: Edward H. Fickett

BUILDING STYLE: Mid-Century Modern

CURRENTLY: Marriott Hotel

IN 1948, KEN HANSEN OPENED SCANDIA WITH HIS SISTER-IN-LAW, TEDDY, WHO WORKED AS THE RESTAURANT'S HOSTESS. With sleek lines, a rock floor, and flowerbeds of greenery between its levels, the building was unlike any other on the Sunset Strip. Stars could slip into the covered parking lot unnoticed and ride up the elevator to the top floor, where the curtains could be drawn for privacy.

The interior included red leather chairs and booths, dark paneling, and copper and brass accents illuminated by huge windows in the dining room. Near the front entrance was a dark and moody bar that looked as if someone from the Rat Pack should be sitting there, enjoying a martini. Above the bar, beer mugs were displayed with the names of Scandia's notable "Club of the Vikings" guests, including Errol Flynn. It is said that the Hungarian-born Peter Lorre ate there every Saturday. In 1981, Barbra Streisand celebrated her thirty-ninth birthday in style at Scandia; the Cake Walk, a bakery on Third Street, provided her Pistachio Cream Sherry Cake.

Scandia's menu was eclectic, with dishes from Scandinavia and well beyond. The items were given names like Hamlet's Dagger (fried lobster with tartar sauce) and Viking Sword (a large brochette of broiled turkey breast, Châteaubriand steak, smoked pork chop, tomatoes, and mushrooms, all served on a flaming sword). Scandia had its own butcher shop, where whole carcasses of beef were cut and prepared. Fish was brought into the restaurant whole (today, fish is pre-portioned for most restaurants). In the spring, shad roe was served as a special.

At Scandia, waiters prepared dishes like sizzling steak Diane and crisp Caesar salad tableside as their guests looked on. The restaurant also served cold soups with flavors like cucumber mint—a very new and exciting type of dish at the time. For more than thirty years, *Holiday* magazine awarded Scandia many honors for its cuisine and 30,000-bottle wine collection, which boasted top-grade French and California reds.

As exacting as the chefs were, the impeccable service was what Scandia was known for. If you dropped a napkin, six waiters would run to pick it up and tuck a new one into your lap. You only had to visit once to be remembered by Frode Benedictus Christensen, the restaurant's maître d' from 1955 to

Above: **Postcard featuring a sketch of the Scandia dining room, 1957.**

1975. Christensen had a gift for recalling his guests' allergies and favorite items on the menu.

In the late 1970s, Robert and Margie Peterson of Peterson Publications purchased Scandia from the Hansens. The Petersons closed the restaurant in 1989, when the area began to deteriorate and its customers started to visit new establishments. For years after Scandia closed, the Petersons sat on the restaurant's wine collection, which had grown to 40,000 bottles. They had moved the collection to a temperature-controlled storage facility across town. In October of 2002, the famed New York wine auction house Zachys (which had split from its partner, Christie's) auctioned off 199 lots out of the 1,574-lot sale at Daniel, a famous restaurant in Manhattan. The rest of the wines were offered at a later date. This was Zachys' first sale, and it launched the auction house into the business. ✕

Scandia on the Sunset Strip, 1967.

Confrerie de la Chaine des Rotisseurs

In the year 1248 under St. Louis IX, King of France, the Guild "Des Ayeurs" was founded. This Guild expanded during the centuries and in 1610 by Royal Consecration was granted the Coat of Arms of Maitres des Rotisseurs. In 1950 gastronomists and professionals took the oath to revive the Society and the Coat of Arms of the Rotisseurs were again raised to its full and just rights. The Brotherhood Chain of the Rotisseurs has for its purpose to unite gastronomes and professionals fervent of good living and the Cuisine of "De la Broche" in particular.

STAND

Cold Cucumber Mint Soup

This soup was served in a chilled sterling silver bowl. The waitstaff had to be vigilant and count the bowls to make sure all were returned, and then painstakingly polish the vessels after their last guest had departed.

Serves 6

2 tbsp. unsalted butter, softened
3 medium cucumbers, peeled, seeded, and thinly sliced
1 medium leek, cleaned and chopped
2 bay leaves
1 tbsp. all-purpose flour
2 cups chicken broth

1 tsp. sea salt
1 tsp. mint, chopped fine
1 cup half-and-half
2 tsp. freshly squeezed lemon juice
chopped dill
sour cream

1. Melt the butter in a large Dutch oven over medium heat, then add the cucumbers, leek, and bay leaves. Cook slowly until tender but not brown, 8 to 10 minutes. Discard the bay leaves.
2. Add the flour and mix well. Add the chicken broth, salt, and mint, bring to a boil, and then reduce the heat and simmer for 20 to 25 minutes, stirring occasionally.
3. Transfer to a blender and purée until smooth (or use an immersion blender in the pan). Chill until cold.
4. Add the half-and-half, lemon juice, and chopped dill to taste.
5. Serve in bowls with a dollop of sour cream and a sprinkle of dill.

Chicken Salad Kon-Tiki

This salad contained what were, at the time, presumed to be the flavors of the Pacific Islands. It had a coconut-curry flavor and was served inside a melon.

Serves 4

2 cups cooked chicken, diced
¾ cup diced celery
½ cup grated coconut
1 tbsp. chutney
½ cup Curry Dressing (recipe follows)
2 medium cantaloupes, cut in half and seeded

1. In a large bowl, combine the chicken, celery, coconut, and chutney and mix well. Add the Curry Dressing and toss to combine.
2. Fill the cantaloupes with the chicken mixture and serve immediately.

Curry Dressing

Makes about 1 cup

½ cup mayonnaise
½ cup sour cream
1 tsp. curry powder
1 tsp. freshly squeezed lime juice
dash of sugar
dash of sea salt
dash of freshly ground black pepper

1. Whisk all the ingredients together in a medium bowl. Refrigerate until needed.

Vinaigrette Dressing

Scandia created this dressing in-house to be used on simple greens. Because the egg whites, chives, parsley, and pepper were already in the vinaigrette, the salad it was poured on could be served quickly.

Makes about 1½ cups

1 cup canola oil
½ cup white wine vinegar
2 tbsp. crushed ice
2 large egg whites, hard-boiled and diced
2 tbsp. chopped chives
1 tbsp. chopped parsley
½ medium onion, minced
1 tbsp. granulated sugar
dash of sea salt
dash of freshly ground black pepper

1. In a medium bowl, whisk the oil and vinegar with the ice. Add the eggs, chives, parsley, onion, sugar, salt, and pepper and whisk to combine. Refrigerate until needed.

French Dressing

This house dressing was Scandia's most requested salad topper.

Makes about 1½ cups

1 cup canola oil
¼ cup white wine vinegar
3 tbsp. water
2½ tsp. granulated sugar
1 tsp. dry mustard
1 tsp. freshly ground black pepper
2½ tsp. sea salt
1½ tsp. Worcestershire sauce
1½ tsp. Hungarian paprika
1 tsp. grated onion
2 oz. blue cheese crumbles

1. In a bowl, whisk together the oil, vinegar, and water until blended. Add the sugar, mustard, pepper, salt, Worcestershire, and paprika and whisk again until blended. Add the onion and blue cheese and stir to combine.

Caesar Dressing

Makes 5½ cups

6 oz. anchovy fillets, drained and chopped
3 tbsp. Worcestershire sauce
3 tbsp. wine vinegar
3 tbsp. ketchup
3 tbsp. freshly squeezed lemon juice
5 tsp. ground black pepper
1 large egg
3 tsp. garlic powder
2½ tsp. dry English mustard
2½ tsp. sea salt
2 tsp. steak sauce
3 dashes of hot sauce
4 cups canola oil

1. Blend all of the ingredients except the oil in a food processor or blender. Pour in half of the oil while the machine is blending. Add the remainder of the oil.
2. Cover and refrigerate until needed, for up to 2 weeks.

"VELKOMMEN TILBORDS!"

HORS D'ŒUVRES

Our individual "COLD CABARET" served at your table and consisting of all the delicacies for which the smörgåsbord is famous. Served for no less than 2 persons, per person 6.50

Smörgås Bricka, *for two or more,* per person 2.35

Shrimp Cocktail ..... 2.15   Lobster Cocktail 2.50

Avocado Cocktail, Russian Dressing 2.00

Marinated Herring 1.35

Iceland Matjes Herring, Sour Cream 1.50

Danish Liver Pate 1.25

Herring Filets in Cherry Heering 1.75

Herring Filets in Sherry 1.60

Assorted Herring Appetizer (Silde Anretning), per person 2.00

Gravlaks with Dill Sauce 2.75
The great Salmon of the north cured in the old Viking manner.

Shrimps in Dill 2.50
Mediterranean Shrimps cooked with aquavit and dill.

Louisiana Oysters on the Half Shell 2.65

Cherrystone Clams on the Half Shell 2.25

Cracked Fresh Dunguenes Crab *(in season)* 2.50

Fresh Smoked Baltic Salmon *(in season)* 3.50
"Via S.A.S. over the Pole."

Papaya with Crab, illumine 2.75

Iranian Smoked Sturgeon .... 2.75   on Smörgås 2.25

The Cured Ham with Golden-Ripe Melon 2.25

For appetizers only—additional service charge added

APPETIZERS THE HOT DELIGHTS

Viking Plättar 2.25
Miniature pancakes flavored with aquavit and served with sour cream and Danish caviar.

The Coquille 2.25
Small Norwegian lobster tails, white wine sauce, peeled stoned grapes.

The Crepe 2.25
Thin pancake wrapped around tiny coral-pink Shrimps in Dill and Hollandaise, glaced under fire.

The Great Hamlets Dagger 2.25
Tiny lobster tails deviled and broiled on the skewer, served with an ice-cold sauce made with caviar and aquavit.

The Mushrooms with Deviled Crab 2.00
Fresh crabmeat cooked with shallots and mustard and stuffed in mushroom caps.

The Mushrooms with Snails 2.25
Tender vineyard snails cooked in mushroom caps with garlic and walnut butter.

THE SHELLS:

Oysters 2.00
Baked in their shell with a fine herb puree, seasoned with aquavit.

Clams 2.00
Minced and Cooked with Butter, Garlic and Shallots and White Wine, Stuffed in Their Own Shells and Baked.

AQUAVIT SERVED ICE COLD WITH BEER

Aalborg	1.10	Tuborg Bottle	.90
O.P. Anderson's ..	1.10	Carlsberg Bottle	.90
Kron-Brännvinn ...	1.10	Olympia Bottle	.65
Löitens	1.10	Schlitz Bottle	.70
Tuborg or Carlsberg Draft	.85	Budweiser Bottle	.70

FISH AND SHELLFISH

Danish Sole, *Specialty of the House* 4.95
Cooked in chablis, stuffed with coral pink shrimps in lobster sauce, glaced with white wine sauce.

Danish Plaice (Rödspätter) 4.50
The flounder of the North Sea breaded and sauteed in butter. Sauce Remoulade a part.

The Danish Trout 4.65
Filets of the rainbow sauteed with tiny lobster tails and peeled grapes.

The Virgin-Lobster Tails 4.65
Tiny Norwegian lobster tails breaded in fresh crumbs and fried with fresh parsley and sauce remoulade.

Broiled Fresh Lake Superior Whitefish (Boned) 4.85
With Cucumbers in Sour Cream.

Poached Danish Turbot *with Horseradish Hollandaise* 4.75

SALADS

Our Special Salad Bowl *with Crisp Mixed Greens*
   and French Dressing 1.00
   with Danish Bleu Dressing 1.25
   our own Caesar Dressing 1.25

Scandia Salad 1.50

Ice-Cold Sliced Tomatoes .... .85

Avocado Salad 1.50

Heart of Iced Lettuce 1.00

Caesar Salad Bowl *for two* 3.00

Cold Green Asparagus, Vinaigrette 1.50

Large French Asparagus, Hot or Cold,
   Vinaigrette 1.75

Imported Belgian Endives 1.65

Wilted Bib Lettuce 1.50

Wilted Spinach Salad 1.50

Orders served for more than the specified number,
will be charged accordingly.

VEGETABLES

Fresh Tender Broccoli	.85
with Hollandaise	1.25
Freshly Cooked Green Asparagus	1.25
with Hollandaise	1.45
Lyonnaise, Hashed Brown Potatoes	.75
Souffle Potatoes	1.50
Au Gratin Potatoes, Cottage Fried or	
Anna Potatoes	.75
Puree of Fresh Peas	.95
Carrots Vichy	.95
Creamed Spinach	.95

SOUPS

Swedish Pea Soup	.85
Curried Turtle	1.00
Vichyssoise	.85
Suedoise	.85
Gazpacho	.85

Sales Tax Will Be Added To The Above Prices of All Food and Beverage Items Served At The Tables in This Room.

LORD MENU CO., L.A.—MA 4-7631

STEAKS AND CHOPS

Our Regular Cuts of U.S.D.A. Prime Beef

New York Cut Sirloin	7.25
Filet Mignon	6.50
Two Double French Lamb Chops	6.25
A Special Tournedo, Bearnaise	5.00
Top Sirloin Steak	6.00
Sirloin Steak a la Minute—(Husets Specialitet)	6.25
Butterfly Steak Saute a la Minute	6.00

Above served with large baked or French Fried Potatoes.

PLANKED STEAKS

Special cuts of Sirloin or Tenderloin *for two or more persons, charcoal-broiled and finished on Oak Plank with potato border and many kinds of vegetables, served with fresh mushrooms and bearnaise sauce, per person* 8.00

Planked Chopped Sirloin Steak with Mushroom Sauce 4.50
Served as above
Chateau-Briand for 2—Potatoes Souffle 15.50

Bordelaise Sauce 1.25

Sauce Bearnaise 1.25

French Fried Onions 1.00

SCANDIA SPECIALTIES

Kalvfilet Oskar 5.85
(Veal cutlet saute, garnished with asparagus tips, crablegs, sauce bearnaise)

Böf Med Lög 5.75
(Tenderloin steak with onions fried in butter)

Biff Lindström 3.75
(Chopped sirloin steak mixed with chopped beets, onions and capers, topped with fried egg)

Dansk Hakke Böf 3.75
(Chopped sirloin fried in butter, smothered in fried onion sauce)

Kålldolmar 3.75
The tender leaves of white cabbage filled with a veal and pork stuffing with rice. Braised in the Swedish manner and served with cucumber salad and Lingon.

Spring Chicken Saute, Louise 4.25
(Unjointed, sauteed in butter with shallot and fresh mushrooms, finished with fresh cream and a dash of old sherry)

Tournedos Theodora 6.00
(Two small filet mignons garnished with gooseliver, bouquets of fresh vegetables, sauce madeira)

Lammesaddel *for 2 or more* .... *per person* 5.85
(Young filet of lamb, roasted and prepared in the Scandia way, carved and served at your table)

"Viking Sword" *(Served for no less than 2 persons) per person* 6.85
(Large Brochette of Broiled Breast of Turkey, small Chateau-Briand, center of a Smoked Pork Chop, Tomatoes and Mushrooms served on a Flaming Sword with many kinds of vegetables and Sauce Bearnaise)

DESSERTS

Rödgröd med Flöde	.75
Danish Rum Pudding	.75
Svenska Plättar med Lingon	1.25
Danish Pancakes with Strawberry Jam	1.25
Iceland Pancakes	1.75
Crepe of the Amourous Viking	2.00
Home-made Ice Cream and Sherbets	.50
Baked Alaska, for 2	3.00
Souffles for 2 or more, per person	2.25
Assorted Pastries	.75

BEVERAGES

Pot of Tea or Coffee	.45
Demitasse	.35
Expresso	60
Café Diablo	1.75
Café Brulot	1.50

"VELBEKOMME!"

Orders served for more than the specified number will be charged accordingly. For service during dinner hours (5:30-10:30 P.M.) $3.00 minimum will be charged.

MAY WE SUGGEST..

OLD FASHIONED GIBLET SOUP .85
VIA S.A.S. FRESH SMOKED COPENHAGEN EEL 2.50
GRAVLAX WITH DILL POTATOES 2.75
STEAMED LITTLENECK CLAMS 2.50
BROCHETTE OF CAPE COD SCALLOPS 2.50

Fresh Maine Lobster Tidbits, Victoria 6.00
(Medallions of Lobster, Mushroom and Truffle with Sauce Nantua Glace, Served with Saffron Rice)

Filet of Chinook Salmon, Francaise 4.95
(Poached in White Wine, Garnished with Tartlet with Mussels and Truffle, Sauce Vin Blanc with Taragon)

Broiled Filet of Corbina, Nicoise . 4.75
(Served with Sliced Lemon, Anchovy Filets and Fresh Stewed Tomatoes)

~~Filet of~~ *Fresh Mountain Trout, Facon du Chef* 4.75
(Stuffed with Crabmeat and Sauteed in Hazelnut Butter)

Chef's Special: Breast of Capon a l'Estragon 4.85
(Served with Wild Rice and Broccoli Spears)

From Our Spit: Roast Sirloin of Beef 5.50
(Served with Braised Celery Roots and Croquette Potatoes)

Via S.A.S.: Swedish Snowgrouse in the Danish Manner . . . 6.75
(Served with Wild Rice Croquette and Artichoke Bottom Stuffed with Chestnut Puree)

TODAY'S SPECIALS

Miceli's

OPEN: 1949–present

LOCATION: 1646 N. Las Palmas Avenue
Los Angeles, CA 90028

ORIGINAL PHONE: HO 3-0311

CURRENT PHONE: (323) 466-3438

BUILDING STYLE: 1940s Storefront

CUISINE: Italian

IN THE LATE 1940S, CARMEN MICELI PACKED HIS BAGS IN CHICAGO AND TOOK OFF FOR HOLLYWOOD, DRIVING DOWN ROUTE 66 ALONG WITH THE OTHERS HEADING OUT WEST AFTER THE WAR. There he met and married his wife, Sylvia, and the couple sent for Carmen's siblings to join them in Los Angeles and help fulfill their dream of opening a pizzeria in the city.

The family found a small building on Las Palmas Avenue, down the street from several motion picture theaters, and opened their pizzeria there. Around the corner on Hollywood Boulevard, the Pig 'n Whistle (see page 69) was closing and selling off its furniture, so the Micelis purchased all of its dark wooden booths and installed them in their new restaurant. The booths are still at Miceli's today, complete with wooden carvings of dancing pigs.

At the time, most Angelenos did not know what a pizza was, let alone a pizzeria. Nevertheless, lines of hungry customers were soon spilling out of the Miceli's front door and down the block.

The Micelis used recipes that had been passed down to them from their Sicilian mother, Maria, who had immigrated to Chicago with her husband in 1921 and opened an Italian fast-food stand in front of her home. In 1952, she moved to California to help her children run their restaurant in Hollywood.

The most popular items on the menu that have stood the test of time are the chicken parm, cheese garlic toast, spaghetti and meatballs, and Aunt Angie's Original Lasagna. Another crowd favorite is the Miceli Special, made with hand-tossed pizza dough, homemade tomato sauce, mozzarella cheese, pepperoni, meatballs, salami, mushrooms, onions, and bell peppers.

Right: Miceli's billboard, 1970s. ▪
Opposite: Sammy Miceli in the window of Miceli's on Las Palmas Avenue.

In the '50s, the Micelis installed a jukebox in the pizzeria and filled it with Italian songs. The restaurant became known for its singing waiters and waitresses; when customers put a nickel in the jukebox, their servers would sing along to the tune of their choice. Today, the jukebox has been replaced by a piano in the center of the dining room, and the waitstaff play and sing everything from Italian operas to show tunes. They recently added Disney music to their repertoire for the little ones.

Another lasting tradition at Miceli's is its collection of Chianti bottles hanging from the ceiling. Even today, if you polish off a traditional wrapped Chianti bottle at the restaurant, you can write a message on it to commemorate the evening and the staff will hang it from the ceiling.

Because of its close proximity to theaters and film studios, Miceli's has had its share of fame. Prior to filming the *I Love Lucy* episode "Visitor from Italy" in 1956, Lucille Ball spent spent a few days at Miceli's learning how to toss pizza dough from Carmen's brother, Sammy. They even filmed the segment on location in the Miceli's kitchen. The story goes that Ball got so good at throwing the dough that, after filming, she made pizza for the entire cast and crew.

In 1960, John F. Kennedy ate at Miceli's after giving his presidential nomination acceptance speech at the Democratic Convention downtown. The Beatles also paid a visit to the pizzeria in 1964, while they were in town to play at the Hollywood Bowl. Over the years, it was not uncommon for Frank Sinatra, Marilyn Monroe, and Joe DiMaggio to be seen at Miceli's.

Today, Miceli's and its sister location on Cahuenga Boulevard are still going strong, both run by Carmen and Sylvia's sons, Joe and Frank. ✕

FIRST IN PIZZA   SINCE 1949

© Miceli's ®

Garlic Butter Cheese Bread Loaves

Because the Miceli family's recipes are sacred, I was not able to obtain the original recipe for their delicious bread. This Garlic Butter Cheese Bread, which I used to make in Hollywood in the 1980s, is my personal homage to the Miceli's Cheese Garlic Toast.

Serves 10

1 large loaf of Italian bread, cut lengthwise
½ cup unsalted butter, room temperature
4 cloves garlic, minced
4 oz. Romano cheese, grated

1. Preheat the oven to 350°F.
2. Place bread on a baking sheet and set aside.
3. In a bowl, combine butter and garlic. Spread half of the mixture on each side of the bread. Sprinkle cheese on top.
4. Place in preheated oven and bake until light brown, about 15 to 20 minutes. Serve hot.

Carmen Miceli (*standing, far right*) and his wife, Sylvia (*seated, second from left*), with guests at Miceli's, late 1950s.

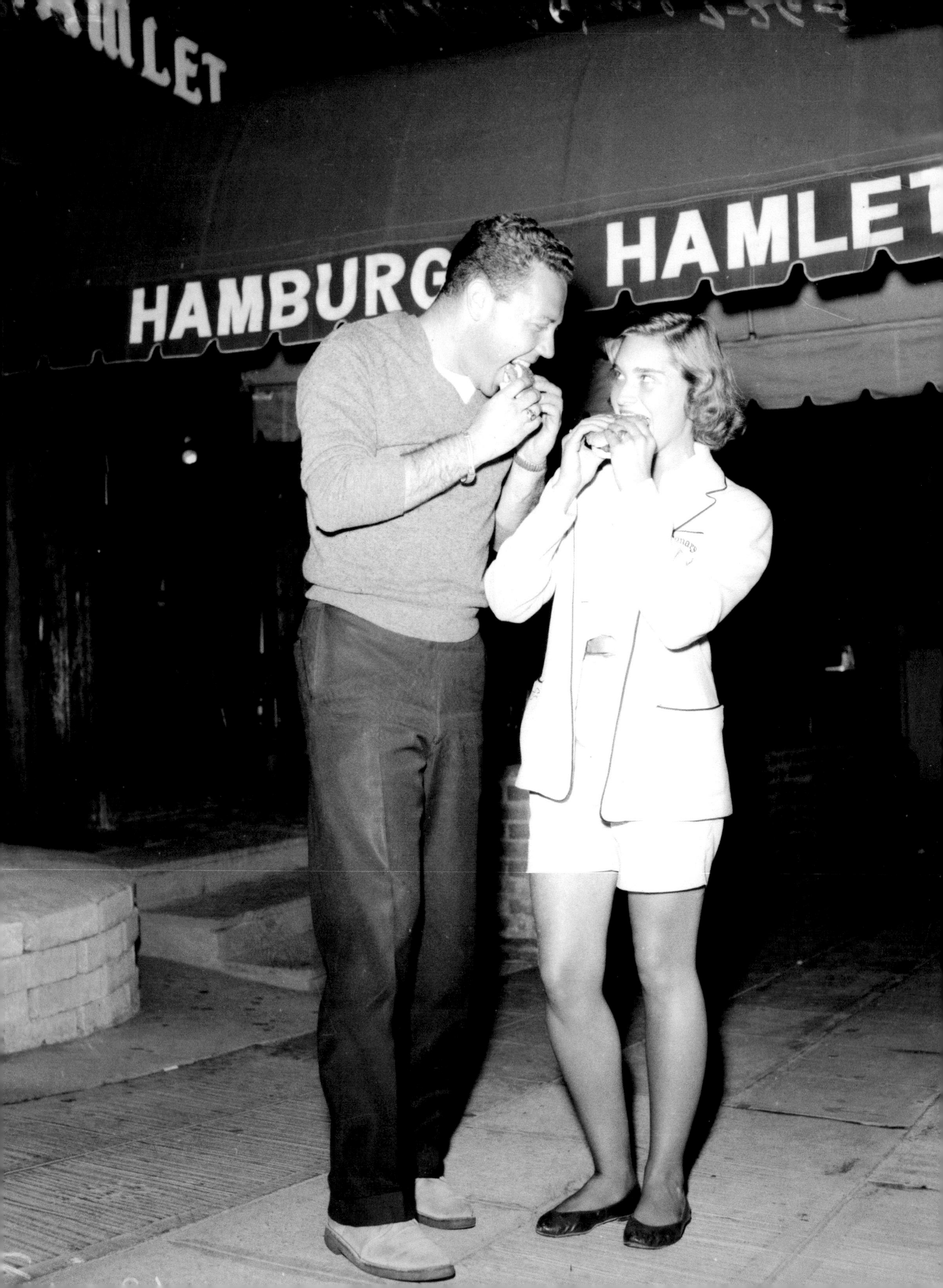
HAMBURG
HAMLET

Hamburger Hamlet

OPEN: 1950–2011

LOCATION: 9201 Sunset Boulevard
Los Angeles, CA 90069

ORIGINAL PHONE: OL 2-1993

CUISINE: American

BUILDING STYLE: 1950s Storefront

CURRENTLY: Roku Restaurant

IN 1950, MARILYN LEWIS, GIRLFRIEND OF ACTOR HARRY LEWIS, SPENT HER DAYS OFF SCOURING THE HOLLYWOOD AREA FOR A PRIME LOCATION TO OPEN A RESTAURANT. That year, the couple put down a deposit on a little place on the Sunset Strip, where they would run their restaurant for eighteen years. They named the place Hamburger Hamlet, after the role every actor wanted to play: Hamlet.

At the upscale hamburger/steak house, Harry was in charge of the kitchen and Marilyn waited tables and trained the staff. The Hamburger Hamlet training manual, which Marilyn wrote herself, could have been a textbook on how to treat restaurant customers. The manual touted what were known as the Nine Commandments, which decreed, for example, that servers should never use the word "fried," but say "sautéed" instead, to sound more classy and European.

Hamburger Hamlet's first chef was Marcelion Martinez, a Zapotec Indian from the highlands of Oaxaca, Mexico. Harry was impressed by his work ethic, and urged him to find more people from his area of Mexico to join the business. Martinez recalled that he had never seen so many black people in one place; it was the first Westside restaurant to break the color barrier. At twenty-four years old, Martinez became the director of the chain's kitchens.

Above: **Wall menus at the original Hamburger Hamlet.** ▪ *Right:* **Hamburger Hamlet on the Sunset Strip, next door to the Opera House, Golden Violin, and Whisky A Go Go, 1962.** ▪ *Opposite:* **Customers digging into their burgers outside the Hamlet, 1958.**

He traveled to Washington D.C. to open the East Coast locations and even visited the White House.

Just two years after the Lewises opened the Hamlet, Tony Curtis, Sammy Davis Jr., and Jeff Chandler made a touching offer—they would run the restaurant and cook for the customers for a couple of nights so that Marilyn and Harry could drive to Las Vegas and officially get married. The three stars took orders and made hamburgers while the couple tied the knot in a Vegas wedding chapel. A few years later, the three men got back behind the counter to run the place when Marilyn gave birth to the Lewises' first son.

One late night in 1953, actress Sarah Churchill (daughter of British prime minister Winston Churchill) paid a visit to the Hamlet and demanded that Harry serve her a glass of beer. Since it was after 2:00 AM—the deadline for public drinking in California—Harry refused. Churchill reportedly proceeded to call him a "dusty American" and criticize American laws. Someone at the next table called the story in to the *International Herald Tribune*, and it ran the next morning in every paper in the nation and even in some foreign countries. The publicity was golden for the Lewises and helped attract stars to the restaurant. Notable celebrities like Ronald Reagan, Frank Sinatra, Dean Martin, and Al Pacino began coming in for the Hamlet's burgers. When Sammy Davis Jr. performed at Ciro's on the Strip, he would often head to Hamburger Hamlet for dinner after his closing number at 1:30 AM. It was not uncommon for him to pour sugar onto one of the restaurant tables and and do a soft-shoe tap routine on top of the table for late-night diners.

Publicity continued to soar for the eatery—so much so that Marilyn had to call Hollywood reporter Sidney Skolsky and ask him to stop writing about the restaurant's success. Crowds of people were overflowing outside the Hamlet and lining up around the block. Some customers were even sitting on the restaurant's stoop to eat their food.

But competition on the Strip was fierce. Former disc jockey Larry Finley opened a restaurant down the street called My Own Place and broadcast *The Larry Finley Show* from the location, taking business away from the Hamlet. Harry and Marilyn did not take this lying down. Marilyn, who had just finished a twenty-six-week contract for a TV series called *The Farmer's Daughter*, talked to radio station KGIL and set up sponsors ranging from Muntz TV showrooms to Triumph sports cars. The Lewises installed a radio wire and, between making burgers and soups, began to broadcast their own show every night, from midnight to 2:00 AM. Sometimes they interviewed patrons eating at the restaurant, but mainly the show centered around the life of the married couple. It was unscripted—"reality radio" for the 1950s.

Hamburger Hamlet had its share of troubles. One morning in January of 1964, the manager opened the restaurant in the morning and was surprised to find a former employee waiting for her inside. Carrying a sawed-off shotgun, he ordered the manager to open the safe, but found that it was on a timed lock. Frustrated, he took her keys and ordered her to her car, where he shot her in the back and took the $10 that was in her purse. The manager survived, but the disgruntled former employee shot and killed a maintenance worker and a deliveryman who happened upon the scene. The suspect was arrested the following week in West Hollywood.

In 1968, the Lewises moved the Sunset Boulevard Hamburger Hamlet to a new location four blocks down the street. They also opened a trendier restaurant on Wilshire Boulevard called Kate Mantilini. Eventually, the Lewises were able to open twenty-four different restaurant locations. In 1987, they sold the entire company for $33.1 million, with a deal stating that, after five years, they could buy back the Kate Mantilini brand. The Lewises' sons, David and Adam, ran the day-to-day operations at the Wilshire and Woodland Hills locations, both of which closed in 2014.

When Harry Lewis passed away in 2013, a memorial service was held at the Samuel Goldwyn Theater of the Academy of Motion Picture Arts and Sciences. Over three hundred people were in attendance. Adam Lewis said his father had a "relentless drive that never extinguished."

The Pasadena Hamburger Hamlet, one of the last two locations in the Los Angeles area, closed in January 2014 and was transformed into a Du-Par's. In September 2014, Kevin Michaels and partner Brett Doherty of Killer Shrimp restaurants purchased and reopened the last remaining Hamburger Hamlet in Sherman Oaks, keeping the original burgers, shakes, and other specialties—like its party brisket and onion soup fondue—on the menu that Hamlet fans love. ✕

Below left: **Inside Hamburger Hamlet.** ▪ *Below right:* **Jeff Chandler and radio star Byron Kane working behind the counter while owners Marilyn and Harry Lewis got married in Vegas, 1952.** ▪ *Opposite:* **Customers outside the Hamlet, 1953.**

Onion Soup Fondue

This deep, dark onion soup is topped with a cheese-covered round of French bread—just the way they serve it in France.

Serves 12

¾ cup unsalted butter
4 to 6 large onions, thinly sliced
64 oz. beef broth
1 tsp. chicken-seasoned stock base

white pepper
1 baguette, cut into 12 slices
12 slices Monterey Jack cheese

1. Melt the butter in a large Dutch oven over medium heat, then add the onions and sauté until transparent (but not browned), about 15 minutes. Add the beef broth and chicken stock base. Cover and simmer for 2 to 3 hours, until the onions are completely limp. Remove from the heat, let cool for a few hours, then refrigerate overnight.
2. The next day, use a slotted spoon to remove and discard the fat that has floated to the top. Heat the soup and season to taste with pepper.
3. Meanwhile, lightly toast the bread slices and cover each with a slice of cheese. Ladle the soup into individual oven-proof bowls and top each with a bread slice. Place the bowls on a baking tray and place the soups under the broiler until the cheese melts and bubbles and becomes soft (but not brown). Remove from the oven and serve.

Party Brisket

Marilyn Lewis, who created this recipe, says the dish goes back to her childhood.

Serves 10

5 to 6 lbs. beef brisket
2 large onions
2 tsp. salt

2 tsp. celery salt
Pungent Sauce (recipe follows)
1 cup Brisket Broth (recipe follows)

1. Place the brisket in a roasting pan or Dutch oven and add water to cover. Peel the onions and add to the pan. Add the salt and celery salt. Bring to a full boil on the stovetop over high heat, and skim off any fat that rises to the top. Reduce the heat, cover, and simmer for 3 hours.
2. Remove the meat, strain and reserve the broth, and let cool. Brush the meat with the Pungent Sauce. Cover and let stand overnight in the refrigerator.
3. The next day, preheat the oven to 275°F.
4. Slice the brisket, cutting across the grain. Place the slices in the Dutch oven and add the Brisket Broth. Cover and bake for 1 hour.

Dorothy Malone, Arthur Kennedy, Harry Lewis, Zachary Scott, and Ronald Reagan at Hamburger Hamlet.

Pungent Sauce

Makes about ¾ cup

½ cup ketchup
2 tbsp. brown sugar
2 tbsp. Worcestershire sauce
1 tsp. black pepper
1 tsp. instant coffee powder
2 dashes of bottled onion juice
2 dashes of bottled garlic juice

1. In a medium bowl, combine the ketchup, brown sugar, Worcestershire sauce, black pepper, coffee powder, and onion and garlic juices.

Brisket Broth

Makes about 2 cups

brisket broth (reserved from Party Brisket)
1 bunch carrots, cut diagonally
1 bunch celery, including leaves, cut diagonally
3 tbsp. chopped parsley
1 large leek, sliced (white part only)
5 beef bouillon cubes
1 cup hot water

1. Let the broth stand overnight in the refrigerator. Skim off the fat and discard. Place the broth in a large pot and add the carrots, celery, parsley, and leek.
2. Dissolve the bouillon cubes in the water and add to the broth. Cover and simmer on low for 1 hour.
3. Use to reheat the brisket, as directed.

Custard Lulu

This custard, created by Marilyn Lewis and loved by all, was Hamburger Hamlet's specialty dessert.

Serves 6

4 large eggs
1 cup granulated sugar
2 cups whole milk
½ tsp. freshly ground nutmeg

1½ tsp. pure vanilla extract
6 tbsp. prepared caramel fudge ice cream topping

1. Preheat the oven to 400°F.
2. In a medium bowl, whisk the eggs and sugar together until they turn pale yellow, about 5 minutes. Add the milk, nutmeg, and vanilla.
3. Place 1 tbsp. of the prepared topping in the bottom of each of 6 custard cups. Divide the milk mixture among the cups and place the cups in a large pan of hot water.
4. Bake until a knife inserted into the center comes out clean, about 30 minutes. Let cool, then chill in the refrigerator.
5. Serve cold in the custard cups.

Below: Sally Forrest and James Craig on the set of *The Strip* at Hamburger Hamlet, 1951. ▪ *Opposite left:* Marilyn and Harry Lewis (*top left and right*) broadcasting their radio show on KGIL with guests Hugh O'Brian and Sammy Davis Jr. ▪ *Opposite right:* Harry Lewis with a cook in the Hamburger Hamlet kitchen, 1953. ▪ *Opposite bottom:* The Hamburger Hamlet on Hollywood Boulevard.

Ben Frank's

OPEN: 1952–1996

LOCATION: 8585 Sunset Boulevard
West Hollywood, CA 90069

ORIGINAL PHONE: (213) 652-8808

CUISINE: Diner

DESIGN: Lane and Schlick

BUILDING STYLE: A-Frame Googie

CURRENTLY: Mel's Drive-In

ARTHUR SIMMS LEARNED ABOUT THE RESTAURANT BUSINESS FROM HIS FATHER, WHO RAN SMALL HOTELS AND CAFÉS IN CHICAGO DURING THE 1920S AND '30S. After serving in World War II, Simms moved to the Los Angeles area and ran the commissary at MGM Studios in Culver City.

In 1952, Simms partnered with Bob Ehrman and opened a coffee shop on Sunset Boulevard named Ben Frank's. Located in the heart of the West Hollywood club scene, Ben Frank's drew many stars, from Andy Warhol, to the Rolling Stones, to the Go-Go's. After the clubs closed for the night, music fans hung out at neighborhood establishments like Ben Frank's that were open twenty-four hours.

In the early 1960s, Simms opened two more Ben Frank's locations in the Los Angeles area and managed two other coffee shop chains, the Copper Penny and the Wooden Shoes. After Simms's son, Thomas, graduated from UC Santa Barbara in 1970, he decided to join his father's coffee shop business, the SWH Corporation.

In the mid-1970s, the father-and-son team realized that there was a market for quality dinner-house food served in restaurants with a coffee shop ambience. In 1974, they brought in partners Brian Taylor and Paul Kurz and opened French Market, a sidewalk café in West Hollywood about two miles from the original Ben Frank's—close enough for them to keep an eye on both locations. Two years later, they also acquired the Kettle, located three blocks from the pier in Manhattan Beach.

SWH used the success of French Market as a template to create a chain of restaurants, the first of which was placed in Anaheim, close to Disneyland. It opened in 1978 as the first Mimi's Café, reportedly named after a girlfriend of the elder Simms. The restaurant was a success, so they opened another

Above: **Ben Frank's on Sunset Boulevard.** ▪ *Opposite:* **Ben Frank's, 1995.**

location in the neighboring Garden Grove. For the next several years, the company opened a new Mimi's Café about every eight months. They continued to operate the other brands while expanding the Mimi's Café locations, testing and marketing products and services at the French Market and the Kettle. By 2001, the company had forty-nine Mimi's Café locations in five states.

After the death of his father in 2000, Thomas realized that it was unrealistic to manage such a large chain by himself. In the previous year alone, Thomas had opened four new locations in Texas. So he hired Russ Bendel to serve as president and CEO, while Thomas served as chairman of the board. In the first three years, Bendel took the company from fifty-three locations to eighty by moving into Midwestern markets.

In 2004, Bob Evans Farms bought SWH, and the company sold the original Ben Frank's on Sunset Boulevard at the end of the year. The restaurant remained empty for a few months until it was transformed into the kitschy, 1950s-themed Mel's Drive-In, which kept the original A-frame Googie building mostly intact. Today, the Ben Frank's legacy lives on through the Mel's menu, which offers the same type of fare: patty melts, fried chicken, and cream pies. Mel's became famous when their "South of Market" location in San Francisco was used in the 1973 Oscar-nominated film *American Graffiti*. ✕

Below: Ben Frank's Googie-style exterior. ▪ *Opposite:* The inside structure of the restaurant remains mostly intact today at Mel's Drive-In.

French Toast Princess Anne

This breakfast favorite was only offered on the weekend menu at Ben Frank's; it was too time-consuming to make on weekdays.

Serves 8

1 lb. egg bread, such as brioche or challah, pulled into pieces
2 medium apples, thinly sliced
1 cup heavy cream
1 cup whole milk
8 large eggs

¼ cup pure maple syrup
2 tbsp. light brown sugar
2 tsp. ground cinnamon
1 tsp. ground nutmeg
1 tsp. pure vanilla extract
¼ tsp. salt

1. Preheat the oven to 350°F and butter a 9 x 13-inch baking dish.
2. Place half of the bread pieces into the prepared baking dish, layer the apples on top, and then cover with the remaining bread pieces. Set aside.
3. In a large bowl, combine the cream, milk, eggs, maple syrup, brown sugar, cinnamon, nutmeg, vanilla, and salt. Pour the batter over the bread and let it soak in, submerging the bread. Bake until a knife inserted into the center comes out clean, 22 to 28 minutes.
4. Serve with fresh fruit and maple syrup.

Lawry's California Center

OPEN: 1953–1992

LOCATION: 570 W. Avenue 26
Los Angeles, CA 90065

ORIGINAL PHONE: (213) 224-6850

CUISINE: Mexican

DESIGN: Saul Bass and Associates

BUILDING STYLE: California Garden Mission

CURRENTLY: Los Angeles River Center and Gardens

IT ALL STARTED WITH A SEASONED SALT. Lawrence "Lawry" Frank created the now-famous Lawry's Seasoned Salt for the Tam O'Shanter Inn (see page 45), which he had opened with his brother-in-law and business partner, Walter Van de Kamp. The two men went on to open Lawry's The Prime Rib and began selling Lawry's Seasoned Salt in stores.

By then, Frank and Van de Kamp had become restaurant royalty. In 1953, they opened Lawry's California Center, a garden oasis close to downtown Los Angeles and a few blocks from Dodger Stadium. Over the years, the center grew into a seventeen-acre site that included three restaurants, a wine store, and gift shops. It was also the home of the Lawry's general offices and a factory for packing Lawry's brand spices—including Lawry's Seasoned Salt.

Because of its proximity to downtown, Lawry's California Center became a favorite spot for business lunches. If it was sunny, like most California days, the Los Portales Patio was the perfect place to bring colleagues from the East Coast. In the 1960s, businessmen could enjoy a few margaritas there before heading back to the office. On Sundays and mid-evenings during the week, live mariachi bands played traditional music tableside at the Fiesta Dinner and La Cocina restaurants. In the 1960s and '70s, weddings were held at the California Center gardens almost every weekend.

In the 1970s, Lawry's opened a cooking school at the California Center to boost the sale of the products in its test kitchen. Most of the dishes prepared at the school used at least one of the Lawry's spices.

In 1979, Thomas Lipton (of Lipton tea) bought the Lawry's Spice brand and the California Center. In 1992, Lipton closed the center and moved the manufacturing facility to San Jose, California.

Lawry's Seasoned Salt can still be found on the tables at the Tam O'Shanter and Lawry's The Prime Rib. ✕

Above: A mariachi band serenades diners at Lawry's California Center. ▪ *Right and opposite:* The California Center's lush gardens, circa 1985.

Above and opposite: The restaurants at the California Center were surrounded by beautiful scenery.

Discover

Lawry's California Center™

Gardens | Dining

Shops | Tours

A GARDEN OASIS JUST MINUTES FROM DOWNTOWN L.A.

Mexican Lasagna

The restaurants at Lawry's California Center were surrounded by exquisite gardens and bubbling fountains. The Fiesta Dinner Mexican restaurant, which served this dish, was one of my favorites.

Serves 12

1½ lbs. lean ground beef
1 oz. taco seasoning
½ tsp. seasoned salt
1 cup diced tomatoes
16 oz. tomato sauce

4 oz. diced green chiles
1 cup ricotta cheese
2 large eggs, beaten
10 corn tortillas
2½ cups shredded Monterey Jack cheese

1. Preheat the oven to 350°F. Grease a 9 x 13-inch baking dish.
2. In a skillet over medium heat, cook the beef until browned, about 8 minutes. Drain off the fat. Add the taco seasoning, seasoned salt, tomatoes, tomato sauce, and green chiles. Mix well and simmer, uncovered, for 10 minutes.
3. In a small bowl, combine the ricotta cheese and eggs. Set aside.
4. Spread half of the meat mixture on the bottom of the baking dish, arrange 5 of the tortillas on top, and spread half of the ricotta mixture on top of the tortillas. Sprinkle with half of the Monterey Jack cheese, then repeat the layers with the remaining ingredients.
5. Bake, uncovered, until the cheese is melted and lightly browned, 20 to 30 minutes. Let stand for 10 minutes before serving.

Black Bean Salad

This side dish was often served with lunch at the Fiesta Dinner restaurant.

Serves 6 to 8

1 lb. dried black beans
10 slices applewood-smoked bacon, julienned
1 medium red bell pepper, seeded and diced
1 medium yellow bell pepper, seeded and diced
1 medium green bell pepper, seeded and diced
1 medium onion, diced

1 clove garlic, minced
2 sprigs cilantro, minced
1 tbsp. ground cumin
1 tsp. cayenne pepper
64 oz. chicken broth
sea salt
freshly ground black pepper
1 cup Italian salad dressing

1. The day before serving, place the black beans in a bowl, cover with cold water, and refrigerate overnight.
2. The next day, drain the beans and rinse with cold water. Place in a large pot with fresh water to cover. Cook the beans over medium heat until tender but still slightly firm, about 1 hour and 30 minutes. Drain in a colander. Rinse again in cold water to stop the cooking. Return the beans to the drained and cooled pot.
3. Meanwhile, in a skillet over medium heat, cook the bacon until about half-cooked, and then drain the fat. Add the peppers, onion, garlic, cilantro, cumin, and cayenne pepper and sauté for about 6 to 8 minutes, until tender but slightly crisp. Add to the beans.
4. Add the chicken broth and simmer the mixture until most of the liquid is absorbed but the bean mixture is still moist, about 30 to 40 minutes. Season with salt and pepper.
5. Add the dressing and toss. Chill in the refrigerator. Stir well before serving.

Creamed Corn

This was a staple recipe at all of the Lawry's restaurants, from the first day of their operation.

Serves 4 to 6

1½ tbsp. unsalted butter
1½ tbsp. all-purpose flour
½ tsp. sea salt
1½ cups heavy cream, at room temperature
2 tbsp. granulated sugar
2 cups whole-kernel corn, canned, fresh, or frozen

1. Melt the butter in a heavy saucepan over medium heat. Add the flour and salt, stirring to blend. Slowly add the heavy cream, stirring constantly until thickened. Add the sugar and corn and heat through.

L'Escoffier
at the Beverly Hilton

OPEN: 1955–1993

LOCATION: 9876 Wilshire Boulevard
Beverly Hills, CA 90210

ORIGINAL PHONE: CR 4-7777

CUISINE: French

DESIGN: Welton Becket and Associates

BUILDING STYLE: Mid-Century Modern

CURRENTLY: Stardust Restaurant

IN 1953, HOTELIER CONRAD HILTON HIRED ARCHITECT WELTON BECKET TO DESIGN HIS LATEST CREATION, THE BEVERLY HILTON. Becket had designed eleven other Hilton properties around the world between 1949 and 1975, all with his signature Mid-Century Modern look. The finished hotel sat on a prime piece of property at the crossroads of Wilshire and Santa Monica Boulevard.

On August 11, 1955, Vice President Richard Nixon raised the U.S. flag at the corner of Wilshire and Santa Monica to declare that the Beverly Hilton was open for business. The hotel boasted 450 air-conditioned rooms—many with private balconies—as well as sunken swimming pool cabanas, tropical landscapes, shops, and parking spaces for over a thousand cars. It also offered four restaurants and cocktail lounges, including L'Escoffier, an elegant French restaurant on the eighth floor of the hotel. The menus described the man who inspired the restaurant—French master chef Auguste Escoffier:

THIS "L'ESCOFFIER" RESTAURANT IS DEDICATED TO THE TEACHINGS OF THE GREAT MASTER, AND TO THE GLORIFICATION OF A LIFE CONSECRATED TO THE ART, WHICH IS CLOSEST TO EACH ONE'S HEART, AND MOST IMPORTANT TO HUMANITY.

For L'Escoffier's opening night, Conrad Hilton flew in French singer Paula Desjardins from Paris to entertain the attendees. Between courses, guests were also treated to a fashion show like no other outside of Paris, featuring beautiful clothing from Christian Dior, Balenciaga, and Balmain.

L'Escoffier was one of the most romantic restaurants in the city, with beautiful views stretching all the way to the Pacific Ocean. Over the years, many chefs worked in its kitchen to create the finest meals imaginable. In 1979, Roy Yamaguchi traveled to the area and apprenticed at L'Escoffier to hone his skills. Today, he owns over thirty restaurants, has published four cookbooks, and is on the United Airlines Congress of Chefs.

In 1987, Merv Griffin purchased the Beverly Hilton (rumor has it that he bought the hotel so he would always have a table at L'Escoffier). Griffin spent millions to completely refurbish and renovate the hotel. In 1994, L'Escoffier was closed and rebranded into a new restaurant named the Stardust. ✕

Cappuccino Soufflé

What's a French restaurant without a soufflé? This dessert contains a perfect balance of chocolate and liqueur.

Serves 4 to 6

3 tbsp. unsalted butter
¼ cup granulated sugar
¼ cup all-purpose flour
1 cup whole milk, heated
1 tsp. pure vanilla extract
1 oz. unsweetened chocolate, chopped fine
1 tbsp. espresso powder

1 oz. orange-flavored liqueur
½ oz. cognac
1 pinch salt
¼ cup granulated sugar
4 large egg yolks, room temperature
5 large egg whites, beaten until stiff

1. Prepare one 1½-quart soufflé dish or six small 3-ounce dishes by brushing with melted butter and sprinkling with granulated sugar to coat the bottom and sides of the soufflé dishes. Set aside.
2. Melt the butter in a small saucepan over medium heat, then add the flour. Cook for 2 minutes, stirring with a whisk. Gradually add the hot milk, continuing to whisk until blended. Add the chocolate, espresso powder, orange-flavored liqueur, and cognac. Add the sugar and salt, stirring continuously. Bring to a gentle boil and cook until the mixture has thickened, about 2 minutes. Remove the pan from the heat. Stirring constantly, add the egg yolks one at a time.
3. Beat the egg whites until slightly thickened. Fold them carefully into the mixture, in three parts.
4. Pour the mixture into the molds. Bake at 350°F for 30 to 45 minutes, depending on the size of your baking dish.
5. Serve hot, right out of the oven.

Below: The dining room at L'Escoffier, 1967. ▪ *Opposite top:* The Beverly Hilton, late 1950s. ▪ *Opposite bottom:* The views from L'Escoffier were unparalleled, 1958.

Trader Vic's at the Beverly Hilton

OPEN: 1955–2007

LOCATION: 9876 Wilshire Boulevard
Beverly Hills, CA 90210

ORIGINAL PHONE: CR 4-7777

CUISINE: Polynesian

DESIGN: Welton Becket and Associates

BUILDING STYLE: Tiki

CURRENTLY: Waldorf Astoria Beverly Hills

IN 1934, A YOUNG ENTREPRENEUR NAMED VICTOR J. BERGERON OPENED A SALOON NAMED HINKY DINKS IN OAK-LAND, CALIFORNIA. After taking trips to Cuba and Hawaii, Bergeron returned with new ideas and recipes for drinks, and added the tropical flavors of daiquiris and planter's punch to the Hinky Dinks menu. In 1937, he visited Don the Beachcomber (see page 117) in Hollywood and decided to turn his Hinky Dinks into a Polynesian restaurant, with tropical drinks and a Chinese-flavored menu. Bergeron's wife suggested that he also change the name of the restaurant to reflect the new menu and drinks. Trader Vic's came to mind, since her husband loved to barter and make deals.

After his success in the East Bay, Bergeron opened the first franchised Trader Vic's in Seattle in 1940. Locations in Hawaii and San Francisco followed, and Trader Vic's began to evolve into a chain of what would become fourteen franchised restaurants. In 1955, Bergeron's fourth location was installed in the brand-new Beverly Hilton Hotel, under the name The Traders. The restaurant was officially renamed a few years later to reflect its parent company, Trader Vic's.

The Trader Vic's chain was well-received in the 1950s, which were flooded with movies and music about the faraway islands of the South Seas, Polynesia, and Hawaii. *From Here to Eternity* and *Blue Hawaii* were playing in movie theaters, and *South Pacific* was running on Broadway. Tiki bars and restaurants were all the rage, with rum drinks galore.

The food at Trader Vic's was largely fantasy, with no real basis in Chinese or island traditions—such as crab rangoon, a mixture of crabmeat and cream cheese stuffed into a wonton and then deep-fried. The menu included twenty different

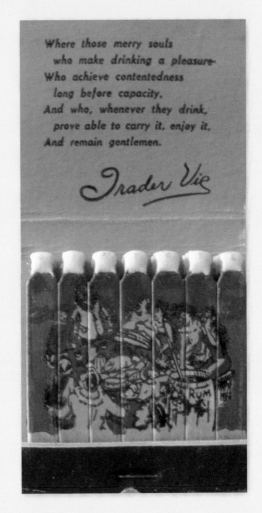

seafood dishes, all cooked in a specially built oven, as well as suckling pig. Oyster appetizers were also abundant, including Oysters San Juan, Oysters Casino, and the traditional Oysters Florentine.

Bergeron introduced green peppercorns, morel mushrooms, and kiwi fruit to Los Angeles cuisine. He also helped popularize snow peas and salmon caviar, and pioneered the contemporary use of wood-burning ovens in restaurants. The entire dining experience at Trader Vic's was a show, from the tiki god glasses, to the flaming drinks, to the wall hangings of tribal masks and flat-bottomed riggers hanging from the ceiling.

The Beverly Hilton Trader Vic's became a favorite watering hole for Dean Martin, Walter Pidgeon, and Ronald Reagan—before and after he was elected to be governor of California. The hotel served as a sort of western White House for John F. Kennedy and his administration. Miramax often used Trader Vic's as a gathering spot, and the Weinstein Company held parties there to celebrate the Golden Globes.

In the 1960s, as many as twenty-five Trader Vic's locations were in operation worldwide, some under other names like Trader Vic's Island Bar and Grill, Señor Pico, and the Mai Tai Lounge. In 1972, United Airlines hired Bergeron to design and implement the food and beverage service aboard the Boeing 747s and McDonnell Douglas DC-10s, from the mainland to Hawaii and back. Bergeron signed on with the pay of a bank president, along with free travel passes and publicity for his restaurants. A month later, he delivered his plan, which proposed new ideas like fruit-flavored salad dressings, hand-shaken drinks with fresh ingredients, and a rack of lamb dish. At the time, United Airlines had also partnered with Western International Hotels, several of which housed a Trader Vic's in their lobbies.

When Bergeron died in 1984, his chain was worth an estimated $50 million a year. However, during the 1980s and '90s, the chain began to shrink as a result of poor location choice and declining popularity. In 2007, Beny Alagem, the new owner of the Beverly Hilton Trader Vic's, shut the restaurant's doors and opened Trader Vic's Mai Tai Lounge, a poolside bar at the hotel that served cocktails and a few of the appetizers from the original menu. Soon after, the original Trader Vic's location was demolished to make way for a Waldorf Astoria hotel. The Hilton's poolside Mai Tai Lounge closed in 2017.

Today, there are two Trader Vic's locations left in the United States, as well as sixteen others worldwide. ✕

Below: The tiki-themed Trader Vic's, 1962. ■ *Opposite:* The entrance to Trader Vic's, 1996.

Indonesian Rack of Lamb

A version of this dish was served as an appetizer aboard the United Airlines Boeing 747s. The recipe can be doubled to make it a hearty main dish.

Serves 6

⅓ cup celery, finely chopped
⅓ cup onion, finely chopped
1 clove garlic, minced
¾ cup canola oil
¼ cup vinegar
2 tsp. steak sauce
3 tbsp. curry powder
2 dashes hot pepper sauce

3 tbsp. honey
1 tsp. dried oregano
2 bay leaves
½ cup prepared mustard
2 tbsp. lemon juice
2 tbsp. lemon zest
1 rack of (6) lamb chops

1. In a skillet over medium heat, sauté the celery, onion, and garlic in the canola oil for 2 minutes. Add the vinegar, steak sauce, curry powder, hot pepper sauce, honey, oregano, bay leaves, mustard, lemon juice, and zest and stir to combine. Bring to a boil, reduce the heat, and simmer for 2 minutes. Chill in the refrigerator.
2. Add the chops to the mixture and marinate for about 4 more hours in the refrigerator.
3. When ready to cook, preheat the oven to 400°F.
4. Drain the chops, reserving the marinade. Arrange on a shallow baking pan and cover the exposed bones with foil. Brush the meat with the marinade and bake for 20 minutes total, turning once and basting the other side with the marinade. The chops should be browned on the outside, with a light pink center.

Pake Noodles

When Merv Griffin, owner of the Beverly Hilton, was in town, this was his favorite appetizer. It makes a great side for any spicy dish.

Serves 2

1 cup freshly cooked lo mein noodles
3 tbsp. unsalted butter, softened
1 tbsp. seasoned breadcrumbs
1 tbsp. sesame seeds, toasted
sea salt
freshly ground black pepper

1. In a large bowl, toss together the hot noodles, butter, breadcrumbs, and sesame seeds. Season to taste with salt and pepper.

Crab Crepes Bengal

This popular dish was one of the most requested appetizers at Trader Vic's.

Serves 6

1 lb. crabmeat, picked over for shells
4 tsp. minced shallots
2 tbsp. unsalted butter, softened
1 tsp. curry powder
½ tsp. sea salt
⅛ tsp. freshly ground black pepper
⅛ tsp. Chinese five spice

½ tsp. Worcestershire sauce
1 cup dry white wine
2½ cups béchamel or white sauce
12 crepes
½ cup hollandaise sauce
¼ cup heavy cream

1. In a saucepan over medium heat, sauté the crab, shallots, and butter for 1 minute. Add the curry powder, salt, pepper, Chinese five spice, Worcestershire sauce, and wine and stir to combine. Bring to a boil over high heat and boil for 3 minutes, until half of the wine has evaporated. Stir in 2 cups of the béchamel sauce.
2. Place a heaping tablespoon of the mixture in the center of each crepe. Roll up and place side by side on a buttered baking pan, seam side down.
3. Combine the remaining ½ cup béchamel, the hollandaise, and the heavy cream in a bowl. Spoon over the rolled crepes.
4. Place under the broiler until the sauce is glazed and tinged with brown, 3 to 4 minutes.

La Scala

Good Music...

    Good Food...

        Good Liquors...

*The largest selection of Liquors
and Imported Wines*

*The finest domestic Champagnes and Wines
at Popular Prices*

9455 Santa Monica Boulevard
BEVERLY HILLS, CALIFORNIA
CRestview 5-9436

La Scala

OPEN: 1956–present

LOCATION: 9455 S. Santa Monica Boulevard
Beverly Hills, CA 90028

ORIGINAL PHONE: CR5-9436

CURRENT PHONE: (310) 275-0579

BUILDING STYLE: 1950s Storefront

CUISINE: Italian

IN 1918, CEFERINO CARRION WAS BORN IN SANTANDER, A CITY ON THE NORTHERN COAST OF SPAIN. When he was nineteen years old, he stowed away on a merchant vessel bound for New York City. Like so many immigrants, Carrion started working at a restaurant in the city, making four dollars per day busing tables. Worried that he would be found without papers and forced to go back to Spain, Carrion headed west. When the Korean War offered him an opportunity to legalize his status with only two years of service, he jumped at the chance.

Carrion changed his name to Jean Leon and, after his service, moved back to Hollywood, where he felt he could make something of himself. He landed his first job at Villa Capri, a restaurant off of Hollywood Boulevard. Over time, Leon became friends with all of the restaurant's star patrons, including Frank Sinatra, Joe DiMaggio, Marilyn Monroe, Gene Kelly, and James Dean. Leon and Dean began making plans to go into business together and open their own high-end Italian restaurant. Together, they chose the name La Scala, which they thought sounded rich.

On September 30, 1955, Leon received word that Dean had died in an automobile accident in Cholame, California. Leon and Dean had planned to sign a contract for the new restaurant the following Monday. However, Leon decided to follow through with the plans for La Scala. He took out a loan and, on April 1, 1956, opened the restaurant in Beverly Hills.

La Scala was an instant success in the Hollywood circles. Fred Astaire, Marlon Brando, Humphrey Bogart, and all of Villa Capri's clientele were fans. Robert Wagner proposed to Natalie Wood over pasta at the restaurant. Leon reportedly delivered an order to Marilyn Monroe's house at 12305 Fifth Helena Drive in Brentwood on August 4, 1962—the night before her death.

In 1962, Leon took a trip back to his homeland, where he bought a beautiful estate and winery in the Catalan wine-growing region of Penedes. They still produce the wine that bears his name (Chateau Leon) and serve it at La Scala.

Above: **The dining room at La Scala, 1962.**

Presidents John F. Kennedy, Richard Nixon, Gerald Ford, and Ronald Reagan were also regulars at the restaurant. President Reagan chose Leon's wine to serve at his inaugural gala in 1981, and President Kennedy frequently had Leon and his chef, Emilio Nunez, flown in for state dinners in Washington.

In 1985, Leon opened La Scala Trattoria in Brentwood. This location was more family-friendly, with lower price points. In 1987, La Scala received a top rating from the *Los Angeles Times* for its unique bread. While many of the restaurants in the area served Pioneer Bread, La Scala served a very special Italian bread called pane di campagna ("bread of the peasants who work in the fields"). They created three different styles of the bread: pane-filone (baguette-style), ciabatta (a wide, flat loaf), and pagnota (a round loaf). The restaurant was also known for its chopped salad, which is still the number-one lunchtime salad at La Scala today.

In 1989, Leon moved La Scala to 434 Canon Drive in Beverly Hills, which is about a six-minute drive east from the original location. Today, celebrites still flock to the restaurant. Everyone has been spotted there, from Barbra Streisand and Gwyneth Paltrow to Rihanna and Justin Bieber. In 2014, the paparazzi closed down Canon Drive just to get pictures of a pregnant Kim Kardashian exiting the restaurant and crossing the street.

La Scala's rule that an entire party must be present in order to be seated caused some conflict in 2013, when Diana Ross came into the restaurant and said that her daughter would be joining her soon. The La Scala staff informed Ross of their rule, but she went to the corner booth and sat down anyway. Leon's daughter, Gigi, explained to Ross that, at La Scala, they treated everyone the same way, whether they were famous or not. "If people jump the line, we don't serve them," she told the singer. Ross waited until her daughter arrived and then stormed out of the restaurant.

Jean Leon died in 1996. Today, La Scala is owned and managed by Gigi. The quality of the restaurant's ingredients has never faltered in its long history, and it continues to set the bar for fine Italian fare in Beverly Hills. ✖

Below: **Guests at Janet Leigh's birthday party, including Tony Curtis (*center, standing in white jacket*) and Sammy Cahn (*seated, wearing glasses*), 1958.** ■ *Opposite*: **John McGiver, Paul Ford, Lewis Charles, and Dean Martin on the set of *Who's Got the Action* at La Scala, 1962.**

Leon Chopped Salad

This is the most-requested lunchtime salad at La Scala.

Serves 4 to 6

1 head iceberg lettuce, finely chopped
1 head romaine lettuce, finely chopped
4 oz. Italian salami, cut julienne-style
4 oz. mozzarella cheese, shredded
15½-oz. can garbanzo beans, drained
Leon Dressing (recipe follows)

1. Combine the iceberg and romaine lettuces, salami, cheese, and beans in a bowl. Toss with Leon Dressing and serve.

Leon Dressing

Makes ½ cup

¼ cup canola oil
2 tbsp. white wine vinegar
1 tsp. dry mustard
½ tsp. salt
½ tsp. freshly cracked black pepper
¼ cup grated Parmesan cheese

1. Combine the oil, wine vinegar, mustard, salt, pepper, and Parmesan cheese in a glass jar and shake well.

Cyrano

OPEN: 1958–1985

LOCATION: 8711 Sunset Boulevard
West Hollywood, CA 90069

ORIGINAL PHONE: OL 5-9836

CUISINE: American

BUILDING STYLE: Renaissance Storefront

CURRENTLY: Diva Rocker Glam

BEFORE CYRANO OPENED ON THE SUNSET STRIP IN 1958, THE BUILDING AT 8711 SUNSET BOULEVARD HAD SEEN ITS SHARE OF CONTROVERSY. In 1942, during World War II, the U.S. government listed thirty bars, clubs, and restaurants that our men in uniform were not allowed to frequent. Café Internationale, as it was called then, was one of them.

"These taverns and bars are not safe or proper places for servicemen to patronize," a naval commander told the *L.A. Times*. "Firm handling is necessary to eliminate that undesirable fringe of the industry."

The precise nature of the "unsafe" and "improper" activities at these nightspots was left unstated, but Café Internationale was known to feature cross-dressing performers. As a result of the military ban, the Department of Alcoholic Beverage Control revoked the café's liquor license. In 1942, the owner, Elmer Wheeler, sued to have the license reinstated, but he passed away the following December and the club closed for good.

Cyrano breathed life into the building again in 1958, when it opened as a small coffee and sandwich shop. Bob Fidler, a young millionaire stock trader, could see from his office window across the street that the little place had potential. He bought the café and gave it a new look and attitude. He wanted it to be equally inviting for everyone, whether they were dressed up or in jeans and a T-shirt. This was a new concept on the Strip, where restaurants and clubs usually catered to clean-cut, well-dressed customers.

The restaurant faced Sunset Boulevard, with inviting bow windows and tables surrounding a fireplace. On warm days and summer evenings, diners sat outside on the patio, people-watching beneath tall trees and hanging ferns.

Fidler knew quality food and cared deeply about where the Cyrano ingredients came from. At one point, he raised his own cattle for the restaurant's beef. The lunch and dinner menus at Cyrano featured veal, steak, and escargots, as well as what reviewers called one of the best-tasting garlic breads in the city. Saturday's soup of the day was always cold vichyssoise. The most popular time to eat at the restaurant was late at night, if you could get a table. On weekends, the kitchen was open until 3:00 AM, so revelers could drop in after the clubs closed. After-dinner fare was lighter, with an offering of crepes, omelets, and cappuccinos.

Opposite: **Cyrano on the Sunset Strip, 1966**

Young stars like Sal Mineo, Troy Donahue, Suzanne Pleshette, and Natalie Wood started to gravitate to the late-night spot. Music greats such as Elton John, Rod Stewart, Neil Diamond, and Elvis Presley came in after playing gigs at Gazzarri's, Pandora's Box, and the Troubadour.

Staying true to his "come one, come all" mentality, Fidler installed motorcycle parking spaces right in front of the restaurant to cater to the "rough" crowd. Fidler also kept "house accounts" for his regulars, and simply invoiced them at the end of every month. This system made things much easier for all parties involved, and also resulted in higher sales, since no one noticed how much they were spending.

In 1968, the *Los Angeles Times* declared that the Sunset Strip restaurants were dying, having been choked off by the music scene and higher-end diners. Fidler, who had become president of the Sunset Strip Restaurant Association, responded that there were twenty-six establishments within a two-mile stretch on the Strip that brought in over $20 million in business. The real issue, he argued, was that parking on Sunset caused traffic problems. This issue was settled with a new rule: no parking on the Strip after 8:00 PM.

Just as he had spotted the little place across the street from his office and knew it could be a winner, Fidler continued to recognize good concepts and moneymaking ideas in the restaurant industry. In his later years, he was one of the prime investors in California Pizza Kitchen and Baja Fresh. Fidler went on to open more Cyrano locations in beachside cities. ✂

Outside Cyrano, 1965.

Cold Vichyssoise

This flavorful French leek and potato soup was served at Cyrano every Saturday, along with little round toasts.

Serves 6

2 tbsp. unsalted butter
1 lb. leeks, cleaned and minced
  (white parts only)
1 medium onion, peeled and minced
8 oz. russet potatoes, peeled and diced

16 oz. chicken stock
salt
freshly ground pepper
¼ cup mascarpone cheese
fresh basil

1. In a Dutch oven, melt the butter over medium-low heat. Add the leeks and onion and cook for 10 minutes. Add the potatoes and stock, cover, and bring to a boil over medium-high heat. Lower the heat and simmer for 35 minutes, partially covered.
2. Put the liquid through a food mill or purée in a blender. Return it to the pot, and season with salt and pepper to taste. Bring the liquid back to a boil, and whisk in the mascarpone cheese. Remove from the heat and let cool.
3. When the soup has cooled, refrigerate for at least 6 hours. Serve cold, sprinkled with basil.

Chez Jay

OPEN: 1959–present

LOCATION: 1657 Ocean Avenue
Santa Monica, CA 90401

ORIGINAL PHONE: EX 5-1741

CURRENT PHONE: (310) 395-1741

CUISINE: American

DESIGN: Britton S. Shriver

STYLE: Nautical

HOW CAN A BAR/RESTAURANT WITH ONLY TEN TABLES AND TWELVE BARSTOOLS HAVE SO MUCH HISTORY AND COMMAND SO MUCH POWER?

Two words: Jay Fiondella.

In the late 1950s, Fiondella was a bartender at Sinbad's, a bar on the Santa Monica Pier. Before his shift, he would sometimes have breakfast at the Dawn Café, a small eatery on Ocean Avenue. One morning, the café's owner, who was tired of working there, said to Jay that he would sell the place to anyone for a dollar. Fiondella took the offer seriously and jumped at the chance. He took out a loan and renamed the café Chez Jay—an homage to Chez Joey, a restaurant in the Frank Sinatra film *Pal Joey*.

Chez Jay's opening night on July 4, 1959, was a circus—literally. Fiondella had a circus tent erected on the south side of the building, and hired Vegas-esque showgirls to entertain his guests. He even had a live elephant there (it ended up denting the bar with its massive trunk; the dent can still be seen to this day).

The interior of Chez Jay has a homey, inviting feel. Red-and-white-checked oilcloth tablecloths cover the tables, and red-and-white awnings hang over the booths. The cement floor is covered with a layer of sawdust and peanut shells. Every wall in the place is packed with ephemera from Fiondella's past adventures, as well as a vast collection of photos of all the stars who have visited the restaurant.

A few years after the restaurant opened, Sinatra himself became a regular at Chez Jay. Table 10 was his favorite—and the favorite of many other high-profile guests. Located in the back of the restaurant, table 10 was in its own room, separate from the rest of the place, with a curtain that could be drawn for privacy. The curtain remained closed for many years until Jay's mother, Alice, removed it to prevent Warren Beatty from "entertaining" so many of his female friends. Jay named table 10 "The Kissinger Room" after Henry Kissinger, who often dined and hosted meetings there. Marlon Brando reportedly left with a waitress after sitting at table 10. It is also said that, in 1971, Daniel Ellsberg passed the Pentagon Papers to a *New York Times* reporter at table 10. In the '90s, Ben Affleck and Matt Damon wrote parts of their Academy Award-winning screenplay *Good Will Hunting* at the table.

The first celebrities attracted to Chez Jay—such as Vivien Leigh, Peter Finch, Vanessa Redgrave, Richard Burton, and Peter Sellers—were mostly British. In the early years, jazz musicians such as Chet Baker and Slim Gaillard performed at the restaurant every week.

Above: Guests—and a live elephant—enjoy peanuts and drinks at the circus-themed grand opening of Chez Jay, 1959. ▪
Opposite: Jay Fiondella at the helm of Chez Jay, circa 1960s.

Chez Jay's celebrity anecdotes are endless. Lee Marvin once drove his motorcycle through the front door to order a drink, helmet and all. Peter Lawford allegedly met a certain blond actress at the restaurant to take her up to his Pacific Palisades beach house, where President Kennedy was waiting. In 1966, after winning an Academy Award for his performance in *Cat Ballou*, Lee Marvin walked into Chez Jay with his entourage, celebrated all night until closing, and then forgot his Oscar at the restaurant; he had to come back the next day to retrieve it. Michelle Pfeiffer met her

Above: Jay Fiondella, his mother, Alice, and Apollo 14 commander Alan Shepard examine the Chez Jay peanut that Shepard took with him to the moon, 1971. ▪ *Opposite:* Fiondella outside his restaurant, early 1960s.

husband, producer and director David E. Kelley, at the restaurant. After a night of drinking, Richard Harris sang songs from his 1967 award-winning movie *Camelot* to the other diners at the restaurant. In 1996, Quentin Tarantino used one of the restaurant's back rooms to rehearse his cast for the movie *Jackie Brown*. It is said that Beach Boy Dennis Wilson's ghost haunts the bar from time to time.

In 1971, Alan Shepard, the commander of Apollo 14, took a peanut from the bar at Chez Jay, hid it in a film canister, and took it with him to the moon. When he returned from the mission, he brought the peanut back to Chez Jay. Once, Fiondella was showing the peanut to Steve McQueen when the actor jokingly popped the entire nut into his mouth and pretended to eat it. After that, Fiondella kept the peanut in a safe deposit box.

Fiondella was something of a playboy. He owned a small house in Malibu that he called "Jay's Sugar Shack." In 1970, his profile in *Los Angeles Magazine* was accompanied by a photo of Fiondella in front of the shack with women in bikinis. He was also featured as the bachelor of the month in *Cosmopolitan* magazine and appeared on ABC's *The Dating Game* and the long-running show *To Tell the Truth*. He often partied into the wee hours of the morning at the Playboy mansion.

Chez Jay made an appearance in many films, including *Lethal Weapon*, *Bad Influence*, *Two Shades of Blue*, *Last Light*, and *A Single Man*. The restaurant was also the inspiration for the Regal Beagle Pub on the hit show *Three's Company*.

When Fiondella passed away in 2008, Chez Jay's manager, Michael Anderson, and Jay's daughter, Anita, became co-owners of the restaurant. In 2012, the Santa Monica City Council officially named Chez Jay a historic landmark, preventing its demolition to make way for new development.

After Fiondella's death, Leonard Nimoy, who had roomed with Fiondella in the early 1950s, told the *Los Angeles Times*: "He was a gregarious, great guy. . . . I ate at his place occasionally. Always had great stories and good food." ✕

La Jolla Potatoes

This signature dish has been served at Chez Jay since the late 1960s.

Serves 6

8 x 8-inch baking pan, buttered
2 lbs. russet potatoes, peeled and cut into
   large chunks
2 large cloves of garlic, minced
2 tbsp. unsalted butter

1½ cups half-and-half
2 tsp. salt
½ tsp. freshly ground black pepper
2 large, ripe bananas, peeled and sliced
4 oz. Jarlsberg or Gruyère cheese, grated

1. Preheat the oven to 350°F.
2. In a large pot of salted water, boil the potatoes until just tender (about 15 minutes). Drain into a colander and allow the potatoes to steam for 5 minutes.
3. Meanwhile, wipe out the pot, add the garlic and butter and return to the heat. Allow the garlic to turn golden, then add the half-and-half, salt, pepper, bananas, and potatoes.
4. Using a hand masher, roughly mash the potato mixture. You want to have a textural contrast of smooth and rough pieces. Season to taste, then transfer the potatoes to the baking pan and top with the grated cheese. Place in the oven to heat through and brown the cheese, about 15 minutes.
5. Serve at once or set the oven at 220°F and keep warm until ready to serve.

Tana's

9071 SANTA MONICA BLVD. CR 5-9444

Your Host Dan Tana

Dan Tana's

OPEN: 1964–present

LOCATION: 9071 Santa Monica Boulevard
West Hollywood, CA 90069

ORIGINAL PHONE: CR 5-9444

CURRENT PHONE: (310) 275-9444

CUISINE: Italian

BUILDING STYLE: Clubhouse

IN 1964, SERBIAN EXPAT AND FORMER PROFESSIONAL FOOTBALL PLAYER DAN TANA (BORN DOBRIVOJE TANASIJE-VIC) OPENED THE RESTAURANT DAN TANA'S ON SANTA MONICA BOULEVARD, FOLLOWING IN THE FOOTSTEPS OF HIS RESTAURATEUR FATHER. At the time, that unincorporated area of L.A.—now known as West Hollywood—didn't have much to offer.

Tana got his start in the restaurant industry while playing on a California league football team. Since he was not legal, the team arranged for his papers and a job as a packer at the StarKist Tuna factory in San Pedro. After that, Tana worked as a dishwasher at Miceli's (see page 181), and then as the maître d' at La Scala (page 211). He was working in the Professional Soccer League offices in Los Angeles when he noticed a hamburger restaurant called Domenico's going out of business down the street. In 1964, Tana bought the place and hired Chef Michele Diguglio to run the kitchen.

Above: Dan Tana's on Santa Monica Boulevard, 1964. ▪ *Below:* Owner Sonja Perencevic (*center*) with the staff at Dan Tana's.

Dan Tana's has remained virtually unchanged since its opening day. The rounded neon sign outside has been there since the restaurant was Domenico's. The walls are still painted a deep red, with matching red leather banquettes and tables covered by red-and-white-checkered tablecloths. Clusters of Chianti bottles hang from the ceiling. Known for its delicious Italian food and steaks, the restaurant offers classic pasta dishes such as fettucini, lasagna, and eggplant parmesan.

Dan Tana's draws a broad range of celebrities. Both Paris Hilton and her mom, Kathy, have celebrated birthdays at the eatery. Johnny Carson said it was his favorite restaurant in Los Angeles. George Clooney's 2006 Oscar party was held there. It was the first restaurant Cameron Diaz ate at when she arrived in Tinsel Town, and she still eats there often with her agent and manager. Drew Barrymore visited many times when she was a toddler, and today she still comes in. In 2011, Ryan Phillippe told *L.A. Magazine* that he and his friends had eaten at either Dan Tana's or Craig's every Thursday for four years straight.

Because of its close proximity to the Troubadour, Dan Tana's has also hosted some of the greatest musicians of our time, such as the Byrds, the Mamas and the Papas, Frank Zappa, Elton John, Bette Midler, and the Eagles, who wrote their 1975 hit song "Lyin' Eyes" at the restaurant.

In 2008, restaurateur Sonja Perencevic bought Dan Tana's. Even under the new ownership, Dan Tana's has maintained the same look, and the menu has retained many of its original items. ✕

Below: **Pacific Red Cars rumbled past Domenico's, which Dan Tana bought and transformed into Dan Tana's, 1940s.** ▪
Opposite: **Chianti bottles cover the ceiling at Dan Tana's, 1965.**

Chicken Piccata

Serve this flavorful dish on a bed of rice or butter noodles.

Serves 4

4 chicken breasts, 6–8 oz. each, skinless and
    boneless, pounded to ¼-inch thickness
1 cup all-purpose flour
½ cup canola oil
1½ cups chicken stock
½ cup white wine
¼ cup freshly squeezed lemon juice
4 cloves garlic, minced
1 tbsp. unsalted butter
1 tbsp. capers, drained
sea salt
freshly ground black pepper

1. Place the flour in a shallow dish. Dredge
   the chicken through the flour.
2. Heat the oil in a skillet over medium-high
   heat. Add the chicken and cook until
   lightly browned on both sides, about
   2 minutes on each side. Drain off the oil.
   Add the chicken stock, white wine, lemon
   juice, garlic, butter, and capers. Cook
   until the sauce thickens slightly. Salt and
   pepper to taste.

RICARD

david hockney
14. Feb. 1976.

Ma Maison

OPEN: 1973–1985

LOCATION: 8368 Melrose Avenue
Los Angeles, CA 90069

ORIGINAL PHONE: (213) 655-1991

CUISINE: California-French Fusion

DESIGN: C. Taylor

BUILDING STYLE: 1920s house

CURRENTLY: Strip Mall

THE NAME PATRICK TERRAIL CHOSE FOR HIS MELROSE AVENUE RESTAURANT WAS SIGNIFICANT. Ma Maison ("my house") was meant to feel welcoming, as if diners were coming to his own home for a meal.

Terrail was bred for the restaurant business. His great-grandfather, M. Burdel, had been the last proprietor of the great Café Anglais in Paris. His grandfather, André Terrail, had made dining at La Tour d'Argent in Paris "a beautiful and graceful ceremony," according to the press, and his uncle, Claude Terrail, had kept that tradition alive, earning La Tour d'Argent a three-star Michelin rating. Terrail's father also managed a restaurant, as did his other uncle and two of his aunts.

Terrail's new undertaking was planned with the utmost attention to detail. Its menus, prepared by chef Elie Cortez, featured simple yet delicious French fare, such as croque-madame sandwiches, peach soup, two-pound lobster tails, and various crepes. The house specialty was brochettes of beef that had been marinated for twenty-four hours. The restaurant had a cheese table for after-dinner tastings. Also on the menu were fondue and raclette, a traditonal cheese dish from Switzerland. All of the pastries, croissants, and breads were made from scratch. French newspapers were flown in for guests to read while they ate.

Located on Melrose Avenue, a few blocks down from La Cienega, Ma Maison was inside a peculiar-looking house situated away from the street. The restaurant's decor was made up of a hodgepodge of random items. The patio was covered with green artificial turf and decorated with umbrellas and plastic flamingos. Low-hanging air ducts and sliding glass doors completed the feeling that the place had been thrown together. But somehow, it all worked; Terrail had a gift for creating a unique ambiance.

Crossing the parking lot in front of the restaurant was like walking through a Rolls-Royce or Bentley dealership. Many

Above: Patrick Terrail with Joel Grey outside Ma Maison, circa 1980. ▪
Right: Terrail and Orson Welles, circa 1980. ▪ *Opposite:* Ma Maison's menu cover by artist David Hockney, 1976.

Ma Maison

Françoise Gilot

actors and industry professionals dined at Ma Maison. In 1974, while convalescing at St. John's Hospital in nearby Santa Monica, Richard Burton grew tired of the hospital food, so he took two nurses and Terence Young, who directed his film *The Klansman*, to Ma Maison for lunch. Burton ordered "water on the rocks" to drink. In his later years, Orson Welles dined at the restaurant on a weekly basis, dressed all in black and accompanied by his toy poodle, Kiki, and his friend, writer and director Henry Jaglom (who was working as Welles's unoffical agent at the time). Welles always entered the restaurant via the kitchen, and ate at his favorite table inside the restaurant, never on the patio.

In 1975, Wolfgang Puck moved to Los Angeles to become the chef and part owner of Ma Maison. Seven years later, after publishing his first cookbook based on his Ma Maison recipes, Puck opened Spago on Sunset Boulevard (see page 261). More and more of Ma Maison's former chefs and staff also established their own eateries: Claude Segal opened Bistango, Mark Peel opened Campanile, and Susan Feniger opened City Restaurant.

In 1982, Ma Maison's sous chef, John Sweeney, was charged with the murder of actress Dominique Dunne. After his prison sentence, Sweeney came back to the area, landing a job at Santa Monica's Chronicle restaurant. He was fired, however, after Dunne's mother and brother showed up at the restaurant and handed out flyers to the patrons that read: "The food you will eat tonight was cooked by the hands that killed Dominique Dunne." Sweeney changed his name to John Maura and moved to the northwest.

On November 14, 1985, Ma Maison served its last meal. The 22,000-foot property, which sold for over $2 million, was leveled and a three-story office building was erected in its place. Terrail also sold the rights to the name Ma Maison to a hotelier, who built a restaurant with the same name in his $26 million Sofitel Hotel less than a mile away. Unfortunately, the hotel's version of Ma Maison failed.

Terrail, who was ready for a change, left Los Angeles for Hogansville, Georgia, where he runs the magazine *85 South* (named after the highway that runs through Hogansville). ✖

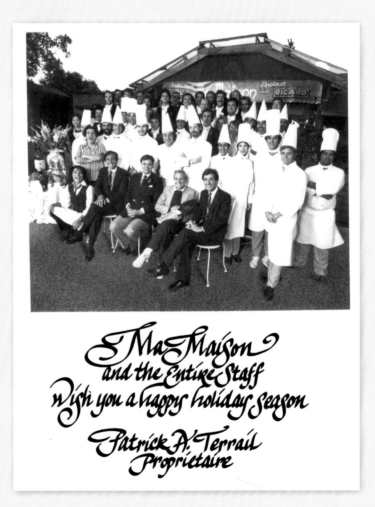

Ma Maison and the Entire Staff wish you a happy holiday season
Patrick A. Terrail Proprietaire

Quiche à la Ma Maison

This quiche was a favorite on Ma Maison's lunch menu.

Serves 6

14-inch prepared pastry pie dough, rolled out
8 oz. applewood-smoked bacon,
  cooked and diced
6 oz. cooked ham, diced
¼ cup fresh chives, chopped
½ cup Gruyère cheese, grated
3 cups half-and-half or heavy cream
7 large eggs
½ tsp. white pepper
¼ tsp. ground nutmeg
¼ tsp. salt

1. Preheat the oven to 350°F. Line a 10-inch quiche pan with the pastry dough.
2. Bake the crust until light brown, about 12 minutes. Set aside.
3. Sprinkle the bacon, ham, chives, and cheese on top of the pastry.
4. In a bowl, whisk together the half-and-half, eggs, white pepper, nutmeg, and salt. Pour on top of the bacon mixture. Bake until puffy and browned, about 30 to 40 minutes. Serve hot with a side salad.

Below: **Barry Krost with Doug and Tina Sinatra, late 1970s.** ▪ *Opposite:* **Holiday greetings from the Ma Maison staff, 1975.**

Above: Bianca Jagger, Jade Jagger, and Alana Stewart, late 1970s. ▪ *Opposite left:* Patrick Terrail with Jack Lemmon, late 1970s. ▪ *Opposite right:* Terrail with Suzanne Somers, late 1970s.

Chicken Salad

Ma Maison served this salad on a bed of greens or homemade bread.

Serves 4

3 lbs. roasting chicken, cooked and deboned
1 medium Golden Delicious apple,
   peeled, cored, and diced
1 stalk celery, diced
1 tbsp. capers
2 tbsp. Dijon mustard
½ cup mayonnaise
salt

freshly ground black pepper
freshly squeezed lemon juice
2 small heads Boston lettuce,
   washed and torn
vinaigrette dressing
2 large hard-boiled eggs, sliced
2 medium tomatoes, sliced

1. In a large bowl, combine the chicken, apple, celery, capers, and mustard. Add enough mayonnaise to lightly coat. Add salt, pepper, and lemon juice to taste.
2. Season the lettuce with the vinaigrette and place in the center of a serving platter. Top with the salad and garnish with the eggs and tomatoes.

Chicken Roulade

This Ma Maison staple is a popular dish in the south of France.

Serves 8

4 whole skinless chicken breasts,
   pounded thin
3 tbsp. unsalted butter, melted
4 sheets dry seaweed (8 x 8-inch square)
2 large carrots,
   peeled and cut into matchsticks
1 large cucumber,
   peeled and cut into matchsticks

1 bunch cilantro, trimmed and chopped
salt
freshly ground black pepper
4 tsp. extra-virgin olive oil
4 flour tortillas (10-inch)
Salsa (recipe follows)
boiled new potatoes, for serving

1. Brush both sides of the pounded chicken with butter. Grill in a frying pan or over coals for 10 to 15 minutes, turning once, until the internal temperature reaches 165°F.
2. Place one whole chicken breast on each piece of seaweed to cover the entire sheet. Arrange 2 sticks of carrots and cucumbers on the lower third of the chicken. Sprinkle with the cilantro and season with salt and pepper to taste. Drizzle with the olive oil. Roll up tightly. Place the seaweed roll on a flour tortilla. Trim the ends to match the length of the roll. Roll tightly in the tortilla.
3. Secure each roll with plastic wrap, tying a knot at each end. Place in a steamer basket with simmering water underneath without touching. Cover and steam for 15 minutes, or until heated through.
4. To serve, remove the plastic wrap and slice into ½-inch slices. Overlap the slices on a plate and serve with salsa and boiled new potatoes.

Menu Designed by:
David Hockney

One in a series of
other menus created
for us by artists:

Francoise Gilot
Joan Worth
Putzie Nutzel
Steve Verona
Michael Heindorff
Kostabi and
Vicky Thiel
Diane Laurence

8555 Beverly Boulevard
Los Angeles, CA 90048
(213) 655-1991

Ma Maison

Since 1973

Above: Patrick Terrail with Governor Jerry Brown, 1981. ▪ *Opposite top:* David Hockney's 1978 menu cover for Ma Maison. ▪ *Opposite bottom:* Terrail with Burgess Meredith and Gene Kelly, 1974.

Salsa

Serves 8

1 large tomato, peeled, seeded, and squeezed
½ small jalapeño chile, minced
¼ medium onion, diced
¼ medium avocado, diced
1 tbsp. cilantro, minced
2 tbsp. white wine vinegar
2 tbsp. extra-virgin olive oil
1½ tsp. tomato juice
sea salt
freshly ground black pepper

1. In the work bowl of a food processor fitted with the metal blade, process the tomato, chile, onion, avocado, cilantro, vinegar, olive oil, tomato juice, sea salt, and black pepper for 10 seconds. Chill in the refrigerator. Serve cold.

Note: For a chunkier salsa, only pulse the ingredients until the salsa reaches your desired texture.

Carlos 'n Charlie's

OPEN: 1975–1996

LOCATION: 8240 Sunset Boulevard
West Hollywood, CA 90046

ORIGINAL PHONE: (213) 656-8830

CUISINE: Mexican

BUILDING STYLE: Whimsical

CURRENTLY: Vacant Office Space

IN 1975, THE SUNSET STRIP'S POPULAR MARQUIS RESTAURANT CLOSED AND WAS TRANSFORMED INTO A CLUB AND RESTAURANT NAMED CARLOS 'N CHARLIE'S. The building retained its whimsical style, complete with turrets, a wraparound porch, and a sunroom.

Unlike most of the clubs on Sunset, Carlos 'n Charlie's served lunch. The restaurant's taco tray was the most popular item on the menu, offering a choice of chicken or beef, homemade guacamole, two types of cheese, chorizo, and grilled veggies. At dinnertime, the club's signature dish was the sole medrazo, a fillet of sole with a spinach and cheese topping. The menu was eclectic, including local dishes, fresh fish, and catches from south of the border. Barbecued ribs, tequila shrimp, and spicy tuna dip were also favorites on the menu.

At one time, twenty-eight different Carlos 'n Charlie's locations were in operation, mainly in Mexico, where the franchise had first been established in 1963. All of the restaurants in the franchise incorporated part of the original Carlos 'n Charlie's name into their own names. But at the time, the similarities stopped there; each restaurant created and followed its own recipes. Today, the Carlos 'n Charlie's brand has only eight locations, mostly in Mexican tourist spots, and all of the menus are identical.

Bernice and George Altschul owned the Carlos 'n Charlie's location on Sunset and ran it with a genuine fondness for their employees, making most of them feel like they were part of a family. The club's disco, El Privado, was a busy place, showcasing new talent on Tuesday nights and featuring everyone from Joan Rivers to Donna Summer. One night in 1977, the rhythm and blues singer Teddy Pendergrass threw himself a birthday party at El Privado that cost him $10,000. On another night, Tommy Smothers of the Smothers Brothers sat down at the bar, ordered a drink, and asked to run a tab. The bartender, J. Lynn McCall, was very busy but continued to replenish his drink. When it came time to close out, Smothers paid the bill and thanked McCall for the conversation. McCall was amused, since they had only spoken about starting the tab and paying the bill.

Above: Carlos 'n Charlie's on the Sunset Strip. ▪ *Right*: Bartender Linda Guillemette. ▪ *Opposite*: Carlos 'n Charlie's owner Bernice Altschul, 1988.

"The drinks had a heavy pour," McCall said. "Sometimes fights broke out."

In the summer of 1988, singer El DeBarge was hospitalized after a man allegedly struck him from behind with a champagne glass at the club. He was treated for neck wounds and underwent surgery.

Despite some rough moments, Carlos 'n Charlie's won more than its fair share of accolades. In 1979, it was named one of the best singles bars in the United States by Playboy Clubs International, and in the early 1990s, Bernice was honored with the West Hollywood Chamber of Commerce's Woman of the Year award.

After the original Carlos 'n Charlie's location closed in 1996, an Irish pub named Dublin's took over the location for a few years. The building was then razed to create Sunset Beach, a restaurant in a modernistic building with white "sails" coming out of its roof, as if it were on the ocean. The location is now slated for redevelopment. ✂

The annual Halloween party at Carlos 'n Charlie's, 1978.

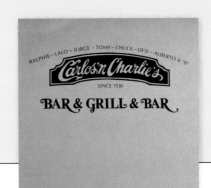

Spicy Tuna Dip

This fantastic dip, served with fried corn tortilla chips, will spark your taste buds.

Serves 4

12½ oz. canned tuna, drained
2 medium jalapeño chiles, seeded and chopped
2 green onions, chopped (green part only)
1 stalk celery, diced
½ cup mayonnaise
sea salt
freshly ground black pepper
¼ cup cilantro, chopped

1. In a food processor fitted with the metal blade, pulse the tuna, chiles, green onions, and celery about 10 times. Add the mayonnaise and salt and pepper to taste, and pulse 5 more times.
2. Transfer to a serving dish and sprinkle with the cilantro.

Charlie's Freeze

A favorite at Carlos 'n Charlie's, this creamy beverage was touted as one of the top 100 drinks in the nation in 1979 by Benson and Hedges.

Serves 1

¾ oz. Mexican coffee liqueur
¾ oz. California brandy
5 oz. vanilla bean ice cream
whipped cream
ground nutmeg

1. Place the Mexican coffee liqueur, brandy, and ice cream in a blender. Blend until thick. Pour into a 9-inch wine glass. Top with a swirl of whipped cream and garnish with a sprinkle of fresh nutmeg.

Spanish Martini

This signature drink was popular in the disco during the 1970s.

Serves 1

1½ oz. dry gin
½ oz. dry Spanish sherry
1 green olive or lemon peel strip

1. Pour the gin and sherry over ice cubes in a cocktail shaker. Stir 20 times. Strain into a chilled martini glass. Add the olive and serve.

L'ERMITAGE

L'Ermitage

OPEN: 1975–1991

LOCATION: 730 N. La Cienega Boulevard
Los Angeles, CA 90029

ORIGINAL PHONE: (213) 652-5840

CUISINE: French

DESIGN: L. J. Murishek

BUILDING STYLE: French Vogue

CURRENTLY: Koi Restaurant

WHEN JEAN BERTRANOU OPENED A RESTAURANT NAMED L'ERMITAGE ON LA CIENEGA BOULEVARD IN 1975, HE REVOLUTIONIZED THE PRODUCE AND FOOD INDUSTRY. At a time when the produce and fresh herb selection was limited in American grocery stores, Bertranou blazed new trails to get his beloved fresh ingredients grown in Southern California, just as they were in his native France. Today, many of the items we take for granted at the local supermarket are there because Bertranou worked hard to make them available.

When Bertranou arrived in Los Angeles from France, he noticed that the weather was similar to France's southern coast. He wondered if the soil could produce the same vegetables. Bertranou began looking for suppliers to grow the food he wanted—and if he couldn't find a supplier, he decided to grow his own. Many of these produce companies started to market their newfound vegetables to grocery stores in the Los Angeles area, including haricots verts, baby carrots, white asparagus, arugula, lamb's lettuce, and fresh Chanterelle, Shiitake, and Enok mushrooms. Dissatisfied with the ducks in the States, Bertranou launched a farm to raise his own.

L'Ermitage was located on L.A.'s Restaurant Row—the stretch of La Cienega from Santa Monica Boulevard to Wilshire that boasted an eclectic collection of over thirty-five restaurants. L'Ermitage set a standard that the other French restaurants in the area still strive to match but rarely succeed.

In 1979, Bertranou learned that he had a brain tumor. He died the following year. At the time, L'Ermitage was so high in

Chef Jean Bertranou outside L'Ermitage with a furry customer.

demand—reservations were booked three months in advance—that the restaurant even stayed open on the day of Bertranou's memorial service.

In 1990, *Los Angeles Times* food editor Ruth Reichl named L'Ermitage one of her top 40 restaurants in Los Angeles. "This is the last bastion of really correct French cooking in L.A.," she wrote. "It makes you feel that French food has remained unchanged for centuries."

Many stars frequented L'Ermitage, including the Reagans, Elizabeth Taylor, Johnny Carson, Betsy Bloomingdale, Paul Newman, and Joanne Woodward. The restaurant's dining room also appeared in the 1987 John Hughes film *Some Kind of Wonderful*.

In 1991, the owners of L'Ermitage announced that they were planning on either selling the restaurant or reopening it with a different style. However, L'Ermitage remained closed, never to reopen again. ✄

The bar at L'Ermitage.

Lobster Mousse

The most decadent appetizer in all of Los Angeles. Pair with plain soda crackers to enhance the mousse's flavor.

Serves 12

Three 1½ lb. fresh Maine lobsters, cooked and cleaned, with the meat removed
1 lb. cooked shrimp, cleaned, peeled, and deveined
salt
white pepper

4 cups heavy cream
5 oz. pistachios
2 oz. truffles
butter
Tomato Sauce (recipe follows)

1. Place ⅓ of the lobster and shrimp in a food pressor fitted with a metal blade. Process for 10 seconds. Through the feed tube, add ½ of the heavy cream and process until it reaches a paste-like consistency. Add the salt and pepper. Repeat with ⅓ of the lobster, and the remaining shrimp and heavy cream. Add the remaining lobster. Set aside.
2. Slice the pistachios and set aside.
3. Cover the bottom and sides of a 9 x 5-inch loaf pan with plastic wrap. Arrange a row of truffles down the center of the prepared pan. Sprinkle with ½ of the pistachios. Top with ½ of the lobster/shrimp mixture, smoothing to the sides of the pan. Sprinkle the remaining pistachios on top, and then add the remaining mixture.
4. Refrigerate for 2 hours. When ready to serve, unmold onto a plate and top with the Tomato Sauce.

Tomato Sauce

780 N. La Cienega Boulevard, Los Angeles, CA 90069 (213) 652-5840

Dora Fourcade
Jean Pierre Fourcade
Proprietors

Makes 1½ cups

6 large ripe tomatoes
salt
pepper

1. Peel tomatoes, cut in half, and squeeze to remove seeds and juice.
2. Place pulp in a food processor fitted with a metal blade. Add the salt and pepper. Process until the right consistency is reached.

Chocolate Mousse

This rich chocolate mousse dish is lined with ladyfingers and topped with a delicious vanilla sauce.

Serves 6

1½ cups water
2 cups granulated sugar
9 large egg yolks
8 oz. dark Swiss chocolate
2 cups whipped cream
1 package ladyfingers
Vanilla Sauce (recipe follows)

1. In a saucepan over medium heat, combine the water and sugar and bring to a boil.
2. Place the mixture in double boiler over medium heat and add the egg yolks, stirring with a whisk for about 30 minutes, or until thickened. Remove from the heat and whisk in the melted chocolate.
3. Fold in the whipped cream. Arrange the ladyfingers around the inside and bottom of the prepared dish. Fill with the chocolate/cream mixture and smooth. Place in the refrigerator for 2 hours. Serve with Vanilla Sauce.

Vanilla Sauce

Makes 2½ cups

1 cup heavy cream
1 cup whole milk
4 large yolks
½ cup granulated sugar
½ tsp. pure vanilla extract

1. In a double boiler over medium heat, heat the cream and milk until scalding, about 4 minutes.
2. In a large bowl, whisk the egg yolks and sugar until light and pale, about 3 minutes. Whisk into the hot mixture and stir until thickened, about 30 minutes. Let cool before serving.

W E G R I N D I T H E R E!

HAMBURGER	FOR THE PURIST!	3.20
TERIAKIBURGER	BLANKETED WITH A BLEND OF TERIYAKI, GARLIC AND GINGER	3.30
CHEESEBURGER	COVERED WITH A BLANKET OF NATURAL CHEDDAR OR SWISS	3.35
CHEESEBURGER/BACON	SWISS OR CHEDDAR....?	3.75
MENAGE À TROIS	AVOCADO, BACON AND CHEESE (SWISS OR CHEDDAR)	3.95
MEXACALI	TOPPED WITH GREEN CHILI AND ONION	3.40
HAMBURGER SAUTE	SMOTHERED IN GOLDEN BROWN FRIED ONIONS	3.35
SLAM DUNKBURGER	SPREAD WITH SOUR PLUM JAM & FRENCH DIJON MUSTARD. A TASTE DELIGHT!	3.45
PEPPERBURGER	GROUND PEPPERCORNS, DICED ONION FIRED BROWN-BLACK	3.45
PINK PEPPERBURGER	PEPPERBURGER WITH SHERRY WINE DRESSING ON TOP	3.55
POLYNESIAN BURGER	TOPPED WITH GRILLED PINEAPPLE, SWEET 'N' SOUR SAUCE	3.65
FOGGYBOTTOM BURGER	SMOOTHED WITH PEANUT BUTTER AND SOUR PLUM JAM	3.35
BACONBURGER	FOR THE PURIST WITH A FLAIR	3.55
AVOCADOBURGER	A GOURMET TREAT!	3.65
FACTORYBURGER	A BIT OF NOSTALGIA WITH BACON AND CHOPPED PEANUTS	3.55
GOLDEN KAZOO	MUSHROOMS AND GREEN ONIONS COOKED IN RED WINE, FRESH BROCCOLI DRENCHED IN MELTED CHEESE (CHEDDAR OR SWISS?)	3.95
MARIEBURGER	GREEN PEPPERS, ONIONS, TOMATOES, SEASONING, FRIED IN OIL. A CZECHOSLOVAKIAN RECIPE SMUGGLED FROM FREE EUROPE BY OUR COOK, MARIE. 3.40; GREAT WITH MELTED CHEDDAR OR SWISS (Mmmm!)	3.95
WHITEDELIGHT	BACON COVERED WITH BLEU CHEESE DRESSING (HOMEMADE)	3.55
BARBEQUEBURGER	WITH OUR OWN MULE-KICKIN' SAUCE	3.45
CHILIBURGER	TOE-CURLIN' CHILI BY OUR COOK FROM WESTERN CZECHOSLOVAKIA	3.90
MUSHROOMBURGER	SMOTHERED WITH SAUTEED MUSHROOMS. A SAN FRANCISCO FAVORITE!	3.50
ZAPATA BURGER	OUR CLASSIC GUACAMOLE...BY OUR CHEF FROM THE SOUTH	3.70
NELLYBURGER	CREAMED HORSERADISH (SOUR CREAM,GARLIC,ONIONS) & BACON (WHOA NELLY!)	3.65
FRANK'S FANTASY	SOUR CREAM & LUMPFISH CAVIAR	4.05

"HAMPTON'S GIVES GREAT HAMBURGER"....OLD BLUE

AND IF THAT AIN'T ENUFF, Y O U C A N A D D:

Sixty-five cents: AVOCADO OR BACON OR CHEESE OR BLUE CHEESE DRESSING OR SHERRY WINE DRESSING OR DIJON MUSTARD OR ONE OF THE FOLLOWING: PEANUT BUTTER, PEANUTS, GREEN CHILI AN' ONIONS, CHEESE SOURDOUGH BREAD, SOUR PLUM JAM.

Eighty-five cents: BROCCOLI, CHILI SAUCE, OR SAUTEED MUSHROOMS.

F O O T L O N G S A N D W I C H E S O N P A P E R T H I N B R E A D:

TUNA MELT	OUTRAGEOUS! OUR SPECIAL TUNA SALAD, SWISS OR CHEDDAR, RYE OR EGG	3.65
GRILLED HAM/CHEESE	SWISS OR CHEDDAR, RYE OR EGG BREAD....?	3.65
GRILLED BACON/CHEESE	SWISS OR CHEDDAR, RYE OR EGG BREAD....?	3.65
GRILLED HAM/BACON/CHEESE	SWISS OR CHEDDAR, RYE OR EGG BREAD....?	3.90
GRILLED CHEESE SAUTE	SAME CHOICES, BUT WITH GOLDEN BROWN SAUTEED ONIONS	3.50
HOT TUNA/GUACAMOLE	TUNA, GUACAMOLE, CHEDDAR OR SWISS, TOMATOES, ALFALFA SPROUTS ON EGGBREAD OR RYE. THIS IS ONE OF OUR BEST!	4.25

S O U P: FRESH VEGETABLE...HOMEMADE, SERVED WITH HOT CHEESE SOURDOUGH. TERRIFIC!   CUP   1.00
                                                                 BOWL   2.25

S A L A D B A R: 20 ITEMS, 4 HOMEMADE DRESSINGS, PEANUTS, SUNFLOWER SEEDS, TUNA,   3.60
                           GRATED CHEESE, RAISINS, SOY BEANS. CREATE YOUR OWN MASTERPIECE

S O U P 'N' S A L A D: OUR 20 ITEM SALAD BAR, AND A CUP OF SOUP, HOT CHEESE SOURDOUGH   4.30

D E S S E R T S: OUR REALLY SPECIAL CAKES: CARROT AND CHOCOLATE - 1.00
                     CHEESECAKE (NY STYLE) - 1.75   MARJOLAINE - 2.00

BEVERAGES: PEPSI, DIET PEPSI, LEMON-LIME, COFFEE, TEA, ICED TEA...45¢
                   MILK, FRESH HOMEMADE LEMONADE...60¢   PERRIER WATER...1.50

TAP BEER:	MUG	PITCHER
BUDWEISER	.90	3.50
HEINEKEN	1.50	5.50

FRENCH WINES	WHITE	GLASS	BOTTLE	RED	GLASS	BOTTLE
CHARDONNAY		2.10	10.00	CHATEAU LAROSE TRINTAUDON '73	2.25	8.50
MOUTON-CADET '76 (ROTHSCHILD)		1.95	8.20	VALPOLLICELLA (ANTINORI '75)	1.75	6.50
CHASSAGNE MONTRACHET '76		3.75	14.00	CHATEAU LAFITE-ROTHSCHILD '72	4.25	21.00

CALIFORNIA WINES	GLASS	HALF LITRE	LITRE	ISLERO	RED	
WHITE	.80	2.25	3.95	SPLIT	2.15	A nice, light, Spanish
				FIFTH	3.40	table wine.

S P L I T S — $1.50 E X T R A

*Additional charge for take-out   **Minimum Charge $1.50 per person

15% Service charge for parties of ten or more

Hamptons

OPEN: 1977–2002

LOCATION: 1342 N. Highland Avenue
Hollywood, CA 90028

ORIGINAL PHONE: (213) 462-0297

CUISINE: American

DESIGN: M. Jensen

BUILDING STYLE: 1940s House

CURRENTLY: Hampton Arms Condominium Complex

PAUL NEWMAN FAMOUSLY LOVED TO COOK FOR HIS FAMILY AND FRIENDS. In the late 1970s, while having dinner with his friend, writer and artist Ron Buck, Newman boasted about his restaurant-worthy hamburgers. Buck told Newman that he had recently inherited his mother's old house, a property that sat on the busy Highland Avenue in Hollywood, between Sunset Boulevard and Fountain Avenue. Newman and Buck collaborated to transform the Highland Avenue property into a restaurant that they named Hamptons, which opened in 1977.

The restaurant soon became a popular hangout for industry professionals. It felt homey, with maple wood chairs that looked as if they belonged in your grandmother's kitchen, and an enormous old tree dominating the enclosed patio. On the far side of the restaurant was a big, round table used by writers during their working lunches. Actors and anyone with an industry union card automatically received a ten percent discount, while known agents got a ten percent surcharge.

The burgers at Hamptons were truly deluxe. They could be made with the customer's choice of beef, turkey, or a variety of exotic meats including wild game, ostrich, and bison, plus a variety of thirty-four different toppings ranging from peanut butter to caviar. The menu boasted twenty-eight different burgers. The Golden Kazoo Burger had mushrooms, green onions cooked in red wine, and fresh broccoli with melted cheddar. The White Delight Burger was topped with bacon and covered in blue cheese. Frank's Fantasy Burger was garnished with sour cream and caviar. My personal favorite was the Ménage à Trois, which included avocado, bacon, and cheese. Actor Phil Leeds, who had a regular table at the restaurant until he passed away in 1998, had a Hamptons burger named in his honor; it was discounted fifty percent for a full week after he died.

Each burger at Hamptons contained eight ounces of meat that was ground fresh a couple of times a day. The restaurant used a special broiler that cooked the bottom and top of the burger patties simultaneously, so the

Hamptons on Highland Avenue, 1998.

natural juices were sealed in. All the burgers were served with a choice of one of four side salads: German potato salad, green salad, grain salad, or pasta salad. At the time, the *Los Angeles Times*, *Hollywood Reporter*, and *L.A. Weekly* raved about the burgers at Hamptons, calling them the best in Los Angeles. Hamptons also served as the test kitchen for the Newman's Own brand, which launched in 1982.

In 1978, William Hunter and William Countryman, friends of the Newman family from the East Coast who were known as "the Bills," arrived in Los Angeles with a touring production of *Cabaret*. The Bills were frequent dinner guests in the Newman home. One night, they brought dessert with them, a new confection that was sweeping the nation: carrot cake with cream cheese icing. Paul and Joanne loved the carrot cake and asked the Bills if they would make a few for Hamptons. The cake soon became a regular item at the restaurant. The *L.A. Times* ran a story on this new dessert and named the Hamptons version the best in the city. At only a dollar a slice, it was packed with pineapple and pecans and smothered in icing.

After the Bills gave up the stage, they began making cakes full time, opening a bakery called the Cake Walk at 5859 Third Street that continued to sell their famous carrot cake. The Cake Walk also created the Pistachio Cream Sherry Cake featured at Scandia (see page 173). In the early 1980s, I was a Cake Walk employee, delivering desserts to Hamptons on the weekends.

Even as the restaurant changed owners and names (it evolved from Hamptons Hamburger Buffet, to Hamptons Hollywood, to Hamptons Hollywood Café) and moved to another location in Burbank, it continued to offer its extensive gourmet burger menu.

In 2002, the restaurant was closed and bulldozed, along with its famed tree, to make way for a condominium complex named Hampton Arms. The Newman's Own brand has gone on to enormous success, raising more than $400 million for charity. ✕

German Red Potato Salad

This was one of the four types of salads served alongside the burgers at Hamptons.

Serves 8 to 10

4 lb. red potatoes, cut into quarters	¼ cup white wine vinegar
8 oz. country bacon slices	½ cup green onion, chopped
1 tbsp. all-purpose flour	½ tsp. sea salt
2 tbsp. granulated sugar	½ tsp. freshly ground black pepper
⅓ cup water, at room temperature	½ tsp. mustard seed

1. Bring a large stockpot of salted water to a boil and cook the potatoes until tender but still firm, about 15 minutes. Drain and let cool.
2. In a large, deep skillet over medium-high heat, cook the bacon until evenly browned and crisp. Transfer to paper towels to drain. Crumble and set aside.
3. Add the flour to the bacon fat remaining in the skillet and cook, stirring, until lightly browned, about 2 minutes. Reduce the heat to medium. Add the sugar, water, and vinegar. Cook, stirring, until the dressing is thick, about 5 minutes.
4. Add the bacon, potatoes, and green onions to the dressing and stir until coated and heated through. Stir in the salt, pepper, and mustard seed. Serve warm.

Gazpacho with Sour Cream and Dill

This soup, which was served daily at Hamptons, could substitute for the salad that came with your burger.

Serves 8

1½ lb. vine-ripened tomatoes
tomato juice, as needed
1 medium cucumber, peeled, seeded, and
   chopped
½ cup red bell pepper, chopped
½ cup red onion, chopped
1 small jalapeño chile, seeded and minced
1 clove garlic, minced
¼ cup extra-virgin olive oil

1 medium lime, juiced
2 tsp. balsamic vinegar
2 tsp. Worcestershire sauce
½ tsp. ground cumin, lightly toasted
1 tsp. sea salt
¼ tsp. freshly ground black pepper
2 tbsp. finely chopped fresh dill
½ cup sour cream

1. Fill a 6-quart pot halfway with water, set over high heat, and bring to a boil.
2. Make an "X" on the bottom of each tomato with a paring knife. Drop the tomatoes into boiling water for 15 seconds, then remove and transfer to an ice bath. Let cool before handling, approximately 1 minute. Remove tomatoes and pat dry. Peel, core, and seed the tomatoes over a fine-mesh strainer set over a bowl to catch the juice. Press on the pulp and seeds to extract as much juice as possible, then add enough bottled tomato juice to bring the total to 1 cup.
3. Place the tomatoes and juice in a large mixing bowl. Add the cucumber, bell pepper, red onion, jalapeño, garlic, olive oil, lime juice, balsamic vinegar, Worcestershire, cumin, salt, and pepper and stir to combine.
4. Transfer 1½ cups of the mixture to a blender and purée for 15 to 20 seconds on high speed. Return the puréed mixture to the bowl and stir to combine. Add the dill and sour cream, stirring to combine. Cover and chill for 2 hours before serving.

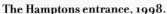

The Hamptons entrance, 1998.

L'Orangerie

RELAIS &
CHATEAUX

L'Orangerie

OPEN: 1977–2006

LOCATIONS: 903 N. La Cienega Boulevard
Los Angeles, CA 90069

ORIGINAL PHONE: (310) 652-9770

CUISINE: French

DESIGN: Valerian Ryker

BUILDING STYLE: Parisian

CURRENTLY: Nobu Los Angeles

NESTLED BETWEEN DESIGNER FURNITURE SHOPS AND CLOTHING STORES ON THE BUSY LA CIENEGA BOULEVARD, L'ORANGERIE WAS KNOWN FOR ITS ELEGANT PARISIAN AMBIENCE. Architect Valerian Ryker had aimed for a light and airy feel in the 120-seat restaurant, which he had achieved with tall, arched windows throughout the place. The high ceilings and pure-white walls lent a refined atmosphere to the interior, and the fabric scheme featured the light colors of a Monet painting: peach, leaf green, light yellow, and apricot. The tables were laid with silver, crystal, Limoges dinnerware, and eighteenth-century French pewter lanterns, all reflected in the many mirrors that hung on the walls. Custom-made panels of blue-and-white Portuguese tiles with illustrations of seventeenth-century orangeries decorated the bar. Outside on the garden patio, the adjacent buildings were hidden by trellises covered with climbing roses and gardenias. A beautiful waterfall completed the idyllic setting.

L'Orangerie's two chefs, Jean Grondin and Jean-Luc Renault, had come from Paris. Their tasting menu, the "Menu Royal," changed with the season and offered eight to ten courses. At $140 per person, it was the most expensive tasting menu in the city at the time. The "Les Viandes" menu featured entrées such as herb-crusted loin of beef, roasted rack of lamb, and steamed chicken and vegetables. A selection of fish dishes was also offered, prepared with simple yet flavorful sauces used in the south of France. The dessert menu featured a "Chocolate Lovers" grouping of four delectable pastries.

In 1992, jeweler Harry Winston and luxury hotelier Relais & Châteaux underwrote an extravagant Oscar party at L'Orangerie. The guest list was a true cross-section of Hollywood, with Billy Wilder, Diane Ladd, Laura Dern, Jacqueline Bisset, Robin Leach, and Joanne Carson in attendance. Jane Seymour took notes on Burgundy wines at her table. Dom Pérignon flowed freely, followed by a consommé of peas, poached turbot, and lamb with truffles. Three desserts—warm chocolate tart, petits fours, and pepper-flavored ice cream with bananas and passion fruit—rounded out the menu. The dress code for the evening specified that men should wear tuxes with polka-dot cummerbunds and women should wear their finest jewelry.

If you wanted to dine somewhere very special in the city, L'Orangerie was the place. President and Mrs. Reagan, Betsy Bloomingdale, and Kirk and Anne Douglas were regulars. In the late 1990s, L'Orangerie was the last of the elegant L.A. restaurants to drop its coat and tie requirement.

Above: L'Orangerie on La Cienega Boulevard, 1980s.

The most difficult years for the restaurant were 2004 and 2005, when it struggled with employee lawsuits over pooled tips and a general drop in demand; diners were seeking out a more relaxed dining experience. In 2005, Chef Nobu Matsuhisa was looking for a new location close to the Beverly Hills-West Hollywood border to open his West Coast flagship restaurant. After almost thirty years in the space, L'Orangerie owner Gerard Ferry sold the restaurant—including its well-stocked wine cellar—for an undisclosed price to Matsuhisa and his investing partner, Robert De Niro.

L'Orangerie served its last meal on New Year's Eve, 2006. Two days later, the Nobu group came in and began to transform the ornate French restaurant into a streamlined stone-and-wood Asian design, similar to the other Nobu locations. ✕

Right: L'Orangerie owners Virginie and Gerard Ferry, Chef Jean-François Meteigner, and maître d' Gilles Lagourgue, early 1980s. ▪ *Opposite:* L'Orangerie was known for its elegant ambience.

Steamed Chicken and Vegetables with Wine Sauce

This dish was one of the most requested items on L'Orangerie's brunch menu.

Serves 4

3½ lb. chicken, cut into smaller pieces
2 large zucchini, thickly sliced
2 large carrots, thickly sliced
2 medium potatoes, sliced
1 stalk celery, sliced
2 sprigs parsley, chopped
1 sprig fresh tarragon, chopped
1 bay leaf
sea salt
Wine Sauce (recipe follows)

1. Place the chicken on a large steamer rack and top with the zucchini, carrots, potatoes, celery, parsley, tarragon, and bay leaf. Season with salt.
2. Cover and steam over simmering water for 45 minutes, or until the chicken and vegetables are tender. Serve in a soup bowl with the pan liquid and the sauce on the side.

Wine Sauce

1 cup dry white wine
1 small shallot, minced
1 tbsp. unsalted butter, softened
1 cup chicken stock
freshly ground black pepper

1. In a small pan, bring the wine to a boil over medium-high heat and cook until reduced by half, about 6 minutes.
2. In another saucepan, sauté the shallot in the butter over medium heat until tender, about 4 minutes. Add the wine and stock. Cook until reduced by one-third, about 5 minutes. Season to taste with pepper.

DOME

Su Huntley 8·80

Le Dome

OPEN: 1977–2007

LOCATION: 8720 Sunset Boulevard
West Hollywood, CA 90069

ORIGINAL PHONE: (310) 659-6919

CUISINE: French

BUILDING STYLE: French Renaissance

CURRENTLY: Vacant

THE BUILDING AT 8720 SUNSET BOULEVARD WAS FIRST BUILT IN 1934 TO SERVE AS THE INTERIOR DESIGN STUDIO OF WILLIAM HAINES, THE FORMER MGM STAR WHO, FOR SIX YEARS, DECORATED FOR THE HOLLYWOOD ELITE. The next occupant was Don Loper, the famous costume and necktie designer. After Loper moved on, the building stood empty for about four years.

In 1977, a new restaurant called Le Dome moved into the first floor of the building. The eatery was the brainchild of Michel Yhuelo and Eddie Kerkhofs, with Elton John as one of its founding backers. The large space featured a bar in its center hub, with smaller rooms radiating out from it. Because of the restaurant's elevation, perched above the Strip, it provided a nice view of the city lights at night.

Originally, Yhuelo and Kerkhofs had different plans for the design of Le Dome. "It would be elegant informality with service of anything, anytime," Kerkhofs said. "No dress code. No minimum orders. Reasonably priced: *la cuisine bourgeoisie*."

But the restaurant soon became an industry hangout, where film stars sat down to large portions of

Below: The entrance to Le Dome, 1988. ▪ *Opposite:* The restaurant's menu cover, drawn by artist Su Huntley, 1980.

Above: Le Dome on the Sunset Strip, 1988. ▪ *Below:* The restaurant's bar, 1988. ▪ *Opposite:* The dining room at Le Dome, 1988.

good, basic French country fare. In the beginning, maître d' Henri Labadie was as kind to the restaurant's unknown guests as he was to the celebrities who visited. However, as the prices climbed and jackets became required, those who weren't "somebody" were seated in an undesirable part of the restaurant that some called "The Hallway." Around Le Dome's tenth anniversary, restaurant critic Ruth Reichl drove this point home with a *Los Angeles Times* article titled "The Best Course at Le Dome? Celebrities!"

The chic French restaurant had a huge star following. Driving past the eatery, you couldn't help but notice the line of limos and Rolls-Royces parked outside. Inside, power brokers preferred the tables to the right of the bar, while celebrities opted for the patio to the left of the bar, where they could be seen.

The most interesting items on Le Dome's menu were listed as "casserole country dishes." The sautéed *boudin noir* (blood sausage) and *boudin blanc* (veal and chicken sausage) were both served with homemade applesauce and mashed potatoes. Roasted wild goose with apricot stuffing became the restaurant's signature dish. The food was pricey, but diners were also paying for the opportunity to sit next to big-name directors, movie stars, and musicians.

In 2003, after twenty-six years of operation, Le Dome reinvented itself with a renovation into what the *L.A. Times* called "Gothic meets Log Cabin." Unfortunately, this was the beginning of the end; in 2007, Le Dome closed for good. A year afterward, Laurent Tourondel, chef and owner of BLT Steak, moved his operation into the space and updated it with a warmer, chain-like ambiance. However, BLT Steak closed after a failed five-year attempt to bring its East Coast flair to Los Angeles. The space has remained empty ever since. ✕

Roasted Wild Goose with Apricot Stuffing

This signature dish was featured on *The Today Show* in the early 1980s.

Serves 6

6–8 lb. goose, cleaned and prepped
kosher salt
2 medium red apples, quartered
3 medium onions, quartered
2 slices applewood-smoked bacon
1 medium carrot, diced
1 stalk celery, diced

1 bay leaf
1 tbsp. chopped fresh thyme
4 cups chicken stock
1 cup red wine
1 tbsp. cornstarch
2 tbsp. cold water
Apricot Stuffing (recipe follows)

1. Soak the cleaned goose overnight in well-salted water.
2. The next day, preheat the oven to 475°F. Rinse and pat dry the goose, then stuff the cavity with the apples and 2 of the onions.
3. Place the goose in a roasting pan, breast side up. Place the bacon on top of the goose and cover with a lid or foil. Bake until the bacon is crisp, about 40 minutes. Discard the bacon.
4. Add to the pan the remaining onion and the carrot, celery, bay leaf, thyme, chicken stock, and red wine. Lower the oven temperature to 375°F. Roast until the internal temperature reaches 170°F on a meat thermometer, about 2 hours.
5. Increase the oven temperature to 475°F. Uncover the goose and brown the skin for 20 minutes. Remove the goose from the roasting pan. Remove the apples and onions from the cavity and discard.
6. Strain the pan drippings into a saucepan. Whisk the cornstarch and cold water together in a small bowl, then add to the pan and cook over low heat, whisking until thickened.
7. Slice the goose and serve with the pan gravy and Apricot Stuffing.

LE DÔME

⚜ Dinner Menu ⚜

Le Dome Restaurant opened its doors in January of 1977.

In 1966, after I graduated from Hotel Restaurant School in Brussels, Belgium I came to America with a dream to fulfill that one day I would own a restaurant that would be dedicated to the highest quality of food and service.

My partner, the late Michel Yhuelo shared that dream with me. We wanted a restaurant that was both elegant and casual. Michel Yhuelo typified both these qualities.

I must express my appreciation to so many people who helped start our restaurant and are still a part of our restaurant staff---
our executive chefs Jean Claude Bourlier and Jean Jacques D'artois.
our Maitre'd Raymond Roy and our General Manager Ramon Ayon.

Last but not least, my sincere thanks to all the wonderful patrons and friends of Le Dome who have supported us these many years.

Your comments on our restaurant are always welcome.

Eddy Kerkhofs

PRIVATE PARTY ROOMS

East or West Sunset Rooms
(with a View of the City)

DINNER 20-70 PERSONS

COCKTAILS UP TO 120 PERSONS

✦

Fireplace Room
(intimate Fireplace setting)

DINNER 30 PERSONS

Apricot Stuffing

The apricots lend a fresh twist to this traditional dish.

Serves 6

2 tbsp. olive oil
1 medium onion, chopped
1 stalk celery, diced
2 ⅓ cups breadcrumbs
6 oz. dried apricots, chopped
3 cloves garlic, minced

1 tbsp. fresh thyme, finely chopped
1 tbsp. fresh parsley, finely chopped
1 tbsp. fresh sage, finely chopped
1 large egg
1 ½ cups chicken stock

1. Preheat the oven to 375°F. Butter a 9 x 13-inch baking dish.
2. In a skillet over medium-high heat, heat the olive oil and sauté the onion and celery until translucent, about 4 minutes. Transfer to a large bowl.
3. Add the breadcrumbs, apricots, garlic, thyme, parsley, and sage to the bowl with the onion and celery.
4. In a small bowl, whisk together the egg and chicken stock. Pour over the mixture and toss to coat.
5. Pour into the buttered pan and bake until firm and top is brown, about 45 minutes. Serve hot.

Chopped Salad

This was a Sunday brunch favorite, especially for those watching their calories.

Serves 6 to 8

Dressing:
¼ cup mayonnaise
1 tbsp. red wine vinegar
½ tsp. Dijon mustard
1 cup heavy cream
dash of Worcestershire sauce
dash of hot pepper sauce
sea salt
freshly ground black pepper

Salad:
¼ head red cabbage, finely chopped
¼ head white cabbage, finely chopped
¼ head iceberg lettuce, finely chopped
2 oz. dry salami
4 oz. cooked ham
½ cup black olives, pitted
½ cup garbanzo beans

1. To make the dressing, whisk together the mayonnaise, vinegar, and mustard in a medium bowl. Add the heavy cream, Worcestershire sauce, hot pepper sauce, and salt and pepper to taste. Whisk until fully blended.
2. To make the salad, combine the cabbages and lettuce in a large bowl. Dice the salami, ham, and olives and add to the bowl, then add the garbanzo beans.
Pour the dressing onto the salad and toss to coat. Serve immediately.

Michael's

OPEN: 1979–present

LOCATION: 1147 Third Street
Santa Monica, CA 90403

ORIGINAL PHONE: (310) 451-0843

CUISINE: California Bistro

BUILDING STYLE: 1930s House

MICHAEL MCCARTY WAS ONLY TWENTY-FIVE YEARS OLD WHEN HE OPENED MICHAEL'S IN SANTA MONICA. He had earned degrees in French cooking, wines, and restaurant management at the Cordon Bleu, and had also studied at the Academie du Vin and the École Hôtelière de Paris. When McCarty arrived in Los Angeles, he joined the group of young chefs making a name for themselves in the city's culinary field.

McCarty wanted Michael's to have a sense of openness, fun, and spontaneity. For his restaurant's location, he chose a three-bedroom house that had been built in the 1930s, just half a block from the busy Wilshire Boulevard and three blocks from the beach. He had the walls painted a creamy color and added French doors that opened out to a lush garden. Today, golden lighting enhances the ambience at Michael's. The food is served on white china, and the staff are dressed in Ralph Lauren pastels.

The food at Michael's is what McCarty calls "modern contemporary French, California style," combining fresh local ingredients with French cooking methods. Michael's was instrumental in establishing this style of cooking, along with Alice Waters's Chez Panisse in Berkeley, California. When diners ask what McCarty's secret is, he always gives the same answer: "The best quality and the freshest ingredients." McCarty also claims that he was the first to bring glass bottles of Evian water to the States.

In 1978, Governor Jerry Brown signed the Direct Marketing Act, enabling farmers to sell their goods directly to consumers. Three years later, the Santa Monica Farmers Market was born, only a few short blocks from Michael's. McCarty took full advantage of the market's fresh ingredients and, today, has established relationships with the farmers who grow for him. Over the years, McCarty and his protégés have given many cooking demonstrations at the market.

McCarty feels that the menu at Michael's has grown organically from his own life experiences and training. Focusing on the freshest farmers market produce, his dishes change to accommodate whatever is being sold in the local market that week. He prefers to serve his customers a progression of flavors with each course, with none of the flavors repeated.

In 1989, McCarty opened a Michael's location in New York, with the same look and menu as the original. It was a hit. McCarty went on to open three more restaurants—Adirondacks in Washington D.C. and the Rattlesnake Club in Detroit and Denver—with his business partner, Jimmy Schmidt. McCarty also dreamed of opening a luxury hotel on the site of the Sand and Sea Club on the Pacific Coast Highway,

Above: Michael's on Third Street, 2011. ▪ *Opposite:* Chefs Michael McCarty and Ken Frank in the kitchen at Michael's, 1976.

Above left: **Inside Michael's, 1979.** ▪ *Above right:* **The patio at Michael's, 1979.** ▪ *Below:* **The opening team at Michael's in 1979:** (*left to right*) **Jonathan Waxman, Michael McCarty, Mark Peel, and Ken Frank.** ▪ *Opposite:* **Michael McCarty with Julia Child at Michael's.**

the former location of an enormous beach house William Randolph Hearst built for his mistress, actress Marion Davies. After McCarty sank millions into the project, the Save Our Beach Committee submitted a petition to ban any beachfront hotels and restaurants larger than 2,000 feet. McCarty was crushed. He ran into a number of financial difficulties after that, including serious earthquake damage and a fire at his home in 1993. McCarty filed for bankruptcy, but soon got back on his feet.

For over sixteen years, mobster "Whitey" Bulger lived down the street from Michael's, in the Princess Eugenia Apartments at 1012 Third Street. Bulger and his girlfriend liked the privacy of a far corner table at the restaurant. The couple once worked up a $192 bill for a steak and lobster dinner, accompanied by foie gras, vodka highballs, and chardonnay. Bulger was on the FBI's Ten Most Wanted list and always paid cash.

In 2012, McCarty renovated Michael's, realizing that his customers in 1979 were very different from the patrons currently dining at the restaurant. He got rid of the restaurant's white tablecloths and fine silver, and ended up saving $100,000 a year just by cutting down his laundry services and simplifying the flower arrangements. ✖

Grilled Chicken with Tarragon Butter

This chicken dish is simple yet flavorful, with delicious tarragon butter sauce.

Serves 6

Three 2½-lb. medium whole chickens
salt
freshly ground white pepper

6 tbsp. unsalted butter
2 tbsp. fresh tarragon leaves, chopped
2 bunches watercress, stemmed

1. Quarter chickens to yield 6 legs attached to 6 boneless thighs and 6 boneless breast halves attached to wing bones, pounded cutlet style.
2. Sprinkle chickens lightly with salt and pepper. Place on grill or broiler with the skin side facing the heat. Cook for 8 minutes per side for thigh-leg pieces, until cooked through, but still moist and slightly pink at the bone.
3. Cook small breasts 4 to 5 minutes on the skin side, then flip and cook 1 to 2 minutes longer, until cooked through but still moist and pink at the bone.
4. For all the chicken, halfway through cooking on the skin sides, rotate 90 degrees to make crosshatched grill marks.
5. 1 or 2 minutes before the chicken is done, melt the butter in a small saucepan over moderate heat. Add tarragon leaves and season lightly with salt and pepper.
6. Arrange a clump of watercress in the center of each heated plate. Place a chicken thigh and leg portion and a breast at the bottom of each plate. Spoon some of the tarragon butter over the chicken.

William's Little Italy

This sophisticated tipple was popular at Michael's in the 1980s.

Serves 1

1 oz. R1 straight rye whiskey
1 oz. Dimmi Liquore Di Milano
½ oz. Amaro Averna
½ oz. Zucca Rabarbaro
3 dashes of Fee Brothers Peach Bitters
orange peel

1. Shake the ingredients together and strain. Pour into a lowball glass over ice. Garnish with the orange peel.

Basil   Shrimps

Basil-
Tomatoe-
Vinaigrette

Spago

Pears California Cuisine

Caramel-Sauce
Puffpastry

Watercress

Vegetables

Baby Lamb

Wolfgang Puck 1981

Spago Sunset

OPEN: 1982–2001

LOCATION: 8795 Sunset Boulevard
West Hollywood, CA 90069

ORIGINAL PHONE: (213) 652-4025

CUISINE: California Bistro

DESIGN: Edward H. Fickett

BUILDING STYLE: Modern

CURRENTLY: Vacant

IN SPAGO'S HEYDAY, IT WAS EASIER TO GET AN OSCAR NOMINATION THAN A RESERVATION AT THE POPULAR RESTAURANT; YOU HAD TO KNOW SOMEONE WITH A DIRECT CONNECTION IN ORDER TO GET IN. Spago was the brainchild of Wolfgang Puck and interior designer Barbara Lazaroff, who was Puck's wife at the time. It was the first upscale, high-end dining establishment serving California cuisine in Southern California. Formerly the executive chef at Ma Maison (see page 227), Puck wanted his restaurant to be sophisticated yet free-spirited.

In 1984, only a few years after opening Spago, Puck was named "Chef of the Year" by the *Los Angeles Daily News*. His menu was unlike any the city had ever seen. For starters, it offered gourmet pizza, which was an oxymoron before it appeared on Spago's menu. Using hand-tossed dough, grilled chicken with goat cheese, and barbecue sauce instead of tomato sauce, Puck transformed the most popular (and pedestrian) dish in the United States into something extraordinary. Handmade pasta was also a specialty of the house. Seasonal dishes, such as pumpkin ravioli, are still on the menu at Spago's Beverly Hills location.

In the early years, dining at Spago was like having a meal at a friend's house, but with celebrities dropping by to visit. Before delivering the eleven o'clock evening news on KABC-7, anchorman Jerry Dunphy and his wife (who was also his makeup artist) would often stop in for dinner. Elizabeth Taylor, Elton John, and Gary Collins (with his wife, former Miss America Mary Ann Mobley) were also frequent visitors.

In 1983, Puck became the official chef for the Governors Ball on Oscar night. That same year, legendary talent agent Irving Paul "Swifty" Lazar moved his annual Oscar party from Romanoff's (see page 153) to Spago, where he continued to hold court every year until his death in 1993.

One brisk evening in 1987, L.A. district attorney Ira Reiner was dining at Spago when his driver was taken at gunpoint and made to hand over his gun and the county sedan. Reiner was not aware of what had happened until later that evening. Reporters swarmed around the restaurant to get the story, asking why Reiner was using the county's resources for a private dinner.

In 1997, Puck opened a second location at 176 N. Canon Drive in Beverly Hills. A month before closing the Hollywood Spago location in 2001, Puck brought back the restaurant's alumni to cook together

Above: Spago on the Sunset Strip. ▪ *Opposite:* The Spago menu cover, hand-drawn by founder Wolfgang Puck, 1981.

again and celebrate the food and place they all loved so much. Puck paired up two chefs per night for the last few weeks of the restaurant's operations.

Many of Spago's executive chefs, line chefs, and pastry chefs have either stayed with the Wolfgang Puck Fine Dining Group (WP Group) or started their own establishments. When Spago Hollywood closed in 2001, the WP Group boasted twelve upscale restaurants and a few dozen locations serving casual fare. Today, the group oversees over a hundred fine dining establishments and hundreds of casual eateries around the globe, including CUT in London, which *The Independent* newspaper reported was operated by "Obama's favorite chef." ✂

Above: Wolfgang Puck at Spago Sunset, 1983. ▪ *Below:* Puck and his staff in the Spago Sunset dining room, 1991.

Goat Cheese Pizza

Wolfgang Puck transformed pizza in America; everyone wanted a taste of the interesting flavors he came up with.

Makes 8 individual pizzas or 2 twelve-inch pizzas

Pizza Dough:
1 tbsp. active dry yeast
lukewarm water
3 tbsp. granulated sugar
2 tbsp. sea salt
5½–6 cups all-purpose flour
¼ cup extra-virgin olive oil, plus more for
    brushing, if desired

Pizza Toppings:
1 cup tomato or pizza sauce
3 medium plum tomatoes, seeded and diced
16 oz. goat cheese, crumbled

1. Preheat the oven to 450°F.
2. To make the dough, dissolve the yeast in about ¼ cup water in a small bowl. Set aside and let bubble.
3. In a separate bowl, dissolve the sugar and salt in 2 cups of lukewarm water.
4. In another, large bowl, combine 3 cup of the flour and 1 cup of the lukewarm water mixture, stirring with a wooden spoon for a few minutes. Add the olive oil and mix well. Add the dissolved yeast mixture and stir for 1 minute. Add 2 more cups of the flour, mixing well, then add the remaining 1 cup of the water mixture.
5. Turn the dough out onto a floured surface and knead until it is smooth and elastic. Cover with a tea towel and let rest for 10 to 15 minutes. Divide the dough into 8 portions for individual pizzas, or 2 for large pizzas.
6. Roll out the dough into 4½-inch rounds for small pizzas, or 12-inch rounds for large pizzas. Brush with olive oil if desired.
7. To top the pizzas: Spread the tomato sauce on the dough and sprinkle with the chopped tomatoes and crumbled cheese. Bake until the top is lightly browned and the crust is crisp, 10 to 12 minutes for small pizzas and 12 to 20 minutes for the large pizzas.

Tip: To make a crispier crust, bake your pizzas directly on a pizza stone that has been heated in the oven for 30 minutes prior to baking.

Spago Sunset, 1993.

Chicken with Garlic

One of Spago's original recipes, this dish is still on the restaurant's menu today.

Serves 4

2 bulbs garlic
¼ cup finely chopped Italian parsley
sea salt
freshly ground black pepper

4 chicken breasts, deboned with skin intact
2 tbsp. unsalted butter
2 tbsp. freshly squeezed lemon juice

1. Place the garlic bulbs in a saucepan and add water to cover, about ½ a cup. Bring to a boil over medium heat. Remove from the heat and drain. Peel the garlic and cut each clove into very thin slices. Toss in a bowl with the parsley, and season with salt and pepper.
2. Loosen the skin on the chicken and stuff about 2 tbsp. of the garlic mixture between the skin and the meat of each breast. Reserve the remaining garlic mixture.
3. Grill the chicken for 5 to 7 minutes on each side, or until the flesh is no longer pink in the center.
4. Heat the butter in a skillet, then add the reserved garlic mixture and sauté for a few minutes. Add the lemon juice and salt and pepper to taste. Heat through. Place the chicken on a platter and spoon the garlic sauce over it.

Macadamia Tart

This delicious tart has received rave reviews and was wildly popular in the 1980s, when Macadamia nuts were considered exotic.

Serves 8 to 10

Pastry:
1½ cups all-purpose flour
1½ cups cake flour
¼ cup granulated sugar
2 cups unsalted butter, softened
3 large eggs yolks
¼ cup heavy cream

Filling:
⅓ cup packed brown sugar
¼ cup granulated sugar
½ cup corn syrup
2 large eggs
2 large egg yolks
1 tbsp. unsalted butter, softened
½ Madagascar vanilla bean, split
1½ tbsp. Frangelico
8 oz. macadamia nuts, coarsely chopped and toasted

1. To make the pastry, blend the flours, sugar, and butter in a mixer bowl with the paddle attachment or dough hook attachment until crumbly. In a pourable container, beat the egg yolks and the cream. Add to the flour mixture and blend until the dough is well mixed.
2. Divide the dough into 3 equal portions and press each into a disk. Wrap each disk with plastic wrap and then with foil. Refrigerate for 10 minutes.
3. Preheat the oven to 350°F.
4. Butter a 10-inch or 12-inch tart pan with a removable bottom.
5. Take one dough disk and roll it out to fit the tart pan.
6. Place in the tart pan and bake until light brown, 20 to 25 minutes. Set aside.
7. To make the filling: In a large bowl, whisk together the sugars, corn syrup, eggs, and egg yolks until light and fluffy. Set aside.
8. In a small saucepan over medium heat, melt the butter, then add the vanilla bean and Frangelico liqueur. Cook until the butter turns brown, about 3 minutes. Discard the bean and add the butter mixture to the sugar mixture. Fold in the nuts. Pour the filling into the prepared tart shell and bake until set, 28 to 32 minutes.
9. Wrap tightly and store in the freezer for up to 2 months.

Note: This recipe makes extra dough that can be used for other purposes. Do not try to cut the recipe down or the chemical balance of the dough will change.

Spago

CHECK NO.
039029
DATE | SERVER

AMOUNT

213 ● 652-4025
8795 SUNSET BOULEVARD LOS ANGELES, CALIFORNIA 90069

72 MARKET ST.
OYSTER BAR & GRILL

BE SAFE CLOSE COVER BEFORE STRIKING

VENICE, CA 90291

72 Market Street
Oyster Bar & Grill

OPEN: 1984–2000

LOCATION: 72 Market Street
Venice, CA 90291

ORIGINAL PHONE: (310) 392-8720

CUISINE: Steak and Seafood

DESIGN: Thom Mayne and Michael Rotondi

BUILDING STYLE: Modern

CURRENTLY: Vacant

IN 1975, LEONARD SCHWARTZ WAS A PSYCHOLOGY MAJOR AT UCLA WHEN HE LANDED A POSITION AS A WAITER AT HAMBURGER HAMLET (SEE PAGE 185) ON SUNSET BOULEVARD—A JOB THAT WOULD CHANGE HIS CAREER PATH COMPLETELY. He soon worked his way up into the management team and kitchen staff, eventually taking on various chef positions at Café California, Le Dome (see page 251), Le Toque, and L'Orangerie (page 247).

Chef Schwartz was approached to become a partner in the opening of a new restaurant venture called 72 Market Street Oyster Bar and Grill, along with co-owners Tony Bill, Dudley Moore, Julie Stone, and Tony Heinsbergen. Installed in a former art gallery, the restaurant was visually stunning. During the day and on warm evenings, the restaurant's large front windows were left open to allow cool ocean breezes to flow inside. The *Robb Report* raved that "the architecture alone is worth the visit," and *Vanity Fair* called it "the place where everyone wants to go."

The food at 72 Market was hearty and filling yet healthy, incorporating local seafood, lots of fresh produce from the farmers market, whole grains, and foods without preservatives. The restaurant was one of the few fine dining locations near the beach.

The restaurant had a loyal clientele of celebrities, including Steve Martin, Alexander Godunov, Jacqueline Bisset, Sally Field, Dennis Hopper, Lisa Bonet, Hugh Hefner, and Bruce Springsteen. In 1987, Oliver Stone used 72 Market to host a delegation of Soviet theater leaders.

The eatery set itself apart by hosting a lecture series and book and poetry readings, featuring such guests as Frank Gentry, George Plimpton, Spalding Gray, E. L. Doctorow, and Raymond Carver. On Sundays, 72 Market also broadcast a live radio show from its location, featuring Dudley Moore and other performers accompanied by the house pianist on the restaurant's grand piano.

The restaurant closed in November 2000, about fourteen months before Moore's death in 2002. ✗

Opposite: **Chef Leonard Schwartz outside his restaurant.**

72 MARKET ST.
OYSTER BAR & GRILL

CHAMPAGNE BY THE GLASS	5.
BEER	2.50–3.
OYSTER BAR MENU	
BLUE POINTS ON THE HALF SHELL	6.
CLAMS ON THE HALF SHELL	6.
JUMBO SHRIMP COCKTAIL	9.75
MARINATED SQUID	6.
CEVICHE OF BAY SCALLOPS & NEW ZEALAND SEA BASS	6.
COMBINATION PLATTER	22.
SOUPS	1/30 –
DAILY SELECTION	5.
KICK ASS CHILI WITH CORN BREAD & CONDIMENTS	
BOWL	10.
CUP	6.

Meat Loaf

This recipe was created by 72 Market's first chef, Leonard Schwartz. It was the most requested dish at the restaurant.

Serves 6 to 8

1 tbsp. unsalted butter, softened
¾ cup green onion, minced
1 small yellow onion, minced
2 large carrots, diced
½ medium red bell pepper, seeded and diced
½ medium green bell pepper, seeded and diced
4 cloves garlic, minced
1 tsp. sea salt
1 tsp. freshly ground black pepper

½ tsp. cayenne pepper
½ tsp. ground nutmeg
½ tsp. ground cumin
3 large eggs, beaten
½ cup ketchup
½ cup half-and-half
1½ lbs. lean ground beef
½ lb ground pork sausage
¾ cup dried breadcrumbs

1. In a skillet over medium heat, melt the butter and add the onions, carrots, celery, bell peppers, and garlic. Cook, stirring for 10 minutes or until the moisture has evaporated. Allow to cool.
2. In a large mixing bowl, combine the salt, pepper, cayenne, nutmeg, cumin, and eggs. Mix well. Add the ketchup and half-and-half, blending thoroughly.
3. Add the ground beef, pork, breadcrumbs, and vegetable mixture, combining the ingredients with your hands.
4. Place mixture into a large loaf pan. Place loaf pan in a larger pan filled with 1 inch of boiling water. Cook in preheated oven for 45 to 60 minutes. Let rest for 10 minutes prior to serving.

Co-owners Leonard Schwartz, Dudley Moore, Julie Stone, Tony Bill, and Tony Heinsbergen at 72 Market Street Oyster Bar and Grill.

Spicy Corn Soup

Enjoy this hearty soup with fresh-baked bread on the side.

Serves 6

6 ears of fresh corn, with silks removed and husks reserved
2 quarts water
3 tbsp. canola oil
1 large red bell pepper, seeded and diced
1 small onion, diced
3 stalks celery, diced

¾ tsp. fresh thyme, chopped
¾ tsp. fresh parsley
¾ tsp. fresh ground pepper
½ tsp. cayenne pepper
¾ tsp. sea salt
dash of paprika
sour cream

1. Cut the corn kernels from the ears of corn and set aside. Reserve 2 of the husks and corncobs, and discard the rest.
2. In a large stockpot, boil the reserved corncobs and husks in 2 quarts of water for 15 minutes. Strain and reserve the liquid. Discard the husks and cobs.
3. In the same stockpot, heat the oil and sauté the pepper, onion, and celery until tender, about 7 minutes.
4. Add the reserved corn. Stir in the thyme, parsley, pepper, and cayenne pepper.
5. Add the reserved cornhusk liquid and bring to a boil. Season with salt and paprika.
6. Serve in dishes with a swirl of sour cream.

Ceviche

This delicious ceviche was made with freshly caught fish.

Serves 6

1 lb. bay scallops
1 lb. sea bass, deboned and cut into pieces
1½ cups freshly squeezed lime juice
5 medium Roma tomatoes, peeled, seeded, and diced

1 medium onion, diced
½ bunch cilantro, chopped (leaves only)
½ cup oregano, chopped (leaves only)
shredded lettuce

1. Slice scallops in half and place in a shallow dish. Add the sea bass pieces (which should be cut to the same size as the scallop halves). Pour lime juice over the meat, then cover and refrigerate for 2 to 4 hours, or until no longer opaque. Drain and discard the lime juice.
2. Place the scallops and fish in a bowl and mix them with the tomatoes, onion, cilantro, and oregano. Chill and serve on a bed of greens.

Acknowledgments

MANY PEOPLE HELPED WITH MY RESEARCH AND LED ME IN THE RIGHT DIRECTION TO GET THE ANSWERS I NEEDED FOR THIS BOOK.

Thank you to my mother, Patty. Honestly, I probably first started writing this book in the 1970s, when I would drag my mom to historical venues with me. In 1978, I recall taking her to C. C. Brown's for a hot fudge sundae and knowing deep inside that it would be my last time there. I also took her to auctions at places like the Ambassador Hotel—not to bid on items at the auction, but to soak in the history within those walls. I thank my mom for spending all of those hours with me.

My family and friends: Neil for always supporting every endeavor I think up. Dad for the lifetime support and guidance. Monica and Pattie for being great sisters. Jonathan for being a true friend. Trina, the greatest publicist ever. Also, Karen Tripson, my longtime friend who helped with this project (and many others), from its inception through its many transformations. Karen, I thank you for the many hours you helped me on this.

The entire *Los Angeles Times* family, past and present. Louella Parsons and Hedda Hopper: if it weren't for these two "nosy" columnists (they were the TMZ of the day), I would not have had half of the information in this book. Russ Parsons: besides being a terrific food writer, Russ has a knack for telling the life story of chefs, which I needed many times in my research. Ruth Buzzi: Ruth contributed her knowledge of the 1980s in Hollywood when I was looking for answers and only finding walls. It pays to remember whom you are introduced to when you're twenty-one.

All of the restaurant families I consulted, especially the Carlos 'n Charlie's staff. So many provided stories and pictures from their life in the 1970s, especially Jenni Sisk, Susan Ross, Linda Guillemette, and J. Lynn McCall. Marje Bennetts, former publicist for Chez Jay's, was a wealth of knowledge.

The Los Angeles Conservancy, Los Angeles Department of Building and Safety, Los Angeles Public Library (especially Emma, for all the hours spent in the menu collection and rare books room, and Christina Rice in the *Herald Examiner* collection), the City of West Hollywood, and Sue Mossman at Pasadena Heritage. Also Deborah Brackstone, archivist for the Paul Revere Williams Project at the University of Memphis.

All of the cooking schools and cruise ships that allowed me to test the recipes to see if they would work in a classroom setting and if the book idea was feasible, including Wendy and Mary at the Cook's Warehouse stores in Atlanta, Georgia, Larry Oats at Kitchen Art in West Lafayette, Indiana, and Erica Lamoureaux, former manager of the Culinary Arts Centers aboard the Holland America Line ships. Also Christopher Spano, the best librarian in the seven seas, and cruise director Gene Moimoi Young, whom I have sailed with around the world.

My great news family at XETV's *San Diego Living*: the greatest producer, Tiffany Frowiss; my current anchors, Lynda Martin, Clint August, Renee Kohn, Laura Cavanaugh, and Jacqueline Bennette; and my former anchors, Marc Bailey, Heather Myers, Kim Evans, and Chase Cain. All of the floor managers that keep the "bumper shots" and my segments looking great, including Brent, Juan, and Jonah.

Lastly, I want to show appreciation to the team at Santa Monica Press: Jeffrey Goldman for his insight and love of L.A. history; Kate Murray for keeping my voice in the editing process and helping make this manuscript perfect; and Amy Inouye for making this book a beautiful work of art, not just a cookbook.

Photo Credits

Ellen Berman Archives: 186

William L. Bird Postcard Collection: 10–11, 23 (top), 39 (top), 123 (top right), 127 (top), 170 (top)

From the Mott/Merge collection, courtesy of the California History Room, California State Library, Sacramento, California: 81, 83, 84, 85 (top)

Courtesy of Cock'n Bull / C-B Beverage: 142, 143, 144 (top, middle left and right), 147 (all)

Courtesy of Dan Tana's: 223 (top), 224

From the ephemera collection of Heather David: 225

Magda Diaz Collection: 45, 65 (top), 108 (left), 201 (bottom), 251 (top)

Courtesy of Gerard Ferry: 247, 248 (right), 249

Courtesy of the Jay Fiondella Trust: 218, 220, 221

From the collection of David and Sharon Franklin (MatchbookMania.com): 176

Historic postcard images from the collection of Elizabeth Fuller: 5 (middle), 20, 59, 96, 159 (top)

From the collection of George Geary: 3, 22 (bottom)

From the private collection of Linda Guillemette: 235 (all), 236

Courtesy of The Hamburger Hamlet: 185 (top), 187 (left), 190 (bottom)

Thomas Hawk (ThomasHawk.com): 54 (top)

Amy Inouye: 128 (top), 133 (bottom)

Frank Kelsey Collection: 30, 43 (bottom left and right), 104 (middle), 205 (all)

Courtesy of Lawry's Restaurants, Inc.: 13, 17, 21, 23 (bottom), 44, 46 (all), 47 (top), 49 (top), 196, 197 (all), 198 (left), 199

Alan Light: 265

Collection of Los Angeles Public Library: 4 (top), 24, 33, 48 (top), 50, 51, 57, 64, 67 (all), 72 (right), 73 (left), 74, 76 (bottom), 88, 89, 97 (top), 100 (all), 101, 108 (middle), 109, 116, 120, 122 (middle), 124, 138, 153, 169 (bottom), 172, 174 (top), 178, 179, 181 (top), 185 (top right), 193 (bottom), 200, 201 (top), 204, 208, 209 (all), 210, 211 (bottom), 215, 222, 228 (top), 232 (top), 237, 238, 239 (top), 240, 241, 242, 248 (left), 250, 254, 260, 264 (left), 266, 267 (bottom), 268, 269, 272

J. Eric Lynxwiler: 5 (bottom), 35 (bottom), 36 (top), 42, 43 (top), 87, 129, 133 (top), 202 (top)

Courtesy and copyright of Ma Maison: 226, 227 (all), 228 (bottom), 229, 230, 231 (all), 232 (bottom), 233

Courtesy of Michael McCarty: 256, 257, 258 (all), 259

Denise McKinney: 15 (top), 22 (top), 23 (middle), 27 (top), 49 (bottom), 53 (all), 54 (bottom), 62, 69 (bottom), 72 (top and bottom left), 92 (top), 95 (all), 97 (bottom), 98 (top), 103 (bottom), 108 (right), 117 (top), 123 (top left and middle), 130, 131 (top), 141 (bottom), 149 (all), 154 (top), 162 (bottom left and right), 163 (top right), 165, 166 (middle left and right), 170 (middle and bottom), 171 (middle left and right), 173 (bottom), 183 (top), 198 (right), 207 (top)

Courtesy of Miceli's: 6, 180, 181 (bottom), 183 (bottom)

From the collection of J. Michael Newlight (MatchbookMania.com): 263, 267 (top)

Edward Padgett: 78 (right)

Chuck Pegot of Captured Souls Photography (San Diego): 26

Fabien Petitcolas: 246

Wolfgang Puck: 262 (all), 264 (right)

Courtesy of Southwestern Law School: 80, 82 (top), 85 (bottom)

Courtesy of the Taix family: 75 (all), 76 (top), 77 (all), 78 (left)

Clifford Clinton Papers, Library Special Collections, Charles E. Young Research Library, UCLA: 127 (bottom)

Los Angeles Times Photographic Archive, Library Special Collections, Charles E. Young Research Library, UCLA: 82 (bottom)

Peter Christiansen Valli: 223 (bottom)

Marc Wanamaker—Bison Archives: cover, back cover, 4 (middle and bottom), 5 (top), 12, 14, 15 (bottom), 16 (all), 25, 27 (bottom), 28, 29, 31 (all), 34, 35 (top), 36 (bottom), 37 (all), 38 (all), 39 (bottom), 40, 41 (all), 47 (bottom), 48 (bottom), 52, 55, 56, 58, 60 (all), 61 (all), 63, 65 (bottom), 66 (all), 68, 69 (top), 70 (all), 71, 73 (right), 90, 91, 82 (bottom), 93 (all), 94, 98 (bottom), 99, 102, 103 (top), 104 (top and bottom), 105 (all), 106, 107, 110, 111, 112 (all), 113 (all), 115, 117 (bottom), 118–119, 121, 122 (top right and bottom), 123 (bottom), 125 (top), 126, 128 (bottom), 131 (bottom), 132, 134, 135, 136, 137, 139, 140, 141 (top), 144 (bottom), 145, 146, 148, 150, 151, 152, 154 (bottom), 155, 156, 157 (all), 158, 159 (bottom left and right), 160 (all), 161 (all), 162 (top left and right, bottom center), 163 (left, middle and bottom right), 164, 166 (bottom), 167 (all), 168, 169 (top), 171 (top left and right, bottom), 173 (top), 174 (bottom), 182, 184, 185 (bottom), 187 (right), 189, 190 (all), 191, 192, 193 (top), 194, 202 (bottom), 203, 206, 207 (bottom), 211 (top), 212, 213, 214, 216–217, 219, 234, 251 (bottom), 252 (all), 253, 261

Photos copyright © Gary J. Wayne (Seeing-Stars.com): 243 (bottom), 245

C. Weiss: 195

Endpapers

PAGE 1 • COLUMN 1 (TOP TO BOTTOM): Courtesy of the Taix family; Marc Wanamaker—Bison Archives; Peter Christiansen Valli; Marc Wanamaker—Bison Archives • COLUMN 2 (TOP TO BOTTOM): Marc Wanamaker—Bison Archives (top three); Denise McKinney • COLUMN 3 (TOP TO BOTTOM): Marc Wanamaker—Bison Archives (top three); Courtesy of the Taix family; Courtesy and copyright of Ma Maison

PAGE 2 • COLUMN 1 (TOP TO BOTTOM): Marc Wanamaker—Bison Archives (top two); Courtesy of Lawry's Restaurants Inc.; Marc Wanamaker—Bison Archives; Denise McKinney • COLUMN 2 (TOP TO BOTTOM): Marc Wanamaker—Bison Archives (top two); Collection of Los Angeles Public Library; Marc Wanamaker—Bison Archives • COLUMN 3 (ALL): Marc Wanamaker—Bison Archives

PAGE 3 • COLUMN 1 (TOP TO BOTTOM): Marc Wanamaker—Bison Archives (top two); William L. Bird Postcard Collection; Marc Wanamaker—Bison Archives (bottom two) • COLUMN 2 (TOP TO BOTTOM): Marc Wanamaker—Bison Archives; Chris Roth; Marc Wanamaker—Bison Archives (bottom two) • COLUMN 3 (TOP TO BOTTOM): Marc Wanamaker—Bison Archives; Courtesy of Dan Tana's; Marc Wanamaker—Bison Archives (bottom two)

PAGE 4 • COLUMN 1 (ALL): Marc Wanamaker—Bison Archives • COLUMN 2 (TOP TO BOTTOM): Marc Wanamaker—Bison Archives; William L. Bird Postcard Collection; Marc Wanamaker—Bison Archives; Denise McKinney • COLUMN 3 (TOP TO BOTTOM): Marc Wanamaker—Bison Archives (top two); Peter Christiansen Valli; Marc Wanamaker—Bison Archives (bottom two)

PAGE 5 • COLUMN 1 (ALL): Marc Wanamaker—Bison Archives • COLUMN 2 (TOP TO BOTTOM): Marc Wanamaker—Bison Archives; Jim Pauley; Collection of Los Angeles Public Library; Marc Wanamaker—Bison Archives • COLUMN 3 (TOP TO BOTTOM): Marc Wanamaker—Bison Archives (top three); Courtesy of Cock'n Bull / C-B Beverage

PAGE 6 • COLUMN 1 (TOP TO BOTTOM): Marc Wanamaker—Bison Archives; Denise McKinney; Marc Wanamaker—Bison Archives (bottom three) • COLUMN 2 (TOP TO BOTTOM): Marc Wanamaker—Bison Archives (top two); Collection of Los Angeles Public Library • COLUMN 3 (ALL): Marc Wanamaker—Bison Archives

Ye Pig'n Whistle Candies

LOS ANGELES
SAN FRANCISCO - OAKLAND
PASADENA

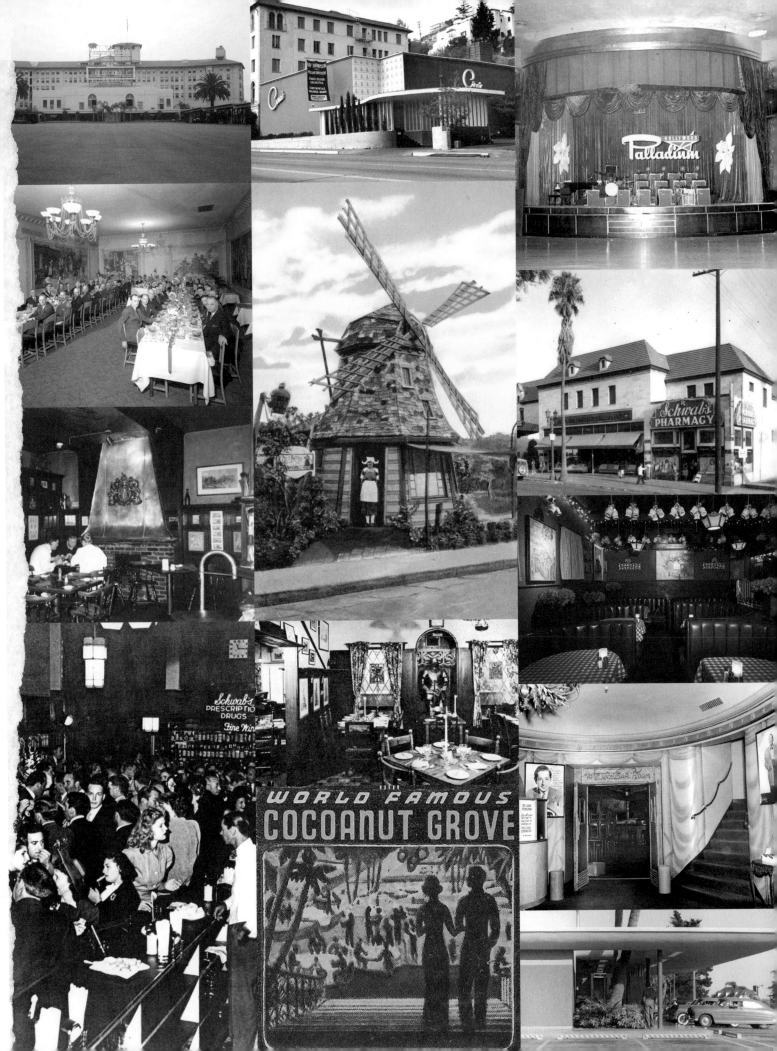

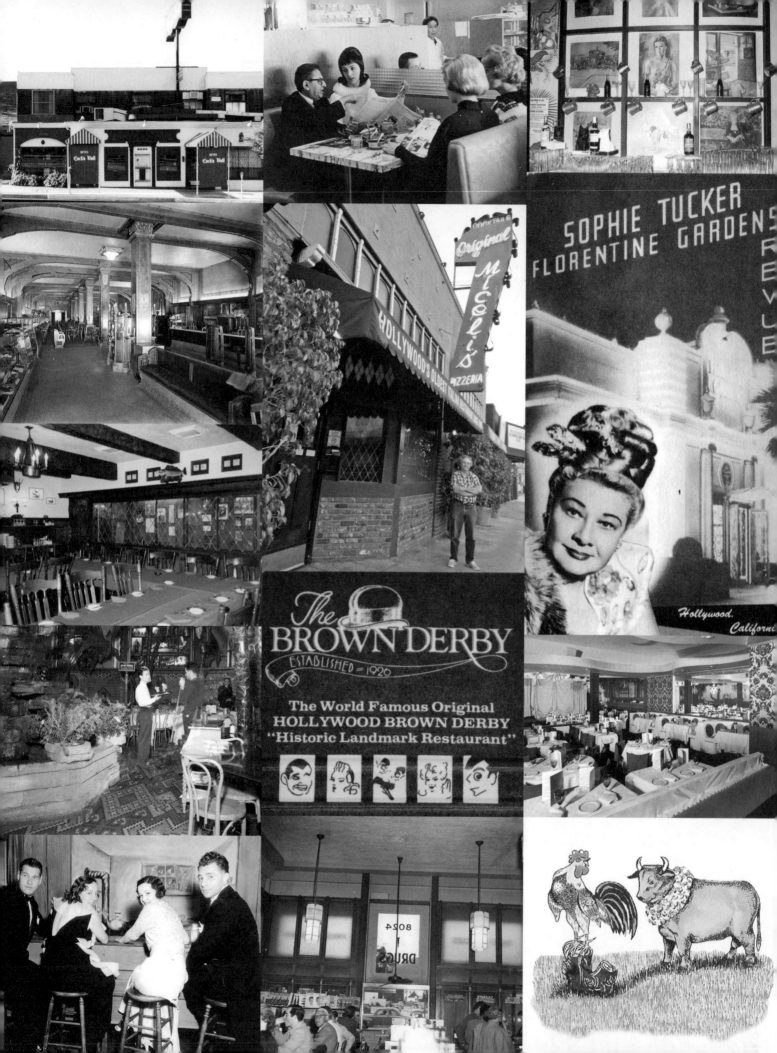